42°   48°   15⁰⁰

178°

N

174°

lington

K STR.

MARLBOROUGH

elson   Pe.

SON
Pe.

Banks Peninsula

Akaroa

Christchurch

L.Ellesmere

CANTERBURY   Plains
Pe.

WESTLAND   SOUTHERN

Pe.

Mt Cook   ALPS

170°

Taiaroa Head

Dunedin

OTAGO Pe.

SOUTH

I.

Invercargill

FOVEAUX STR.

Paterson Inlet

L. Te Anau

Milford Sound

FIORDLAND

Dusky Sound

42°   48°

A SURVIVAL BOOK

Man Against Nature

Survival Books are published in close association with Anglia Television's
Natural History Unit who make the 'Survival' series of television documen-
taries on wildlife.

SURVIVAL BOOKS

Edited by Colin Willock

ALREADY PUBLISHED

*

*

Man Against Nature

R. M. LOCKLEY

A SURVIVAL SPECIAL ON NEW ZEALAND WILDLIFE
Editor Colin Willock

ANDRE DEUTSCH

FIRST PUBLISHED 1970 BY
ANDRE DEUTSCH LIMITED
105 GREAT RUSSELL STREET
LONDON WCI
COPYRIGHT © 1970 BY R. M. LOCKLEY
ALL RIGHTS RESERVED
PRINTED IN GREAT BRITAIN BY
EBENEZER BAYLIS AND SON LTD
THE TRINITY PRESS
WORCESTER AND LONDON
SBN 233 95996 3

for
JEAN FRANCES

Acknowledgements

Among the many who helped in one way or another to make this book possible I would specially thank those who read parts of it, who sent material, and in other respects gave advice and information. These helpers include Sam Chaffey, Roger Duff, A. T. Edgar, Robert Falla, Charles Fleming, John Gibb, Jim Henderson, Fred Kinsky, Ann and Jack Mark, Ken Miers, Chris Robertson, Ronald Scarlett, R. H. Traill, John Tripp, Gordon R. Williams, and Kazimir Wodzicki. I acknowledge with pleasure the help of authorities on the staffs of the Wildlife Branch of the Department of Internal Affairs, the National Parks Authority, the Forest Service, various research stations and other services of the New Zealand Government. The New Zealand High Commission staff in London have been a valuable source of information, as well as providing most of the black and white photographs. To all the above, as well as those unnamed who gave hospitality, practical advice and other assistance, I offer my warmest thanks. Last, but far from least, I must thank my wife who, as a New Zealander, was my best critic and most consistent help throughout.

R. M. LOCKLEY

Contents

Colour Illustrations

Illustrations

ILLUSTRATIONS

TEXT FIGURES

MAP

Preface

New Zealand! New hopeful country, magnificent land of scenic beauty, movement, excitement and open discovery, of nature's own clear rapid changes and slow majestic design as well as the astounding clumsy, sad, ugly wounds wrought by man and his machines, his flocks, his herds, his foolish introductions. A country of gentle pastures and jagged mountains, of tree ferns and honey-eating birds, eroding hillsides, sheets of sudden rain, Antarctic winds, avalanching screes, earthquakes, glaciers, sunlit English paddocks and sleek racehorses, weeping willows, Lombardy poplars, Victorian atmosphere of afternoon tea in drawing-rooms, jam for lunch, volcanic chasms blowing seething steam, barbed wire, brash colonial voices, giant kauri and gum trees, gloomy pinewoods, tussock deserts, concrete posts, gulleys with dead sheep, magnificent manuka gorges, broad lakes, sliding peaks, unwanted deer, chamois, thar, wild pig, opossum, uncontrollable shingle, bursting rivers, man-made saharas, wind-chopped fiords, bubbling mud and bawling geysers, thermal heat and colour, rainbow trout, creeping crayfish, strident Australian frogs, cicadas, wetas, and huhu grubs; goldfinches and skylarks alongside native kingfishers, kea, kaka, kakapo, kiwi, weka, flightless stone-age birds skulking in the butchered bush, prehistoric tuatara dragons and insignificant primitive frogs hiding on unwanted islands; caves which glitter with glow worms; and in the sea, whales, dolphins by the thousand, giant game fish, teeming shoals of all sorts, whiskered crawfish, a thousand tons of trevalli at one haul of the seine, and little delicious whitebait. A land of wooden shacks, corrugated roofs, picture windows, glorious gardens in sprawling suburbs, whirling domestic gadgets, roundabout clothes driers, Maori hill-top pas, whares, bowling greens, speed-boats, water-skis, snow-skis, swags, climbers, fishermen, swimmers, sailing-boats, power-cruisers, rugby football, bar-becues, water-melons, marching girls and helpful people: stout smiling Maori full of Polynesian song, splendid beer, kumara, paua, toheroa, oysters, mutton-birds and genial sang-froid; gracious women and hospi-table dry-witted Pakeha men clipped of speech, driving dusty cars over hedgehog and opossums to get to their beer; little tin-roofed churches and chapels staunch against heathen and earthquake; and always sheep and wool, sheep and cattle, sheep and more sheep.

The atmosphere is clear air, long sunlight, and sudden terrible rain. A down-under, topsy-turvy world to the European, but vivid and liveable; in the north the sun so strong it is apt to dry old people to the consistency of an over-wintered apple, in the south frost and snow and wind and rain and sun give the cheeks a roseate bloom. But there is still vast space to breathe pure air, though New Zealand is an uncrowded country of heedless people moving all the same with blind, headlong eagerness to keep up with the worldly Joneses, and cover the land with get-rich-quick settlers, modern concrete and metal clutter.

Whither goes New Zealand? The aim of this book is to adorn a fascinating tale rather than point an inadequate moral. Nevertheless to show, by describing the disastrous impact of man upon a virgin land of marvellous beauty, how some of us destroy that which we love best. Those first white pioneers – some of them – were Utopians, loving the pristine land dearly, they held high ideals, they saw their mistakes with deep anguish of soul. But others there were who had fewer or no scruples, who paid lip service to God and the humanities, but who lived instead for sordid mercenary gain, squandering the country's natural wealth mercilessly with indiscriminate felling of forest, burning, over-stocking, poisoning the land.

If this book should give food for thought among those politicians, living their town lives, who control the management of the land of New Zealand, and make them pause awhile in their strange plans for the development of 'industrial wealth', and consider that man does not live by bread alone, I shall feel rewarded. If it causes them to give effect to a stronger policy for conservation of natural resources, of trees, plants and animals, to stiffen their resistance to the rage of concrete and over-population, to give priority to the more wholesome way of life of the countryside, I shall feel doubly rewarded. For, as I have tried to show in this book, the riches of New Zealand are not those of her sprawling towns in which half her population is concentrated. In a world on the verge of starvation her fortune is to be a well-fed nation, with abundant farm and forest produce and unlimited fish as her main assets, her principal bargaining point, her only real hope of maintaining her present high standard of life.

But do her leaders know this? I doubt it.

When I hear the foolish voices of men in cities who cry out for more industrial development, more and more metal and concrete, more coins, more paper money, I am saddened. For, as we have discovered in Great Britain, industrial wealth has never made a nation spiritually rich; rather the agglomeration of houses and factories which are destroying England today reduce the inhabitants and workers to a low level of mediocrity and existence, and produce poverty, misery and crime on a vast, increasing scale. It is only in close contact with the care of the land that the abiding virtues flourish.

Let New Zealand pause and take stock and make a supreme effort to save what is left of the beauty of her countryside and protect it from the modern poisons of conurbation, land abuse, overstocking – with humans as well as sheep – while there is still the opportunity. Let her grow more gently, more slowly, learning to live not on her capital resources but on the natural increment of her good husbandry of lands, forests and seas. For as surely as she seeks to overstock her islands with man and animals there must be a corresponding decline in the average standard of living; and an increase in artificiality, a loss of independence and sturdiness of character, the helplessness of the mob, and that general malaise which, as history has shown, precedes the fall of empires. These may sound dramatic words, but they carry the weight of the opinion not of too-busy businessmen – whose only interest is to make money today without thought of the morrow – but of the thoughtful biologists,

2

naturalists and world food experts who have calculated, in practical terms, that New Zealand's cultivable lands and pastoral hills were never meant to be squandered and degraded at the present rate of overbuilding and overstocking. New Zealand can never support at the present level of comfort the tens of millions of people which her businessmen dream of.

Go slow, New Zealand, go slow!

There is still time; much, but not all, has been lost. Glimpses of the Utopia dreamed by your early pioneers may still be had. I have enjoyed scenes in New Zealand beautiful beyond the power of this pen to describe. Vividly do I remember my first pastoral dawn soon after arrival in New Zealand on my initial visit. Sleeping on the balcony of a Hawke's Bay sheep station I woke to the songs of innumerable skylarks, of blackbirds, thrushes, greenfinches and goldfinches, and afar off those of native bellbirds and pipits. Beyond the fruiting walnut above the fragrant flower garden sheep grazed contentedly in paddocks grown emerald after recent rain. Dogs barked, impatient to be off the chain, hens cackled over the laying of our breakfast eggs. A shining cuckoo with pale breast and metallic green back glinting with gold dust dropped its rich pure scale of whistling notes from the top of an eucalyptus, calling and listening, then flying to another blue gum and calling again and listening for its mate.

I got up and wandered down to the cool fast-flowing river, to bathe beside huge weeping willows where fan-tailed warblers sang, flicking with a silver look in the sunlight which filtered through the long, spread white tail-feathers. A yellow bunting stammered from the furze, another sweet reminder of English country lanes. Trout darted around my shoulders as I swam in a pool mossed with the long salmon-pink and green hairweeds, with mimulus and the little white water-crowfoot. Picturesquely atop a young weeping willow an azure-backed kingfisher squawked a wheezing song as I waded ashore, dappled water reflections dancing in the shadows of the eroded cliff of the opposite bank.

What a strange fascinating mixture of contrasts and contradictions New Zealand appeared to me then! Here were native kingfisher and fantail nesting beside English starlings and sparrows in the hanging cliff and its exotic and native vegetation. Here I could watch the happy English goldfinches, whose tinkling song mingled with the rippling notes of the river in deep narrows each side of enisled willows as they fed upon the parachuting seeds of the abundant thistles, while the native banded dotterels – delightful new bird for me – watched me suspiciously from the shingle banks, and idly ran after the swarming white butterflies. A pair of gone-wild muscovy ducks had a brood teetering in the shallows. A white-necked cock pheasant was stripping the seeds from long cocks-foot grass – a riot of gorgeous colour as he stood against the waxy, hairy giant leaves of senecio. Along the dry walls of the bluff above me a string of goats, alleged by the farmer to be useful in controlling weeds, gam-bolled agilely, nibbling alike English furze, New Zealand tree fern, five-finger, mahoe, manuka, and poisonous tutu. I strolled upstream, my rapture somewhat shaken by the sight of an Australian magpie and a native harrier disputing over the stinking carcase of a sheep (it looked like a natural casualty, but I learned later that a shepherd had flung it from the height after it had died in the pasture above). I was to get used to the fact that the gullies from which many farms derive their bathing and drinking water supplies are often the grave of farm animal casualties.

Back in the orchard of the sheep station I gathered ripe fruit. There were orange, lemon, peach, apricot, plum, apple, pear, and walnut trees; passionfruit, vines, watermelons, and soft fruits of every kind. In this land of plenty there were not enough hands or mouths to cope with the yield, or to preserve more than a fraction of this orchard and garden wealth for the winter.

This was my first glimpse of the New Zealand Arcadia. I was in a land of plenty, of sunlight, of a gallant and welcoming country people. A land, of the many I have seen in both hemispheres, worth living in, worth fighting to preserve its Arcadian possibilities. A land I have since learned to love. A land I have explored from north to south, from Cape Reinga to Stewart Island. A land where my daughter lives happily married to a third generation Pakeha (Maori name for the white settlers). To daughter Ann, who drew me to make my first visit, and to her husband John, and to all the many friends I made as a result of this and other visits, I offer this book in humble admiration for the best in the fine character of the New Zealanders; but I do so apologetically, well aware of my own ignorance of that great little country, yet in absolute good faith that the dangers which I have seen and been shown within those shores seem little apparent to so many of the native-born residents. I have felt compelled to emphasise, some will say over-emphasise, these – to me – very real dangers from mismanagement of land and resources, equally in the present as in the past, in relating the history of the onslaught of man upon a virgin land, yesterday and today, as seen through the eyes of a student of animal behaviour. Out of that observation, out of the serious talks I have had with leading scientists and biologists in New Zealand, I long with them to see a stronger policy of conservation of natural resources adopted. These men have told me of their frustration due to the failure of the Government to implement the findings of their research and accept that very advice on conserva-tion which the politicians have demanded of them. This failure is the result of the old familiar mixture of vulgar political expediency, of paying lip-service to the scientist while encouraging a nullifying inter-departmental rivalry, of putting short-term business interests first, and the long-term husbandry of dwindling natural wealth last.

Meanwhile the rape of the fair country proceeds.

1 In the Beginning

In the beginning, before the coming of man, the forests were tall and beautiful throughout the length of the land. Giant kauri dominated the drier slopes of the North Island, the tall white pine kahikatea stood majestically above the flax in the swamps. In the South Island, beneath the eternal snows of the Alps an endless rain-forest of tree ferns and evergreen beech clothed the steep western slopes from the glaciers to the Tasman Sea, a cool jungle of epiphytes and lianes, of glow-worms, and rata and the red pine rimu. Eastwards was a huge alluvial plain where giant moas grazed like herds of giraffes.

Flowers were plentiful, subdued in colour and full of nectar. Bees and butterflies were comparatively scarce. Instead birds rifled the honey tubes of many plants and acted as fertilising agents.

Everywhere there were handsome birds, never seen by man. Many were so free from fear that, like the moas, they had lost the use of their wings. Unafraid, they fluttered from branch to branch, bowing their gaudy heads in movements of courtship and feeding, calling with strange cries never heard by man. Or walked about in the bush, or along the shore, by night as well as by day. Or swam in lake, river and sea. Some water birds – swan, goose, penguin – were also flightless.

There were no land mammals to attack or compete with the birds, and few avian predators. The most formidable was the great eagle, a relative of the Australian eagle, but rather a sluggish bird, slow to fly and preferring to hop over the ground; probably it lived much on carrion, vulture-wise, picking the carcases of moas and other birds which had died from natural causes or become mired in the deep swamps. Much smaller was the harrier, another carrion feeder and opportunist, snatching up anything small, helpless and edible as it floated on leisurely wings over bush and plain. Still smaller but more dashing and powerful on the wing was the falcon, able to strike down birds in flight, even to drive away the harrier. There were two native owls, but they lived chiefly on insects, lizards and bats. They haunted the trees where, in the twilight of the forests, there were hundreds of small bats of two kinds.

Along the shore thousands of seals and sea-lions congregated to rest, moult and breed, unseen, unmolested by man. They were fat, full-fed, gregarious but often noisy with territorial argument. For the seas around were so rich in fish that there was little room for the seals to find hauling out space on the rocks and beaches, so numerous were they. These seas were the meeting place, the point of convergence of two waters, the warm sub-tropical currents of the Pacific, and the ice-cold flow from the Antarctic; in this zone of turbulent upwelling the water was alive with plankton and krill, the basic food of all marine life and supporting vast shoals of small and large fish. Also feeding on these dense layers of krill and fish were enormous schools of migratory whales, dolphins and porpoises.

But of human beings, not a single one. The art and poetry and civilisation of China was five thousand years old; Christ was born and died on the Cross; the Scandinavians had settled Greenland and dis-covered America and ravished western Europe, but still no man had set foot in the isolated islands we now know as New Zealand. One thousand miles to the west the aborigines were in possession of every region of Australia and Tasmania. To the north-east a great chieftain reigned 2,400 miles away, on Tahiti, where it was customary to kill and eat surplus population in intertribal warfare.

So the islands slept, peaceful, virgin, protected on all sides by the barrier of a few thousand miles of the cool fish-abounding waters of the Roaring Forties latitudes, enjoying a million years of freedom unsullied by the wars, politics and religions of *Homo sapiens*.

This land had no name among its innocent, chattering, unnamed birds, its silent tuataras and lizards, its noisy seals. Perhaps the migrating whales and dolphins in their underwater conversations discussed its marine topography which they knew from feeding and travelling around its shores? Their keen eyes could see its great hills with that wise cetacean look which, we now know, does not belie the complicated brain and intelligence of these great sea-mammals. Maybe they had some name for it, some sibilant signal sound – we know that dolphins at least have a considerable code of vocal communication more varied than that of any other mammal save man. And would the delphinic name for New Zealand be as beautiful as that given by the first men to find the land? *Aotearoa* (Land of the Long White Cloud) – a wild, ringing sound, as fitting for and as lovely as the pristine wilderness itself.

'In the beginning [explained the geologist] the earth and the earthly desires which men cherish were not, for as the Bible rightly declares, the earth was without form, and void. But to get nearer the present time, why it's only about five hundred million years ago that the first living creatures appeared on the New Zealand scene . . .' With characteristic disregard for the ticking clock my hospitable friend Charles Fleming, F.R.S., had plunged into a fascinating description of the time scale, deduced from fossil evidence, of the development of life in New Zealand – then part of a huge land mass, possibly of a lost continent, probably a limb of the mysterious Antarctic continent of Gondwanaland. 'This was the Cambrian Period,' he went on, 'with the earliest fossils of sponges, trilobites and brachiopods. The ancestors of our oldest present-day reptiles and land plants appeared in the Triassic Period, two hundred million years ago. Much later came the first birds, the giant penguins of the Oligocene, thirty million years ago. Probably the immense moa or *Dinornis* had already arrived to stalk the land like a mighty ostrich, but we have to wait until the Pliocene for the first birds to be recorded. Then the Pleistocene, virtually yesterday but in fact about two million years ago, produced a large crop of moas, the New Zealand eagle, the giant swan and goose and the still living notornis, for our fossil record.'

While my mind was reeling with this flight through the ages he went on to explain that meanwhile there had long been mammals in the sea – seals and whales – but none on dry land, no earth-bound mammals (for we must except a few bats which had flown across the ocean). These cetaceous creatures could swim away on the approach of the several 'recent' glaciated or Ice Ages which assisted the extinction of land-bound animals and plants on the soil which is now New Zealand. What shape the first island of New Zealand was none can ever know, but during the last Ice Age, fifteen to twenty thousand years ago, it was one long island, and then suffered a severe impoverishment of its birds and plants. We can only guess what species were exterminated by the cold. The ice was once more grinding the highest lands into their present scenic diversity. Then came a re-warming of the climate, a melting of ice, a flowing of rivers, a burgeoning of bird and plant activity, a splitting into new forms which occupied the fresh sun-warmed ecological niches of the land. But no mammals – save in salt water, and the aerial bats.

The seas rose with the melting of the polar ice caps and, combined with the heavy eroding waves and fierce tides of the Roaring Forties latitudes, opened up the present channels to form New Zealand into North, South and Stewart Islands.

Strange. No land mammals on these great islands, not even fossil mammals? Why? When only one thousand miles to the west, a whole new world of unique mammals existed, on an island called Australia.

It is easy to understand how birds arrived in New Zealand. Some evolved from ancestors which must have flown there in the first place from the nearest land masses of Australia and Asia. Because these early immigrants encountered no ground-living mammals to kill or compete with them some of them found it more convenient to walk rather than to fly. Some grew very large and heavy and developed short, stout legs, at the expense of their wings. They were mostly vegetarian, these giants, for it is an advantage to be large. There is greater metabolic efficiency, better conversion of food, less loss of heat if your body surface is small in ratio to bulk weight. A tiny humming bird can consume its own weight in food in 24 hours and may starve to death if kept without food for one day, but an ostrich can fast for several days and its normal maintenance ration each day is equal to only a small fraction of its body weight. At one extreme of this fashion was *Dinornis maximus,* a moa which stood ten feet high on leg bones thicker than those of a cart horse, and which must have had an appetite for grass equivalent to that of a large cow. *Dinornis* lost all trace even of a rudimentary wing. Other birds retained their full powers of flight: one or two even made an annual migration out of primeval New Zealand and wintered (the cuckoos) in warm islands to the north. The golden plover and the godwits, which breed in Siberia, came to feed on New Zealand shores in their winter, the southern summer.

In splendid oceanic isolation the New Zealand land mass, with its varied rock formation of volcanic and sedimentary origin, remained inviolate from man down the centuries far into historic times. When the last Ice Age melted away, leaving only the snowfields above the 6,000-foot contour, most of the moas and some smaller birds had survived. The moas had done so by browsing on grass, shrubs and low-growing trees which had persisted during the cold period. They also ate berries and seeds and, as in domestic fowl and other birds, they ingested numbers of small stones which aided digestion of these.

Wherever the skeletons of moas have been uncovered – in swamps and river beds, in clay or sand – little heaps of gizzard stones have been present, (up to $5\frac{1}{2}$ lbs weight in the case of one single giant moa gizzard) often embedded in the remains of the vegetable food. Farmers in New Zealand have also found these gravelly stones in neat heaps beneath the turf when breaking virgin soil, and no moa bones near by, proving that the moa periodically vomited or passed scores, even hundreds, of pebbles when 'spring-cleaning' its gizzard, possibly also ejecting the old membrane or lining which enclosed them (certain wading birds such as curlews moult and eject the old lining of the gizzard at intervals as a new lining forms).

There are 27 species or forms of moa accepted by the experts on this ostrich-like bird, of which 22 have so far been found in association with the middens and hunting camps of the first Polynesians to occupy New Zealand. Not all of them roamed the steppe-like plains. Some were adapted to life in bush and rain-forest, and one at least seems to have survived into the last, if not the present, century, by so doing. This was

Megalapteryx (which means 'big kiwi'), a small moa about three feet tall. As recently as 1949 some of its feathers and bones were found in a cave in Notornis Valley in the South Island, above Lake Te Anau – a cave I was able to explore in 1962 (page 133).

Recent research has shown that even the giant *Dinornis* was alive as late as about AD 1500; and the Polynesians encountered, slew, and ate it, along with other smaller moas whose bones, and implements made of these bones, have been found in their middens. Another large moa was *Eurapteryx*, no mean size, for it stood on its short massive legs as high as a man (Figure 1). With no vestige of wings the great moas strode about, cropping the tussock pastures. The huge egg must have been a *bonne bouche* for the Polynesian who, after sucking the contents through a small hole, used it for storing water – as the Bushman of Africa does today with the ostrich egg (Figure 2).

The only moa-like bird to survive for certain today is the national bird of New Zealand, the kiwi. Scientists place it in its own family, but it is obviously descended from the same archaic source as the moas. The nearly extinct *Notornis*, like the extinct *Aptornis*, is of a younger stock – the flightless rails. The *Aptornis* was a kind of giant wood hen or weka (page 127) which when erect was about three feet tall, and whose bones have been found in swamps beside those of the giant moa of two thousand years ago. Kiwi bones date back at least before the last Ice Age, but how ancient this primitive-looking bird is we do not know – probably as old as the moa, possibly many million years.

The kiwi survived the glaciation by sheltering in holes, feeding by night and living largely in bush and forest on a diet of worms and insects, probing the ground and rotten vegetation with the long, sensitive bill, guiding itself through the ground clutter with cat-like facial whiskers. Its sight is very poor but senses of touch, taste and smell are acute. The nostrils are situated at the tip of the flexible upper mandible. A system of nerves and muscles connects this sensitive extremity with the brain, and informs the kiwi of the exact nature of the food out of sight below. The egg is enormous for the size of the bird, and not surprisingly, as soon as it is laid, the male takes over all responsibility for incubation from the exhausted female.

HARPAGORNIS   EURYAPTERYX   MOA-HUNTER

PACHYORNIS   DINORNIS MAXIMUS

Figure 1. Moa-hunter and three largest moas. The eagle Harpagornis was also hunted—it
was a poor flier.

(Russell Clark, courtesy of Canterbury Museum)

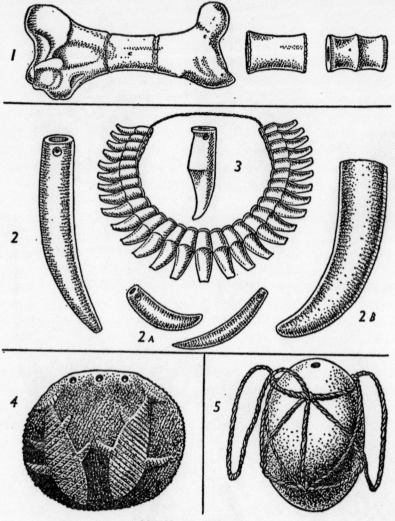

Moa-Hunter Artifacts

Figure 2. Moa-Hunter Artifacts

1. Thigh-bone of moa, scored to break out mid-section; mid-section as broken away; 'reel' worked from mid-section.
2. Imitation, in serpentine stone, of sperm-whale tooth favoured as central pendant in necklaces of moa-bone and ivory 'reels'.
2A. Smaller examples of 2.
2B. Sperm-whale tooth worn as central pendant in 'reel' necklaces.
3. Pendants shaped in moa-bone or ivory in imitation of complete necklace of whale-teeth. Side view of one shows how outward pointing curve of original tooth is imitated.
4. Massive stone breast-plate of black serpentine, with carved fish in relief (from Okain's Bay, Banks Peninsula).
5. Moa-egg water bottle, with Moa-hunter version of string-bag we believe it would be carried in.

(after Russell Clark, courtesy of Canterbury Museum)

A large flightless swan *Chenopsis* also existed in New Zealand, and the goose *Cnemiornis*, whose bones have been discovered in the same layers of sediment as the Pleistocene moas. These water birds arrived originally by air, then settled down to an easy land and freshwater existence, when the wings became redundant. No one knows what they looked like, for they died out before white man arrived, but a bold artist has depicted the goose coloured like the Cape Barren goose of Australia, because of structural likenesses and a probable relationship.

There are good reasons for believing that the powerful New Zealand eagle *Harpagornis* was alive when the Polynesians arrived a thousand years ago, for it figures in Maori legend as the *hokioi*. Awls made from its bones appear in the middens of the Moa-hunters. Its skeleton has been found at rare intervals in the swamps. Probably this great eagle, larger than the Australian wedge-tailed eagle (which can kill lambs), but closely resembling it in bone structure, fed on small moas, *Aptornis*, *Notornis*, swan, goose and other diurnal birds. Its bones have been found entombed in the same swamps with some of these, suggesting that it had pounced on the body of a victim caught in the ooze, and itself had become mired. Examination of the wing bones indicates that it was probably a very weak flier, and like the goose, on arriving in New Zealand (evidently from Australia), it evolved into a large sluggish creature, relying rather on hopping towards and jumping upon its wingless ground prey than on stooping from the air. The tendency towards flightlessness is always fatal to birds in a world inhabited by man; and the eagle quickly became extinct soon after this hunting mammal arrived.

But before he arrived what was the New Zealand scene really like? We can strive to picture it in the late moa age, say about the time of the Roman Empire. The climate would not be very different from today – the Ice Age long past, new small birds arriving, finding unoccupied ecological niches of territory and food, and earlier migrants already far subspeciated, already diverging into new species altogether – some flightless. The same fierce circumpolar westerly winds of today would be prevalent. Striking the fiordland and the alpine zone of the South Island's west coast, the cloud-laden winds would deposit their huge cradles of moisture in the form of rain, or snow on the high peaks. The persistent local precipitation of up to 300 inches a year creates conditions favourable to the broad-leaved trees, ferns and dense undergrowth making up the typical rain-forest of the lower altitudes, producing a climate which, tempered by the cool Tasman Sea air, is mild, never very cold or hot. The sound of running water is never absent on these steep western slopes.

The heavy rain causes erosion of the softer rock, leaving the harder as jagged peaks. The soil and shingle flow to form the Canterbury alluvial plain to the drier east, or tumbles into the deeps of the Tasman Sea on the windward side. By the time the wind has pushed the rain-clouds eastwards over the Alps and down towards Canterbury there is little moisture left. As these cloud masses hang in the air above the Alps they form the 'North-west Arch': their shape and density are a good forecaster of the weather, for those who, from experience, can read them correctly.

The sun shines freely over the plain, and as the wind rushes down the eastern foothills it sucks up the warm air reflected from the lower, level land. In the centre – Otago – the rainfall in some years is under 12 inches, and on the east coast under 30 inches, a year. Enough rain, abundant sunshine, and level or undulating terrain produce ideal conditions for millions of grazing sheep today.

Yesterday the moas enjoyed this vast steppe, as it recovered from the last glaciation. It was probably at first sub-alpine in nature, and only more recently became a treeless steppe. It could have become treeless from fire: during dry weather the first colonists a thousand years ago might have burnt the plain; or even in pre-human times an occasional flash of lightning could have started a great fire amid the summer-dry bush, fires from which the moas fled in terror. But this is speculation. The evidence indicates that moas must have been numerous enough in Canterbury and the tussock lands of the eastern half of the South Island. They were there in their thousands, perhaps millions, to maintain the steppe in good condition by regular grazing, without which it is possible that these plains would revert to bracken, and scrub, and last of all, if unfired, to forest.

In the North Island there were moas of olden time, but due to the warmer climate and as the extent of plain and tableland was less, they seem to have vanished earlier, leaving their plentiful remains in caves, swamps and dunes. They may have adapted themselves somewhat to the new growth of bush and forest as the climate grew much warmer, living on the forest edge, or in open forest, shifting to higher tussock country as dense forest gradually conquered the warm fertile valleys and lower savannas. But with the coming of Polynesian man to populate densely the North Island they were no more than a legend by the time white men set foot there.

Meanwhile new species of birds were arriving on the wing from Australia to flood the islands with song and colour after the long winter of the last glaciation.

Expert naturalists, like Robert Falla, late Director of the Dominion Museum, Wellington, with whom I have shared happy expeditions in the field, have carefully examined the geographical relationships between the land birds of Australia and New Zealand. Of the land and freshwater birds breeding in New Zealand today (and excluding seabirds, and wintering species which do not breed) at least one-quarter are found in Australia. Seven species (spur-winged plover, white-faced heron, coot, royal spoonbill, grey teal, silver-eye and welcome swallow) are known to have arrived to nest in New Zealand within the last century. Eleven more are identical with Australian species, and another seventeen are distinct subspecies of, and closely related to, Australian species. This subspeciation was doubtless achieved after their geologically recent arrival in New Zealand, possibly since the last Ice Age. Subspeciation can be very rapid in isolated islands. The separation of the North and South Islands occurred only about 15,000 years ago, but already certain species have developed colour changes in plumage, and become distinct subspecies in each of the three main islands.

It happens that, in addition to Australia being the nearest land mass to New Zealand the prevailing winds over the 1,200 miles of the Tasman Sea are westerly, favourable to the passage of birds towards New Zealand; but not vice versa. Any such crossing, however, is accidental, storm-induced; if we exclude seabirds and waders – fastest of migrants

– there is no regular latitudinal movement or migration of land-birds west-east or east-west over the Tasman. The very limited regular migration of land-birds to and from New Zealand is all more or less longitudinal. The large majority of the birds do not migrate at all, except within the limits of the islands; they do not need to in the mild climate, and many species are totally sedentary within a few miles of their nesting places.

No land mammals. Was New Zealand, then, never part of another continent? Was it ever an island since the first life began on shores thrown up from the depth of the sea – as Maori legend declares? So the birds were able to fly there and settle down in their paradise; and the plants arrive, floating as seeds through the air, upon the ocean, and in the feathers, claws and bodies of the migrating birds? It is as easy to account for the plants as for the birds, especially the vast numbers of ferns which cover New Zealand. The spores of ferns can travel thousands of miles through the air. The ferns of New Zealand arrived long before the birds, and date back over two hundred million years. I was fascinated to examine some of these, as living fossils, still flourishing: coal-measure ponga tree-ferns or their descendants, the primitive *Psilotum nudum* on volcanic screes, the ancient *Tmesipteris tannensis* hanging from trees in wet forests.

Like the birds and long before them the plants evolved into unique insular forms. Some may have arrived via Antarctica, which at one time was under forest – as we know from coal discovered there; from the disputed Gondwanaland which once joined, or did not join, New Zealand with South America. Significant for this theory are the splendid fuchsias, so characteristic of New Zealand, which originally were native only to South America (and one species in Tahiti, *en route* between); and their variety and beauty indicate the degree of development and speciation that has occurred in oceanic isolation. These and the lovely rata and pohutukawa and other trees unique to New Zealand share a synthesis of living with certain birds with long brush-tipped tongues, the New Zealand honey-eaters – bellbird, tui, stitchbird, the kaka parrot and others. The plants provide delicious nectar in summer and

Eroded landscape, central North Island

Man against forest: North Island. Snow-clad Ruapehu on the skyline

Two examples of specialised evolution

The huia, now extinct, paired for life;
with their different beak forms, each
serving a separate purpose in feeding,
the sexes were entirely interdependent

A North Islar
kiwi, showing
the 'whiskers'
which give th
bird its delica
sense of touch
the dark

edible fruit in winter; in return the birds do the work of bees and trans-
fer the fertilising pollen from blossom to blossom. Later they scatter the
undigested seed far and wide in their droppings.

No land mammals. How then did the earth-bound indigenous lizards
(the skinks and geckos) and the primitive frogs arrive? None of them is
a long-distance swimmer, and even the frogs of New Zealand are not as
fond of water as most amphibians are. It is possible that the ancestors
of the lizards and frogs arrived in this land on flotsam of log and tree
drifted on tide and wind, perhaps from Australia, where related species
lived. It has even been suggested that their eggs could have been carried
accidentally on the feet or plumage of migrating birds.

But the presence of the astonishing dragon-shaped tuatara, a true
reptile found nowhere else in the world, suggests that New Zealand has
been an island for perhaps one hundred and thirty million years. If so,
evolutionally at a full stop, a living fossil, the tuatara was the only
four-footed vertebrate to survive over this period.

This lizard-like animal, two feet long when full-grown, was first
described as a lizard by the British Museum in 1831 from a skull, and
named *Sphenodon* from the large, wedge-shaped front teeth of the upper
jaw. In 1867 Dr Albert Günther discovered, after examining other
specimens, that the skeleton was unlike that of any living reptile and
more closely resembled that of the primitive reptiles of the Mesozoic
era, the beak-head dragons *Rhynchocephalia*, whose fossil remains have
been found in rocks two hundred million years old. I was to enjoy the
remarkable experience of studying at first hand this stem reptile, this
true saurian, whose once numerous cousins the dinosaurs perished from the
earth before man was evolved (so they say) from the same reptilian source!

I saw this little crested dragon on a tiny island in the Bay of Plenty,
where a two-foot male, possibly over a hundred years old, was basking
handsomely in the sun. Tuataras are long-lived, sluggish, white-spined
and dignified-looking, brown and yellow-brown, matching in variable
colour the rocks and holes they share with seabirds. Since man arrived,
bringing European rats, cats and dogs, they have vanished from the
main islands, and are confined to a few small offshore islets, from Cook
Strait northwards.

3

The tuatara evidently adapted successfully to the periods of glaciation in the past, able to fast and hibernate for long periods, living in a semi-trance for months on end. Its processes are slow. Only twelve to fourteen eggs are laid, and these take over a year to hatch; during the winter the unhatched embryos, like the adults, hibernate in a state of torpor, as if dead, their development apparently totally arrested. Other primitive features are the lack of a male copulatory organ, and presence of a third or pineal eye at the top of the head. This is quite an elaborate organ, with a lens and a light-sensitive layer or retina, but no iris. However, it seems to be of no use to the tuatara: the connecting nerve to the brain is degenerate and the eye itself is covered with the scaly skin which clothes the rest of the head. Possibly this third eye is a relic of a second pair of eyes on top of the head (once useful to its ancestors, if they then lived, crocodile-wise, in water?). The modern tuatara has a very fine pair of large eyes, ringed with scales of gold colour and with vertical pupils. Its body temperature at 52° F is the lowest in the reptile world. It feeds on insects, wetas (giant crickets), snails, geckos, skinks, and an occasional petrel or petrel egg.

Whichever way they arrived in New Zealand the geckos, skinks and frogs all have unique characteristics, indicating development in long isolation. The native geckos are ovo-viviparous, that is to say the eggs are retained and hatched within the female. The skinks are more diurnal than the geckos, and also viviparous. The indigenous frogs are extremely primitive, like the tuatara living fossils – of an early amphibian family, and evidently surviving today because of adaptation to, and lack of competition for, their unusual ecological niche. There are three species of this ancient *Leiopelma* frog, all very small, barely 1½ inches long when adult. They have huge eyes, but no ear-drums, and faint voices. They live on cool, moist mountain tops or windy islands, hiding deep under vegetation and stones. Some of them can subsist, without running or pond water, on moisture seeping from above. Two to eight eggs are laid, each in a gelatinous capsule filled with water; here the tadpole develops into a complete tiny-tailed frog before breaking free. These almost silent nocturnal native frogs are rarely seen, and could be in danger of extinction.

Three larger species of frog have been introduced from Australia and are rapidly spreading over the fresh water habitats of New Zealand, where they are extremely vocal in the breeding season. The golden bell frog *Hyla aurea* is commonest, so named from its tinkling call, but it also croaks loudly. The whistling frog *H. ewingi* is small and very handsome; it was introduced about a hundred years ago to provide duck food and for laboratory use. The great green tree frog *H. caerulea* is rarest and so far confined to the North Island.

No land mammals, did I say? Well, are bats really land mammals? To be sure there are two species of New Zealand bats, one so ancient that no one can guess its closest relative, the other a member of a common Australian group and apparently a relatively new colonist. Bats, of course, are capable of flight across the sea like birds, and the presence of these two distinct species only reinforces the evidence of New Zealand's isolation. All things considered, and with apologies to zoologists . . . no *real* land mammals!

Neither were there any snakes in this land. New Zealand, despite the scientific arguments in favour of connections with a fabulous southern continent – Gondwanaland, of the drift of continents, of the wandering of the Poles, must have been a remote South Pacific island long before the first mammals and snakes appeared on earth. But let the palaeontologists argue over the geological history and its biota as they may; my task here is to show how man entered and began to destroy this snakeless Eden.

2 The Arrival of the Maori

In the beginning (explained the Maori *tohunga*) the earth was mother Papa, and the sky was father Rangi. They clung together so inseparably that their children, who were gods, grew up cramped and miserable, denied freedom and light as they groped in the darkness between their parents. When they were old enough to be strong and wilful the children consulted each other; they decided by a majority to force their father and mother apart, so that they could escape into the world. But of all these young gods who tried their strength only Tane, father of the forest, was powerful enough to tear Rangi from the arms of mother Papa and hurl him skywards. But the god Tawheri, father of the winds, who had resisted the separation, joined his banished father in the sky, angry with his brothers and biding his time. The others ranged abroad, for now all was light, and there were many pleasant god-like tasks to complete.

Rangi, far above his beloved Papa, wept tears of rain; the dew and mist of Earth also are the signs of endless weeping of the separated couple. Yet Tane found favour in the sight of his parents as he created tall forests, and beautiful flowers and birds of many colours to enliven them, and to clothe the earth, his mother Papa. The other gods were also busy, each with his own creative affairs; but Tawheri did nothing. He attended Rangi idly, looking down jealously at Tane. He saw that Tane was forever trying to atone for separating his parents so harshly, making beautiful things for both. Having dressed Papa in trees, flowers and singing birds, Tane planted the sun and the moon in the sky for Rangi, to lighten day and night for them all. Tane gave his lonely father a robe of scarlet to put on at sunset; and a basket of stars – the Milky Way – to brighten the hours when Papa was asleep and the moon was out of sight. Tane would lie warmly on his mother's breast and gaze upward with her to admire the great beauty of the sorrowing Rangi.

Tawheri's bitterness grew. Secretly he prepared a great storm. Suddenly he left Rangi's side. The gale of his wrath blasted Tane's trees to the ground. He rushed upon all his brothers. He stirred up Tangaroa, god of the sea, peacefully living with his grandchildren – Ikatere, father of fish, and Tutewehiwehi, father of reptiles – and drove them apart. Tutewehiwehi fled to Tane and the land for shelter, and Ikatere retreated under the water with his brood of children. Only Tu-matauenga, god of future man, refused to bend before his mad brother. Tu stood erect, and at last Tawheri was out of breath and returned to rest beside Rangi, the sky father. But the peace of the world had been destroyed, and the brothers were at war one with another, as their Maori descendants have been ever since. Tangaroa still tries to lure back his grandson Tutewehiwehi, father of reptiles, from Tane's dry dominion. Tawheri willingly helps him in this feud by stirring up the sea with fierce winds; then Tangaroa hurls his waves against Tane, and bites and tears at the land – his mother Papa, who cradles Tane so safely. But when Tawheri is tired at last, and the sea is still again, the children of Tane launch their canoes from the land and capture the fishes which are the great grandchildren of Tangaroa.

The children and grandchildren of the gods are immortal too, the undying creations devised by the gods – trees, flowers, birds, fishes, tuataras, lizards, frogs, etc. But the gods were not satisfied. They decided to make a complete woman from the warm red soil of earth. When this was done Tane gave her life by breathing into her nostrils. They called her Hine-ahu-one, that is, Woman-created-of-earth. Tane mated with her, and so was born the Dawn-maid. When Tane mated with his daughter, another daughter resulted. Then the Dawn-maid, perceiving at last that Tane was her father, fled from further incestuous union. She took refuge in the Underworld, where she forever gathers the spirits of her descendants and is known as the Great Lady of Darkness.

Then Tu, father of men and god of war, created Tiki, the first mortal human male, and so began the generations of man upon earth. These first human beings partook of the god-like nature of their creators. One such was Maui, hero of Maori legend. Thrown into the sea as an unwanted child – like so many surplus Polynesian babies – this half-god survived to achieve miracles. He managed to snare the rising sun in a noose of unbreakable New Zealand flax, and beat Ra into agreeing to travel more slowly across the sky, so that day could be longer. With the same jawbone of a grandparent with which he thrashed Ra into submission, he fished up from the deeps of the sea an enormous stingray, which became the North Island of New Zealand.

Perhaps, after all, there was a real man called Maui, not quite so superhuman, but a Polynesian who had wandered in his canoe, storm-driven, far from his South Sea island home, and reached New Zealand? Who, somehow returning to Tahiti on a change of wind, steering by sun and stars, had told the story of the wonderful huge land he had discovered, full of meaty moas and other edible birds, and the seas around abounding in whales, dolphins and fish? Naturally in time his tale would be embroidered with supernatural events, would be woven into the traditions and myths of the Polynesian religion, which was a stone-age culture and purely word of mouth.

Myth and legend in the dark-skinned aborigine of Australia are scarce, uncollected or lost, but there are vague tales of the 'Dreamtime' which suggest that on arrival in Australia, about twenty thousand years ago, he found giant kangaroos, moa-like emus, and even the 'Bunyip', a terrifying giant beast of the swamps. But these stone-age people, like the stone-age Polynesians who came to New Zealand, knew the use of fire, and both brought with them the dog. In Australia the dog ran wild and became the dingo, assisting the extermination of the larger marsupials such as the giant kangaroo, the diprotodon, and the Tasmanian wolf. Whenever he was able to the aborigine killed and ate it (under pressure of extreme starvation he killed and ate his own young children). Evidently it did not remain domesticated for long; but puppy dingoes could be recovered from the wild and kept in captivity at intervals.

The dog brought to New Zealand was unable to survive in the wild;

there were no mammals for it to live on, although there were flightless birds (and the little Polynesian rat also came with the first settlers a thousand years ago). Moreover it was evidently small and domesticated, having been bred for generations in captivity and fed largely on vegetable food to fatten it for the table. There is no evidence that it ever ran wild and lived for long away from man. It was rare by the time the first white man set foot in New Zealand, and was eaten or died out before the nineteenth century.

The fires of the Australian aborigine were intelligently managed, and confined within small areas, enabling the local tribes to track living creatures over the burnt area for weeks after; and the regrowth attracted the vegetarian kangaroos and wallabies to return, when they could be spotted easily across the cleared ground. Mary Gilmore, quoted by Vincent Serventy, comments that the white man's rashness in burning the bush wholesale upset the aborigines, who were to learn in due course 'that fire, miles wide, would be lit to burn him and his!' Nevertheless the early native firing of the Australian bush, together with the gradual drying up of the climate, helped to create desert, and made it harder for the aborigine and the dingo to flourish on depleted protein sources. Hence the strict division of land into tribal hunting grounds – a pattern to be followed much later by the multiplying natives of New Zealand. Hence the crossing of the windy Bass Strait 150 miles to the cooler island of Tasmania, an island-hopping adventure involving the passage of not less than 50 miles of open sea to the Kent Islands in the first part.

Originally the aborigines were a tropical people. Their dark colour and negroid appearance indicate that they arrived in Australia via the Asian land-bridges, along the equatorial Indonesian chain of islands to Papua, and so via the Torres Strait and its innumerable small coral islands to Cape York in Queensland. They lived much by the sea, using primitive dug-out canoes to cross the narrow sounds in fine weather. Having reached Queensland, they would have multiplied and moved fast southwards along the fertile east coast, rather than westwards against desert barriers. At first there would have been food in abundance: dugongs, reptiles and fish along the shore, marsupials and birds inland. Evidently they were a hunting people; they brought no planted food, unlike the Polynesians who came to New Zealand. Nor was it possible to domesticate any native Australian animal or plant. Even the white man, with all his skill, as Serventy points out, has failed to do this.

It seems, however, that moving south to the cooler latitudes of Victoria and Tasmania, enjoying the abundant marsupial food, the black people gradually gave up seafaring. The archaeological evidence shows that fish was at first an important item of their diet, but by the time white men arrived in Tasmania, the aborigines were entirely dependent on food obtained on land, from insects to the largest kanga-roos, and sea lions in the coastal rocks. There was nowhere to go anyway: to the south lay the cold stormy Antarctic, and in the north, hostile tribes held territory. Already their northern cousins spoke a very different dialect, and still farther north, in the motherland of tropical Queensland, the strongest tribes remained strong to prevent any return of hungry southerners, zealously guarding their hunting grounds where they still speared sea fish, crocodiles, dugongs and turtles, and lived in tropical plenty beside the Coral Sea.

These hardy, still-naked Tasmanian and south-east Australian aborigines would have been ideal colonists for New Zealand, at least climatically, although they would have had to reorientate towards a sea-fish diet in the absence of land mammals. But if they had canoes at all, these were small, poor degenerate dug-outs, unfit for long sea voyages. As Hobart (south Tasmania) to Bluff (south New Zealand), is only 940 miles, and the prevalent winds over the intervening Tasman Sea are westerly, conditions were propitious for an expedition to colonise New Zealand, under 900 miles from land to land. But there is no record or evidence of such a crossing, even of storm-blown aborigines, no trace of their stone-age culture of spear, boomerang, nulla-nulla, or primitive rock paintings in the archaeology of New Zealand. Some Maori legends do, however, speak of strangers arriving from the sea who were dark-skinned, and came from a large hot country to the west. If this was so, they have totally disappeared without trace. As we shall see, the Maori reaction to strangers daring to land on his tribal territory was to attack, kill and eat them.

Unlike the Australian aborigine, the Maori of New Zealand is a true

Polynesian, tall and of distinctive and uniform physical character, with golden-brown skin, brown eyes, smooth (not frizzled) hair, broad but not unshapely nose and prominent but not negroid lips. Young Maori men and women are extremely handsome, as good-looking in European eyes as the finest European types (the scrawny, beak-nosed, lean European specimen is decidedly ugly in Maori eyes). The Polynesian tends to acquire a thick trunk long before middle age, but stoutness is looked upon favourably.

It is generally considered that relatively recently they originated in that home of fair-skinned peoples, Asia, and more particularly eastern India. Structurally they resemble in some degree the Malays and Indo-Chinese. It is supposed that under pressure of population they migrated from India through the peninsulas and islands north of the Equator, where they became expert seamen. Avoiding the tropical jungles of Papua and Melanesia, which were inhabited by extremely hostile dark-skinned, head-hunting cannibals, they sailed eastwards through the Philippines. Probably not earlier than the first century AD they burst forth into the empty uninhabited Pacific Ocean, a mere canoe load or two of hardy, pioneering seafarers in search of virgin territory to inhabit. Down the centuries they colonised and overpopulated one small island after another: the Carolines, the Marshall, Gilbert and Ellice Islands, then reaching the large island of Samoa, next the Fiji group, Tonga and the Cook Islands (Raratonga). It is not to be supposed that each voyage to a new island was deliberate; most new islands were found accidentally, either by explorers or by storm-driven canoe. But these restless migrating people were by now expert at living for days at sea on the fish and birds they caught, drinking the rain from their sails. Season by season, they had learned how to make use of winds and currents. They could steer expertly by the sun, moon and stars, using their acute sense of time.

Figure 3 shows their wanderings and how they colonised all the islands in the central Pacific, covering a vast area of much water and little land, and becoming the Polynesian people as we know them today, speaking the same tongue, though with many insular dialects.

During one of the early voyages the Polynesians found a huge group

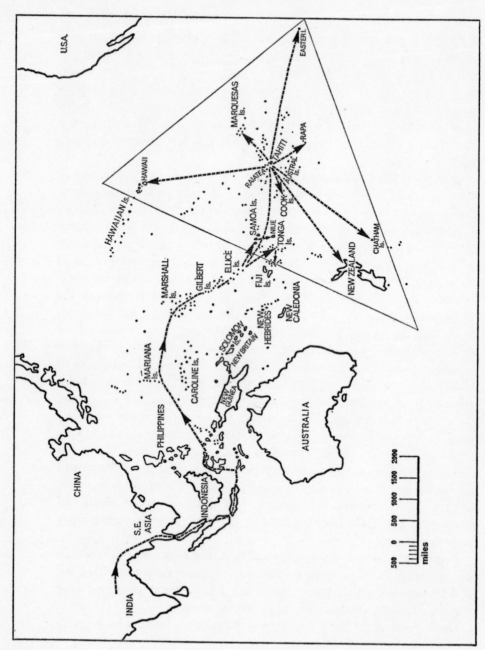

Figure 3. The wandering of the Polynesian people

of coral islands where the stars of the Southern Cross showed low on the horizon, in latitude 18° south. This vast archipelago became the homeland, the *Hawaiki*, of Maori legend and genealogy. Hawaiki was not, as was once supposed, the Hawaiian Islands (which lie 20° north of the Equator), but the Society and Tuamotu Islands, the largest of which is Tahiti. The first settlers were almost certainly a small family party, but they multiplied in ideal conditions of virgin territory in a moist tropical climate rich in fruits and fish. In 1769 Joseph Banks records that the stone-age Tahitians enjoyed the following which 'the earth almost spontaneously produces': bread fruit, coconuts, thirteen sorts of banana, plantains, vi (tropical apple), sweet potato (kumara), yams, tara, jambu, sugar cane (eaten raw), pia root, cabbage tree, pandanus fruit, nono (sour apple), and sundry roots less appetising. Fish were plentiful. The only domesticated animals were 'South Sea hoggs', dogs and chickens, all of which were eaten.

When Cook and Banks arrived in the *Endeavour* in that year, Tahiti was full to overflowing with an organised society, presided over by local chieftains. There was plenty of food at that time, but much talk of war, past and future, against other tribes on nearby islands. Banks describes with horror the considerable infanticide which took place – without understanding the implications of this practice which conveniently if ruthlessly reduced the number of mouths to be fed, and put to death all malformed or cretinous infants. He commended the general happy nature of the Tahitians, while condemning the promiscuity of their love affairs (one has the feeling that the diarist Banks had his tongue in his cheek and was writing to create a favourable impression of his morals for those who would read him at home. He had a warm eye for the ladies!).

We can picture the first inhabitants of this archipelago, which was to become the spiritual homeland of Polynesians living elsewhere, finding peace and plenty for many years. It is necessary to accept that as the pig, dog and chicken are creatures of Asian origin, these were brought all the way, island by island, from the ancestral continent – one more argument for planned voyages in large well-victualled craft. At first there would be no dispersal of population from Tahiti, possibly for a century or two. Then surplus young people, led by sons of chieftains, supported by priests practised in astronomy and navigation, set forth in large, or double, canoes fully equipped for long voyages in search of new islands to occupy, or, if already occupied, to attempt to conquer. Failure to do one or the other would mean a return home, by remembering the outward celestial navigation; perishing at sea from storm or starvation; or death or enslavement at the hands of the hostile occupants of the visited island.

During the first 500 years AD probably every large island within the great Polynesian triangle was colonised; of Hawaii in the far north, Easter Island in the east, and Tonga in the west. The settlers carried with them their common language and religion, the worship of ancestors, the habit of the chiefs to marry within their families, often brother with sister. Incest was normal and necessary where the first humans on a remote island were so few; and therefore it became a custom, and so revered that it became a religion. The credo of the Polynesian was based on a recital of the genealogical tree of their inbred forebears, back to the father of all, the Adam and Eve of the first generation to reach Hawaiki or Tahiti; and his name was Tane, Kane, or Tiki, and in time he was regarded as a god. He was said to be fair-skinned, child of the sun itself.

It was these oral genealogical records, collected from the many Polynesian island tribes, and all agreeing with pleasing exactness both in names and number of generations, that enabled investigators to calculate with some accuracy that the Polynesian homeland was first peopled not earlier than 58 generations ago. Allowing a generation to be 25 years this would fix the first occupation of Hawaiki around AD 500. Supposing the first canoe contained only one fertile woman, and allowing her to raise two procreant daughters, and each daughter in each generation thereafter to rear also two procreant daughters in the new homeland of Tahiti, in the next five hundred years (twenty generations) there would be over a million female descendants alive and procreant! Tahiti and its islands could not have supported even half that number in comfort upon its natural wealth (present population is about 40,000). Emigration, war, infanticide, and cannibalism were the factors controlling numbers. It is not surprising to find that there are oral traditions of several population explosions, in the form of Viking type departures from the homeland. But although these reached all the larger, warmer Pacific islands now known as Polynesia, New Zealand still lay unoccupied by man or land mammal for something like 750 years after the birth of Christ.

At this point we must refer to another opinion on the origin of some of the Polynesian tribes which inhabit the South Sea Islands today. The Norwegian Thor Heyerdahl, in his remarkable book *The Kon-Tiki Expedition*, puts forward the theory that these light-skinned people could not have come from India or Indonesia so late as AD 500 or (a second wave) AD 1100 because there were no stone-age people of that colour at this late date in those continental lands and islands, which were already highly civilised and adept at working every kind of metal. The only neoliths of the first centuries AD in the Far East were the black-skinned native of Melanesia and Australia, who are closer to the negroid peoples of Africa and totally unlike the Polynesians. Moreover, and this Heyerdahl found so significant that it was a main reason for the voyage of the *Kon-Tiki* raft, such a migration over the sea from the west was all against the westward flowing currents and the westward blowing trade winds prevalent in the south-central Pacific, caused by the rotation of the earth. Heyerdahl looked for evidence of fair-skinned people east-wards, in the New World. He sought the source of a vanished island people who were responsible for the stone pyramids and platforms built on Tahiti and Samoa, and for the huge stone statues which still stand, their origin unknown, on Easter, Pitcairn and the Marquesas Islands.

In Peru, amid the stone monuments of Inca and pre-Inca civilisation, he heard of a race of tall, pale-faced men with beards who were formerly considered to be gods because of their wisdom, learning and striking appearance. When the Spaniards arrived and conquered Peru the Inca Indians told of how these white gods had erected colossal stone figures and platforms long before the Incas achieved power. Their high priest was the white sun-king Kon-Tiki. One day . . .

'Kon-Tiki was attacked by a chief named Cari who came from the Coquimbo valley. In a battle on an Island in Lake Titicaca the

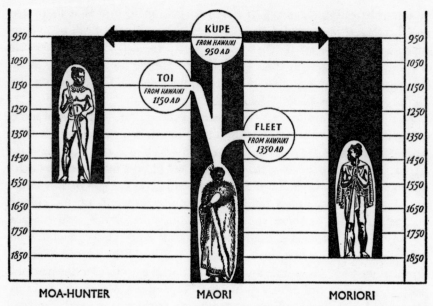

Figure 4. Diagram, based on time scale, showing relationship of Moa-hunter, Maori and Moriori.

(*Russell Clark, courtesy of Canterbury Museum*)

mysterious white men with beards were massacred, but Kon-Tiki himself and his closest companions escaped and later came down to the Pacific coast, whence they finally disappeared overseas to the westwards.'

How? On a balsa raft? Having described how his own raft drifted and sailed in four months over 4,000 miles from Peru to the Hawaiki homeland, Heyerdahl concludes his book with these words:

'My racial theory has not necessarily been proved by the success of the Kon-Tiki expedition as such. What we *did* prove was, that the South American balsa raft possesses qualities not previously known to scientists of our time, and that the Pacific islands are located well inside the range of prehistoric craft from Peru. Primitive people are capable of undertaking immense voyages over the open ocean. The distance is not the determining factor in the case of oceanic migrations, but whether the wind and the current have the same general course, day and night, all the year round. The trade winds and the Equatorial Currents are turned westwards by the Rotation of the earth, and this rotation has never changed, in the history of mankind.'

In support of a westward colonisation from South America is the American origin of the sweet potato or kumara, universally grown as an essential food in Polynesia when the Europeans first identified it there, but then unknown in lands further west or in Asia. It can be dried and stored, remaining edible and viable over a long period. Kumara is the native name for this plant in both Polynesia and Peru. It does not like salt and will not survive drifting hundreds of miles in the sea. Heyerdahl cites a New Zealand legend that it was brought over the sea in vessels which were not canoes, but consisted of 'wood bound together with ropes' – that is, balsa-rafts.

The approximate date for the arrival of the first man in New Zealand was fixed by ethnologists and historians in consultation with responsible Maori chiefs and leaders who had learned by rote the names and generations of their ancestors, handed down as part of their religious discipline. From these genealogies there was general acceptance that New Zealand was first visited 39 to 40 generations ago by the explorer Kupe and his wife in his canoe *Matahorua*. This would mean a date of about AD 950 for the voyage when, accompanied by Ngahue in the canoe *Tahiri-rangi*, Kupe first sighted the land of the long white cloud.

Some accounts declare that he found no human beings or other mammals, but only birds. One version, however, states that Kupe encountered a fairly large native population. Lately the archaeologists have supported this version as the result of recent Carbon 14 analysis of charcoal samples from the ovens of moa-hunting men. These samples have been dated firmly around AD 750.

How did Kupe find Ao-tea-roa? We can conjecture that, if his ancestors had reached Tahiti from the west four or five centuries earlier, it would not be impossible for him, or any other skilled seaman, to know the sailing directions, by sun, stars and trade winds, to reach Raratonga, and Tonga, for the oral records were strictly kept and handed down by the learned tohunga from observations made by the first and subsequent

voyagers. The distance between Tahiti and Raratonga is considerable –
600 miles – but the trade winds were favourable. Having reached
Raratonga, the next island to the west would be Tonga (the Friendly
Isles), a good 800 miles away. To the south-west of Raratonga the
North Island of New Zealand is 1,800 miles distant, with the volcanic
Kermadec group two-thirds south. Knowing from the tribal information
where Tonga was – almost due west from Raratonga, or in the probable
words of advice from the tohunga: 'Keep the (trade) wind from the east
behind you and steer towards the setting sun' – Knowing this, did Kupe
steer too far south, and raise the Kermadecs? Then, finding these islands
too small and barren, did he sail on southwards? If so, unless he was
fortunate in striking a patch of fine weather, he would have sailed at
last into the zone of the westerly winds.

Legend has endowed Kupe with the title of grand explorer. Tradition
records that, storm-driven or not, he landed first in the far north of the
North Island, and made a thorough exploration of the coast southwards.
He found the interior rich in moas and timber; but there were no coconuts, bananas or kumara, no coral, and the climate was distinctly cool.
The forests were full of beautiful birds so unaccustomed to man that
they could be knocked down by hand. The huge stupid moas scarcely
moved out of his way. As on Tahiti there were no snakes, no four-footed
animals to hurt man; and the sea teemed with fish, whales, dolphins,
seals. The explorers coasted south and reached Wellington harbour,
and saw in the far distance the snowy heights of the South Island.
Deterred by the stormy Cook Strait and the cold climate he turned
around the south-west coast of the North Island. Here the westerlies
blew the two canoes rapidly north. Kupe is said to have completed the
voyage around the North Island at Hokianga – 'Kupe's Returning
Place'. Rounding Cape Reinga, he set course for the Kermadecs, for
Tonga or Raratonga, for the homeland.

Returning at last to Tahiti, like Odysseus to Ithaca, the heroic Kupe
gave his people a glowing account of the new land, as well as explicit
sailing directions on how to reach *Tiritiri-o-te-moana* – Gift of the Sea,
another name given to it in Maori incantations. It is said that Kupe
brought back with him dried moa meat and the tough flint-like and

A North Island saddleback
New Zealand pigeon

An introduction from neighbouring Australia, the Parma wallaby has survived on Kawau Island, becoming extinct in Australia until re-introduced from New Zealand. In the hand (left) and photographed at night, showing the strikingly red eyes

handsome *pounamu* or greenstone, so hard that axes made of it were still in use four centuries later, to build the canoes which accomplished the Great Fleet expedition.

The oral records of Maori history do not show that there was any enthusiasm to follow up Kupe's discovery during the next two hundred years. Possibly there were other attempts to reach Aotearoa. But the Toi expedition from Hawaiki, eight generations later, about AD 1150, is regarded as even more authentic than Kupe's discovery. Toi is said to have set out with a retinue of his family and slaves in his great canoe in search of his grandson Whatonga and Tu Rahai, two daring young men who had ventured far to sea during a canoe race, and were blown beyond the horizon in a sudden storm. After fruitless searching he decided to sail by Kupe's route to Aotearoa. By accident he discovered the Chatham Islands, some 450 miles from the east coast of New Zealand. It is possible he left a small party to colonise this group, which abounded in tame flightless birds, sea-fowl and huge herds of seals. The natives of these islands, from archaeological evidence, can hardly be dated later than this century.

Toi sailed on west to reach New Zealand, which he found inhabited by the *Tangata-whenua* (People of the Land), who spoke his language, but were a poor people with no tradition of how they arrived. Were they the descendants of Kupe? They had no kumara or other Tahitian fruits, but subsisted adequately on moas and other birds, fish and bracken root. The moa-hunting Tangata-whenua were said to be a dark people resembling the Melanesian rather than the Polynesian. Radio-carbon analysis of charcoal from their ovens agrees with the date of 1150 for Toi to find these people, but no Melanesian element is evident in the design of the contemporary stone and bone implements, fish hooks, harpoons and ornaments found on these sites. These are all typically Polynesian; the necklaces, for instance, were made of moa bone or the local Serpentine stone fashioned to imitate the sperm-whale teeth of the necklaces of Tahiti. In his old age Toi settled at Whakatane, where, because of his diet of bracken and other roots, he became known as Toi the Wood-eater.

There is next an account, no doubt romantically embroidered down

4

the centuries, of how the storm-blown Whatonga eventually returned to Hawaiki, only to learn that his grandfather, the chieftain Toi, had sailed away to search for him; whereupon it was Whatonga's duty and wish to set out to find him in return. After many adventures Whatonga arrived in Aotearoa in his great canoe *Kurahaupo*, with sixty warriors, and several attendant women. At last he found Toi, amid great rejoicing. He took up land in Hawke's Bay, and his sons Tara and Tautoki founded the settlement of *Te Whanga-nui-a-Tara* (the great harbour of Tara) which is now Wellington.

Although the sea-route was now established between the homeland of Hawaiki and Aotearoa, the 2,400-mile voyage between was a formidable barrier, and there is little satisfactory evidence of any voyages for another two hundred years. The population of the South Sea Islands had meanwhile increased to such an extent that war had become the only means of resisting starvation. Fighting had become the main occupation of the chieftains, their sons and slaves. Massacre and cannibalism of the vanquished was the accepted conclusion of each battle. The insular cults built up on many small Polynesian islands over many decades of peaceful development might be overthrown in a single attack by a war fleet from some far distant island – witness the already mentioned stone platforms and images of forgotten religions which stand in the jungles of islands now deserted or occupied by people who cannot explain them. The most powerful chiefs built splendid war canoes, still without any metal tools, with beautifully carved hull and prow, and maintained their rule over districts and islands by force of spear and club. Replicas of these war canoes can be seen in several museums in New Zealand today.

About AD 1350 a great fleet of canoes is said to have gathered in Hawaiki to colonise the land of Kupe and Toi – Aotearoa. Warriors from whom present-day Maori proudly trace their descent over the intervening twenty or so generations manned the canoes, which had such romantic names as *Te Arawa* (Shark) – the leader; *Tainui* (Great Tide); *Tokomaru* (South Shadow); *Kuruhaupo* (Storm Cloud); *Mata-atua* (Face of a God); and also the *Takitimu, Horouta* and *Aotea* canoes. Compared with these canoes Heyerdahl's balsa raft was incomparably slow and clumsy. The canoes might be 70–100 feet long, driven at such a speed by as many as sixty paddlers that they could ram and split in two amidships an enemy canoe. The long-distance expeditionary canoe was double, a catamaran, with a superstructure holding the two keels apart and providing thatched quarters for the women, children and stores. All the canoes carried tall sails, some almost as tall as the vessel was long, but no proper masts; the sails could be inclined forward to spill surplus wind, or in rain or fierce sun they could be pulled astern by the sheet ropes to provide an awning. We can picture them sailing swiftly through the Pacific swell before the trade wind, or being rowed in calm with a steady rhythm, in perfect time (as was remarked by Cook and Banks), with the supple five-foot paddles, while the men chanted traditional songs, and the priest uttered prayers to the gods of the sea and winds, and the musician played a tune on the *kooauau*, a flute – often made from human bone – with a name like the sound it produces. At double the rate of the *Kon-Tiki*'s dawdling progress the expedition could have made New Zealand, over 2,400 miles, within one month, granted correct navigation.

The *Kon-Tiki* expedition proved that it was possible to live comfortably at sea for an indefinite period on a well-found small vessel. In setting forth on a long voyage, particularly to colonise another island, the canoes were loaded with food stores of kumara, coconuts, taro and many other fruits and roots; also dried pork and fish; and at times live pigs, dogs, chickens, even the Polynesian rat. The last was edible protein; it would equally well have been an acceptable stowaway; it was said to have reached the Chatham Islands with or before Kupe, before Toi left a nucleus of settlers in 1150 – if, indeed, he did. Water would be carried in long bamboo pipes, and gourds or coconuts; also caught in the sails, as well as sucked from (the lymph of) fishes. Edible fish could be had abundantly on these voyages, especially those whose habit was to leap out of the water – flying fish, sardine and dorado – and strike the decks. The smaller fish, of course, were excellent bait for hooking the really large ones, as well as seabirds, on sharp bone fish-hooks carried – or made – on the voyage.

The brown-skinned Polynesian people were happy, carefree, not given to worrying much about tomorrow. They loved the sea and could swim almost from birth. They were expert marine biologists, students of fish, wise in knowledge of weather. The most frightful storms of the Pacific could not soon destroy the well-found canoes which, because of their construction of wood and strong vegetable fibres, were flexible enough to survive the blows of the waves, and were probably far more durable than the balsa raft of Thor Heyerdahl which survived four months at sea without serious strain or major repair. But doubtless many canoes were lost at sea through errors of navigation; and others arrived at the wrong destination.

The wrong destination. It is only fair to add that some investigators are sceptical of the oral genealogical trees, and stories of 'deliberate' voyages from Hawaiki to New Zealand, preferring to believe that all early colonisations were fortuitous, and probably from the nearer Cook Islands rather than Tahiti, that canoes were blown off course on local fishing or marauding expeditions – as not infrequently happened. Surviving meanwhile on fish, birds and rain water, some of these lost seafarers were eventually blown to or washed up against the Land of the Long White Cloud. But this does not explain how the cultivated kumara and the edible dog arrived in New Zealand; or the very strong evidence, in the genealogical story, of the dispatch of the Great Fleet of canoes in the middle of the fourteenth century.

With the arrival of the Great Fleet canoes in New Zealand a new and more vigorous culture arose. The men were trained warriors, determined to acquire land and establish themselves as chieftains. They found that the descendants of Toi had exterminated all the larger moas; but they had brought with them a selection of Tahitian plants, of which the kumara, taro, and yam grew well in summer in the warmer north part of the North Island, where they first settled. Other tropical plants, such as the bread fruit and coconut palm, failed.

Like the Saxons who had conquered and divided England four hundred years earlier the warriors of the Fleet, numerically fewer than the descendants of Toi, were nevertheless able to dominate the scene. The newly arrived tribes from each canoe became established in the several districts they had taken by fighting; in the warm north the Ngapuhi; farther south the Ngatihaua, the Ngatimanipoto and the Waikato; in Taranaki, the Taranaki; and so on.

The South Island climate was less attractive to the warmth-loving Maori; the snow on the distant Alps must have been beyond their knowledge, the cold, rain-filled mountains dread places, haunted, like the high cone of Tahiti, by powerful vindictive gods. The South Island was nevertheless explored and valuable greenstone found for tool-making; but the high southern beech forest and snowgrass country were never occupied except by occasional hunting parties.

Gradually pressure of population in the north forced the weaker tribes and sub-tribes farther and farther south until, about 1700, the last of the weak Ngati-mamoe Maoris were driven across Lake Te Anau into the wet, cold forests of fiordland by the Ngatu-tahi, dominant in South Island. 'Run!' mocked the conqueror. 'Skulk forever in the haunts of the takahe, for you are banished from the world of men and sunlight!' The frightened men and women did so. In 1773 Cook discovered in remote, isolated Dusky Bay a poor native family eking an existence on fish, fowl and seal, but apparently of no fixed abode.

In the process of fixing the boundaries of their petty kingdoms and hunting grounds, the multiplying descendants of the Fleet engaged in the most bloody fighting. Tribal war was increasingly a fashionable necessity, and the young men were early taught to be brave and ready to fight and live – or die and be eaten – in defence of land and tribe. It is doubtful if the Maori at their highest peak of population ever numbered more than 200,000 in pre-European times. At this figure they exceeded the inhabitants of Tahiti, or even of Hawaii at that time, for the land was plentiful even if its productivity was low, due to its climate and mountainous topography. For these reasons they remained largely a fish-eating people, shore-dwellers, and travelled principally by canoe, visiting and raiding along the sea-coast and its islands. And there were some settlements around the large inland lakes. They had no wheeled transport, no draught animals, no pigs, no metals still; yet they achieved a degree of organisation and culture far above that of the Australian aborigine or any other stone-age culture of that late epoch of history.

While the men were hunters, fishers and warriors, the women tilled the patches of soil in the spring for the production of kumara, taro and yam, which, with fern root, was the staple carbohydrate in their diet. Enough was harvested to last over the winter and provide new seed. The women also gathered wild fruits, and searched the rivers and pools for crayfish and eels, and the tidal pools and inshore sea and sands for shell and other fish.

All tools were bone, stone, wood or vegetable in origin. The native flax *Phormium* was stripped of its fibres for weaving into cloth for skirt and cloak, which would be decorated with feathers. Dogskin was only worn by chieftains and important people. (Cook found dogs scarce in 1769, much prized; too many had been eaten.) Wood cutting adze and axe were made of the hard greenstone, grooved to take a wooden haft, and with these tools and the sharp edges of sea-shells they built their splendid canoes and the tribal pa or meeting house. There was leisure to decorate canoe, pa, gateway, fighting sticks and musical instruments with intricate and often beautiful designs in which former Polynesian and newer Maori gods, birds, fish and reptiles figured. Paua and other iridescent shells were inserted to provide eyes or otherwise enliven the wooden carvings. Personal ornaments and charms were made of greenstone, shell and bone, including human bone.

The land belonged to the tribe as a whole, not to the individual, a fact which to this day has bedevilled attempts to buy it by Europeans. Almost all activity was in fact communal, directed by the *ariki*, the paramount chief, a hereditary office. Through the exalted line of his ancestors, remembered by name (and order in time), the chief was invested with a sacred prestige or *mana*, and his person and belongings were *tapu* (taboo), not to be touched or violated without dire results – a convenient religious device by which he held despotic sway over his superstitious subjects, their life and death in his hands. So powerful was tapu that a man who broke it, even unwittingly, might lie down and die out of sheer fear or chagrin afterwards. But while the chief was endowed with a sacred form of tapu, another and evil sort of tapu could be laid upon a foe or transgressor, or especially an inanimate object, the touching of which brought sickness and death – again by the power of auto-suggestion.

The chief had his high priests, the tohunga, and was often one himself, skilled in witchcraft, sorcery and communication with the numerous tribal gods. The tohunga had the power of placing, and also removing, tapu upon persons and property. He was the repository of the sacred legends and genealogies of the tribe, by which they traced descent direct from the ancestral gods, from Maui, Tiki, Kane, and the deities of nature already described. He was therefore a man of great learning and wisdom, to be consulted in every major decision to be taken. He was able to recite the *karakia* – the incantations, prayers and injunctions – which were varied according to each occasion of war, birth, illness, death and burial.

Intimate worship of a supreme God, Io the First, the Parentless, the Life-Giver, was reserved for the initiates of the *ariki* and the tohunga. Io was unapproachable by the lower classes of the tribe, or by the *tutua* men and women slaves taken in war; these were permitted to have inferior gods to appeal to and guide them in their personal and family affairs. Thus while the common people could obtain comfort from their lesser gods, matters of major concern could only be decided by the chiefs and priests in secret communion with the all-highest Io.

The Maori religion did not include the acceptance of original sin, or of supreme happiness in the hereafter following piety in the life on earth. The Maori seized 'joy as she flies' in the present, contented if he could achieve mana through obedience, skill and courage within the community. There was an afterlife but it was not the heaven and hell of Christianity, but simply a place where the spirit lived on. After death the spirit left the body and travelled to the northern end of the land at Cape Reinga, where it drank from the sacred stream there before leaping into the ocean of Kiwa, into the arms of the Great Lady of Darkness (the Dawn-maid) who lived in the Underworld – which lay in the direction of the Hawaiki homeland.

The centre of the tribe was the *marae* or meeting place in the village, often in front of the principal *whare*, the chieftain's house. Here the politics and public affairs of the community were debated with all the ceremony of a modern county council meeting. The chief and tohunga listened to the voice of the people, and pronounced judgement when necessary, and when the case was difficult retired to consult the gods. Debate was one of the chief delights of the Maori. It was often concerned with that major preoccupation, the preparation for and participation in war. Another pleasure in the village was the athletic contest, designed to encourage skill in hand-to-hand fighting.

Strangely enough the use of the bow and arrow was quite unknown, the boomerang and blow-pipe unheard of. The Maori fought exclusively at close quarters with spear, long and short, club, and throwing stone. As the best areas for cultivation in the North Islands became overpopulated, and land for hunting purposes inland more rigidly defined as to tribal boundaries, trespass increased and war became endemic. To avoid surprise and massacre each strong tribe constructed one or more forts upon a strategic site – usually a hill-top. This was known as the *pa*, and closely resembled the early forts of the Romano-British period in Britain. The pa was moated with deep trenches or terraces from which the approaching enemy could be fired down upon; and if the attackers gained these ditches the defenders could retire within the fort, which was a palisade of sharpened stakes and tree-trunks easily defended from within, but extremely difficult to surmount from without. Some pas were on islands or peninsulas, protected by water and swamp. Many such pas, now regarded as 'ancient monuments', can be recognised by their terraced outlines against the skyline of the hills above many a coast road in the North Island, as for instance in the Bay of Plenty, a densely settled area of Maori occupation, both then and now.

The powerful tribes dwelt in the best lands, and their many villages contained well-built houses with framework of the long-lasting totara wood, and roof and sides of reed and rush thatch. Each leading tribe, and some sub-tribes, had a special meeting house, larger than the family dwelling or whare, which was more strongly built, with heavy uprights and roof-trees decorated with carvings of squat conventionalised human and animal forms, generally linked by curvilinear and spiral patterns, and more like the art of the Incas than of Polynesia. These patterns were also used in the characteristic tattooing of the faces and bodies of the men, and upon the lips and chin of the women. Tattooing practice has lingered on into the present century; some grandfathers and grandmothers of today carry the chin tattoo with pride, and their children may wear Maori patterns of tattoo upon breast and limb, sailor-fashion.

Such was the state of culture of the Polynesian people, who had lived for probably a thousand years in the Land of the Long White Cloud, when for the first time the white man encountered the Maori, in AD 1642. It was a state of climax: that is to say, without metals and wheat and the bread grains, without large domesticated meat and milk-producing animals, or native wild mammals, human numbers could not expand beyond a maximum – between one and two hundred thousand persons – without an appropriate increase in food supply. Reproductive capacity was high in this philoprogenitive people, but in the competition for living space and food, life was cheap. The practice of infanticide – the drowning of unwanted babies, chiefly those born with blemishes and babies for whom no man would accept paternity – had been imported with the original settlers from Hawaiki. Incessant war, engendered primarily by shortage of food, but more immediately by the see-sawing of inter-tribal feud, which required *utu*, or head-for-a-head revenge, periodically wiped out surplus adults, sometimes whole tribes.

In the search, the sometimes desperate need for protein, especially in the wet, cold winter, when sea-fish were scarce and the freshwater eels reduced by over-hunting, the Maori ate the last domestic dogs, slew the last moas and hunted to extinction other large birds in the North Island: the cave rail, aptornis, notornis, goose, swan, crow, giant harrier and New Zealand eagle; and reduced several other birds to rarities. Only in the gloomy forests of the South Alps did one or two moas and the notornis survive the hunting forays of the scarcer, more scattered South Island tribes, who nevertheless accounted for the extinction of the little weka, the gallinule, aptornis, coot, Finsch's duck, goose, swan, merganser, snipe, eagle, giant harrier, crow, and all the moas save megalapteryx.

Man continued to hunt man also – for the Maori found human flesh satisfying to eat, and his need for protein was often great, when his belly was empty or only half-full of tasteless fern root and hard-won grass grubs. But there were strict rules and tapu about cannibalism; only an enemy might be eaten, never a member of the same tribe. Maori hunting of Maori was as ritualised as in other animals. As the robin will first threaten an alien robin entering its territory, the Maori tribe might warn another that it would be attacked at a certain time if it did not retire, or pay tribute; there might be a mutual agreement to open hostilities the next day; in the meantime both sides had the opportunity to organise defence and attack. During the fighting a truce might be called to enable one side or the other or both to re-provision and rest, then the fight would be resumed. (This chivalry in battle was to astonish and be admired by British soldiers later.) The victors proceeded to kill any of the vanquished still alive in their hands, sometimes sparing the life of a son of a chief or priest considered to be tapu or for hostage purposes. The common warriors, and women and children not wanted as slaves, were butchered and cut up, and their joints and limbs sorted into baskets, and carried off to the roasting ovens.

As a robin will drive away or fight to the death an alien robin daring to enter its territory, so the hungry Maori who dared to hunt in the land of another tribe might expect to have to fight to the death, or be driven back to hunger and starve at home.

This has ever been the price of overpopulation the world over. It became apparent once more in a new phase to the Maori, whose stone-age civilisation was about to be overtaken by the metal age of the Pakeha – the white invader. Club and lance, heathen incantation and cannibalism, were to clash with musket and sword, Christianity and low cunning, in the same competition exactly – for territory and food. The Maori knew it for what it was, and responded as of old. But the white man gave it a different name. Colonial expansion.

3 Pakeha Poison

Instructed by the Governors of the Dutch East Indies a competent navigator from Holland, one Abel Tasman, was sent from Batavia with two ships to search for the fabulous southern continent (Marco Polo's mysterious land of wealth, *Beach*), a search which had already cost the Spanish, Portuguese and English several fruitless voyages. He was to engage in trade if possible; and take possession in the name of Holland of all new-discovered lands. He sailed on an agreed course in August 1642, first to Mauritius, then south to near 50 degrees. Finding no land in this stormy latitude he turned east, and discovered *Van Diemen's Land*, now known as Tasmania. Leaving the anchorage here on December 4th he sought for the entry to the Pacific and the route to Chile. Westerly gales brought him across the Tasman Sea and he sighted the alpine coast of South Island on December 13th. Coasting north inshore he rounded Cape Farewell and on December 18th came to anchor in what is known today as Golden Bay, at the northern tip of the South Island.

Here the two ships *Heemskerck* and *Zeehaen* were visited by some twenty-two Maori canoes; one was a catamaran, some carried sails, but the first to approach was a war canoe. This 'prau' suddenly, at a given signal, rammed at high speed the Dutch cockboat which had been lowered with the intention of establishing friendly contact and trade; and four of the crew were lanced or clubbed to death before the 'villians' were driven off by gunfire from the ships. Tasman was disappointed with this hostile reception, and with the mountainous appearance and rough climate of *Staten Landt* (in South America), as he thought it to be. This was the name he gave it on the chart he made, inserting the words 'Murderer's Bay' in the appropriate place. The weather continued disappointing; all the way up the west coast of the North Island he was unable to land because of the surf. Passing Cape Reinga at last, he attempted to land on the Three Kings Islands on the twelfth day of Christmas (hence the name), but was defeated by the surf and the appearance of tall men with clubs, who threw stones at the cockboat. Tasman sailed on north – to discover the Tonga and Fiji Islands. He had failed to land in New Zealand.

When it was discovered that the new land was not the east coast of South America after all, it was renamed Nieuw Zeeland, after the island province of Holland. It was written off by the Governor of Batavia as inhospitable and 'without matters of great profit'.

For 127 years after Tasman's visit the islands were unvisited by white man until, with a copy of Tasman's chart on board, Captain James Cook in the *Endeavour* was the first explorer to sight the east coast of New Zealand. On October 8th 1769 he anchored his ship off Poverty Bay, North Island. He was on the same mission as Tasman, to find the fabulous southern continent, after first observing the transit of Venus at Tahiti for the Royal Society. He had been well received by the natives of Tahiti, discovered two years earlier by the English ship *Dolphin*, some of whose crew had returned with the *Endeavour*. From Tahiti Cook carried a Polynesian chief Tupia and his servant boy, of their own free will, to New Zealand. This was fortunate, as it was discovered that Tupia could understand the Polynesian dialect of the Maoris, who proved at first as hostile as those encountered by Tasman.

Before Tupia could parley with them and announce that Cook's intentions were peaceful and his stay temporary, they had attacked four boys left in charge of the ship's boat when Cook and Banks first went ashore to explore. One Maori was shot dead by the white sailors in rescuing the boys. Next day three or four hostile Maoris were killed in further attempts by Cook to make a peaceful landing, and three young men were brought aboard as prisoners. Tupia learned from these Maori youths that their chief fear was of being killed and eaten; but, assured that they would be treated as guests, they relaxed, laughed and ate prodigiously of European food. The humane Cook was far more perturbed over the killings than the Maori, although he thought that they were justifiable because 'I was not to stand still and suffer myself or those that were with me to be knocked on the head.' Banks wrote in his diary: 'The most disagreeable day my life has yet seen. Black be the mark for it.'

From the detailed journals kept by Captain Cook and Botanist Banks, and the sketches of accompanying artists, an admirably full picture of the rediscovery of New Zealand is available to the grateful historian. Thanks to Tupia only a few Maoris were killed. At further landings, as soon as Tupia had explained the peaceable nature of the *Endeavour*'s visit, the amateur scientists went safely ashore to conduct their topographical, ethnological and natural history studies, but with gun in hand. What the Maori thought of the invader was recorded some eighty years later in the tribute by Chief Te Horeta of Coromandel, who as a boy met Cook: 'There was one supreme man in that ship, itself a god. We knew that he was lord of the whole by his perfect gentlemanly behaviour and noble demeanour.' The white lord gave the boy a nail which he treasured as a sacred tool from a god.

Domesticated dogs and native rats (kiore) were the only mammals noted. The dogs resembled those they had seen on Tahiti, were fed on vegetables, and fattened for eating. They had no bark and, except to scent out kiwi and other burrowing birds, were useless for hunting. Their skins were in demand for decorating the cloaks of the superiors of the tribe. They were used as sacrificial offerings to the god of war.

In subsequent visits, in 1773 and 1777, Cook introduced European pigs, and to this day wild pigs in New Zealand are known as 'Captain Cookers'. They have reverted closely to the black hairy wild boar type. He also brought poultry, sheep, goats, and many garden and farm seeds which he thought would be useful to the natives. He reported the soil light and fertile, with excellent stands of timber and fibre (flax *Phormium colensoi*, a flag-leaved plant totally different from European flax, but with fibres equally as tough for rope, sail, and cloth-making). In fact if only this country were 'settled by an industrious people they would very soon be supply'd not only with the necessarys but many of the luxuries of life'. Prophetic words, but Cook was a far-sighted visionary as well as an eminently practical man. He correctly foresaw that the intertribal wars of the Maoris, which he estimated to be around 100,000 in number at that time, would keep them too divided ever to join in opposing white settlement.

Explorers after Cook in this century were never quite so humane and wise in their treatment of the Maori. Through fear and misunderstanding several white visitors shot them down as if they were wild beasts, and, if they dared to resist, ravaged their settlements. As a result, understandably, some parties of white men were ambushed and massacred. But the flow of Europeans into the Pacific was a flood which could not be stopped. Men were lured there by reports of immense schools of whales, and of rookeries of fur seals. Suddenly, before the end of the eighteenth century, whaling stations and traders had set up establishments along the coast.

Fascinated by the new wealth of metal and money the Maori were drawn into the activities of the powerful white gods, who had weapons which could kill at great distances, and fire-water which could fill the brain with joy and forgetfulness. These and other marvellous possessions were promised to them in exchange for native foods, timber, fish, and the gathering and dressing of flax. Natural-born sailors, the Maori men looked with envy on the great sailing ships, but understood well the value of the native timber to renew masts and spars, and that their flax made the toughest ropes and sails. They enlisted willingly in the whalers, mingling on board with unscrupulous, degraded whites, such as escaped convicts from the penal settlement in Australia, as tough as the Maori warrior himself and a good deal less ethical in his relations with native people.

The sweeping east coast of the North Island from the Bay of Islands to the Bay of Plenty was found to grow every kind of English and North American garden, farm and orchard crop. Horses, cattle, sheep and domestic animals thrived. Noble trees grew in the kauri forests and the white pine swamps, ideal for shipwright and store-house building and repair. The whaling ships from the South Island hunting grounds could be refitted and victualled in the North Island, to the material profit of the Maori, operating through the agency of white traders who came to settle among them. Among the articles of early barter guns and women figured prominently; the Maori thought nothing of exchanging by sale or hire one of his wives or daughters for a musket. The visiting seamen, with or without articles of trade, thought nothing of enticing the wahines on board to amuse themselves during the long days and nights of the refit. There quickly arose a low class of white longshoreman who lived by procuring native women, by buying cheaply or as stolen goods native carvings, and stone-age implements, by supplying beer and spirits in grog-shops. Short of crew through the many desertions, death from scurvy or drowning, masters of whaling ships connived with the beachcombing pimps to kidnap Maori men and youths while they were drunk and incapable of resistance. Voyages were long in those days, and a year or more might pass before a whaling ship revisited that shore. (But in matters of insult the Maori had long memories, governed by the tradition of utu.)

There was even a trade in human heads, which, shrunk to fist size by native art, were worth a considerable sum of money in Australia for export to Europe.

From 1800 onwards the new settlements building up along the southeast coast of Australia were the springboard of the white attack on New Zealand. The mountainous south part of the South Island was reported to be virtually an unoccupied land of deep fiords and harbours filled with seals and fish, with schools of whales close inshore. The world demand for oil had increased tenfold. Many British and Australian whalers defied the monopoly of the East India Company which extended to all British ships between the Cape of Good Hope and Cape Horn. If they did not hold a licence from the company they could not legally trade or take whales. This did not apply to foreign ships and in particular the Americans were free to exploit the new source of both. They were soon joined by private firms from England and Sydney in fierce competition to secure the best cargoes. As whales rapidly became more scarce and troublesome to hunt on the stormy southern ocean, the whaling ships put crews ashore in small boats to work the more sheltered waters of the South Island from land bases.

The wholesale slaughter of the seals began. The blubber was rendered down in trypots and the skins rough-cured on frames. It is reported that in 1806 a cargo of 60,000 sealskins was landed at Port Jackson (Sydney), and in one week in 1810 the products of seal hunting brought to that port were valued above £100,000 – by today's values about £1 million.

Crews which landed in the deep-water coves of the south, and of Stewart and Chatham Islands, built rough huts and sheds from native trees and flax, and set up their cauldrons and frames. It was a rough life in a cold, rainy climate. Provisions were poor – sacks of weevilly flour and salt meat, salt and tobacco chiefly. For the rest there was seal meat, occasional fish for the trouble of hooking it – and more seal meat. The land was steep and barren of animals, save the seabirds and penguins in season. Inland there were comparatively few birds large enough to provide a good meal. Already the flightless takahe (notornis) was confined to the high tussock country. Around the camps the large flightless kakapo, a beautiful moss green-yellow ground parrot, quite abundant at first, was swiftly exterminated by hungry men, dogs, cats and rats. Wild pig – Captain Cookers – were still scarce, although spreading and colonising the interior, devouring native ground birds. The absurdly tame kea parrot could be knocked down with a stone if the men desired a slim meal out of this cheeky bird of thieving, magpie habits.

As it is known that the whaling ships were heavily infested with rats, it is certain that these escaped and lived ashore with these crews, as camp followers, thriving on the abundant offal from trypot and seal-skin. There is no exact date for the invasion of New Zealand by both black and brown European rats, but they were plentiful on all three main islands by 1850. The sealing crews were often many months ashore before their ship returned – if it did; for several disappeared at sea, and the abandoned crews suffered the additional hardships of making their way on foot or by small boat along the sheer, mountainous coasts to the nearest settlement, exposed to frost and snow, pitiless rain, hunger, and Maori ambush. Meanwhile the abandoned rats moved off in search of food and cover elsewhere.

The settlement of Port Nicholson (Wellington) by the New Zealand Company, 1839

A small Maori war canoe sailing past Mount Egmont, a snow-capped sleeping volcano 8,260 feet above sea-level, 1847

A Maori matriarch, wearing
the chin tattoo of a woman of
high rank

A typical tattoo pattern of a
Maori warrior

From the Banks and Otago peninsulas in the east to Milford Sound and beyond in the west, between 1790 and 1820, the fur and other seals were butchered to such an extent that they were virtually exterminated in New Zealand waters. Only a shy handful remained to carry on the species amid inaccessible surf-bound rocks. The sealing crews sailed away from the Foveaux Straits to more remote rookeries. Eastwards they devastated the herds on the Chatham Islands, and southwards as far as the sub-Antarctic Macquarie Islands, in the same fierce competitive policy of slaughter of seals of every age – bull, cow and pup. On each island hundreds of thousands were butchered; afterwards the ships moved on, leaving only the bones of their prey to be cleaned up by the abandoned European rats.

Some traders found it profitable, when sealing was reduced to a side-line for lack of skins, to remain in New Zealand, developing the demand for timber and flax. As yet there were no white women, but there was no lack of half-caste children, fathered but seldom acknowledged by the traders, whalers and seamen. There was also a legacy of European sickness, including venereal disease. Sometimes the trader achieved a veneer of respectability by living with the Maori mother of his children, and trading honestly with the Maori people – sensibly aware of the need for tribal protection while enriching his banking account in Sydney. In return he was expected to join in the eternal feuds against other tribes. The first 'safe' settlement for white traders was with the tribes of the Bay of Islands, a centre for refitting and victualling ships. Nowhere else was it really possible for a white man to go about unarmed and alone. More isolated trading posts, and some sealing depots, had been attacked by Maoris for the sake of obtaining muskets and ammunition, or in revenge for unfair dealing, seizure of land or other insults to a proud people.

One often quoted instance of such utu occurred in 1809. A Maori had been brutally treated as a sailor in the whaler *Boyd*. On return of the ship to Whangaroa, he reported the matter to his tribe, who came aboard in force, massacred and ate almost every white sailor and burnt the ship. In reprisal the white crews of sister ships of the *Boyd* burnt a Maori village – the wrong one; but this was utu which the

5

Maori naturally expected. Another feud had been created, and by Maori custom it could never die.

It was now the dream of the Maori warrior to obtain a musket and supplies of ammunition; for with pitiless logic he saw a new, sure and quick road to glory and possessions. Having traded food, timber, flax and his labour for guns, hatchets, knives and other lethal weapons he could roam with impunity in the lands of his stone-age contemporaries, exterminate – and eat – those who resisted, and enslave those who were prepared to work for him getting flax, food and timber which he could sell to the trader for more muskets and ammunition.

As Cook had foretold, the internecine wars between the tribes, now accelerated fearfully, would prevent any co-operation against the white settler. Indeed each coastal tribe wished to have a 'Pakeha Maori', as the white trader within the tribe was called, to advise them, obtain guns and European goods for them, bargain for them, and use every cunning to help them overcome their rivals. He had to be a man of courage, able to take part in battle when required. Some of the poorer types and escaped convicts from Australia so disgusted the Maori that they considered there was no acquirable virtue in killing these whites and eating their flesh. It was better to turn them into slaves; and this was occasionally done.

Early in the nineteenth century the sad history of the Chatham Islands became a sadder one. Isolated some 450 miles east of the South Island, in a cool Antarctic current, these small windy islands were first settled possibly as early as AD 750 or by the explorer Kupe about AD 950 or Toi, two centuries later. Whoever the first settlers were they found a vast abundance of protein food in the immense numbers of seabirds and seals, as well as fish and several large flightless land birds (since become extinct). There were no moas. Seal skins were worn as cloaks, and a *maro* or breech-clout of the same material or of flax, against the cool climate. By 1791, the year of their discovery by white men, they were distinctly darker than the Maori. They were later to be known as the Moriori. They had no oral traditions of a long genealogy, and no training in war or the building of elaborate canoes. There were no tall trees. They rafted from one island to another on bundles of flax and vegetation – a hunting and fishing people who ate fern root and the only land mammal, the little Polynesian rat. Ethnologists now consider that they were from the same stock as the Maori, but, adapted to a cool climate and a different food supply, the descendants of the original settlers there emerged, through the initial inbreeding, and long isolation, as a distinctive type.

When the Foveaux Straits sealers found the Chatham Islands, they reported a primitive people who lived there in peace, and did not resist their assaults on seal rookeries. This information reaching the Maori chief Pomare of the Ngatiawa at Port Nicholson (now Wellington), he tricked the white captain of the brig *Rodney* into agreeing, under pain of death, to convey a raiding party (900 all told) of his tribe to the Chathams in 1835. Then followed a ghastly massacre of the innocent, unresisting Moriori: they were killed in batches and eaten as convenient. Enough were kept as slaves; but many lay down and died as – beaten – rabbits and rats do in extreme despair. The conquerors were subsequently to fight among themselves over the division of property, over women, liquor, and slaves. In 1839, when the French whaler *Jean Bart* called there, the Maoris held a party aboard and became so drunk and quarrelsome on the skipper's liquor that the captain slipped anchor and put to sea. Out of sight of land he ordered his crew to slaughter the drunken Maoris and throw them overboard. In the fight that followed the Maoris sobered enough to find muskets in a store-room below, and retaliated with such effect that the French took to their boats. Steering by the sun the triumphant Maoris returned to the Chathams, ran the *Jean Bart* aground, plundered and burnt her. But the French in their small boats perished in a storm at sea.

In 1842 Britain annexed the islands and set the surviving Moriori free; but it was too late. A people originally 2,000 strong, they had been eaten, or otherwise absorbed by another people – an historic fate often repeated in the Polynesian islands, and not confined to man alone. W. P. Bourne, studying a collection of sub-fossil deposits from the middens of the Chatham Islands Moriori, draws the conclusion that this archipelago was formerly one of the greatest breeding places for petrels in the world, with at least four species of albatross, four species of gadfly petrels, six of shearwaters, three of prions, and single giant and diving petrel species. Penguins abounded. The Chathams are situated on the line of convergence of the two zones of surface water: the cool Antarctic and the warm sub-tropical; their meeting causes that turbulence and upwelling of water rich in plankton and krill already referred to. The coming of the Moriori to the seabird paradise had begun the extermination, to be carried on by the Maori who had eliminated the first human settlers so brutally. But seabirds can escape to sea. More melancholy was the extermination of the birds which could not escape, because they were land birds or flightless or both. Their extinction on the Chathams occurred in two periods:

Moriori: giant rail, weka, little weka, swan, Chatham duck, snipe, kakapo, kaka, falcon, laughing owl, crow.

Maori-Pakeha: Diffenbach's rail (1840), fernbird and Chatham rail (1900), bellbird (1906), bittern (1910), brown teal (1915), shoveler duck (1925).

It is true that if we take the long view of geological time it is seen that species have come and gone unceasingly through each period of a million years or less; that the major effect upon the survival of species has been the changing climate, not the prehistoric activities of man. The dinosaur and the brontosaurus failed to adapt and went out of circulation 200 million years ago. The moas were already dying without the help of man before Christ was born, and man had multiplied to eight figures on the left side of the decimal point. The rhinoceros, hippopotamus and elephant are relics of the age of giant mammals, only able to survive in future at the will of man. But there's the rub: *at the will of man.* For the first time in his whole history, man does have this power. Yet, still blindly, at this stage in the competition for living space, man continues to multiply, and to crowd off the face of the world all wild animals larger than himself, and many smaller, unique and beautiful creatures.

Some think this is melancholy, unethical, avoidable; others shrug their shoulders.

The Pakeha who brought the metal age to the Maori eagerly collected the bone and stone implements of these neolithic people – even the shrunken heads – to send to the museums of the world. The Maori as eagerly sold these simple tools, so inefficient by comparison with the coveted musket, axe, knife, scissors, reaping hook and needle. In placing lethal metal weapons in the hands of a primitive warlike people the white man had incurred a serious responsibility; but the traders were only interested in their profits, and the settlers only in obtaining land. Even the few thinking, religious men who felt a call to spread the Christian gospel were not free of ulterior motives.

Sent to the new Australian penal settlement late in the eighteenth century were a few hardy chaplains instructed in the tough task of administering religion and justice to the convict chain gangs. Here the lash of the whip accompanied the lash of the Word. In order to live in the aboriginal wilderness it was necessary to acquire land and grow crops. Some of these missionaries, and their children after them, were to prosper exceedingly by both operations, for the new farms could be worked at great profit with unpaid convict labour, and the sale of produce to the rapidly expanding settlement. Pushing out in all directions in the search for land for themselves, many freed and escaped convicts began to farm. To do so they freely encroached upon the tribal hunting grounds of the native blacks. The naked neoliths were helpless to resist the ruthless whites and their guns; they were evicted, pressed into slavery to work the land, shot at sight if they persisted in using their seized lands, and their women taken as concubines and servants. Poison was freely dropped into their drinking water-holes. The aborigines of Tasmania were to be exterminated by white settlers as ruthlessly as the Maori exterminated the Chatham Moriori, the only difference being that the whites were not cannibals. The missionaries endeavoured to 'protect' the aborigines from this exploitation by clothing their nakedness, teaching them English, giving them work for a nominal wage, and generally Christianising them, British Empire style. With no thought to restore their lands to them.

Among the chaplains of the New South Wales convict settlement was one Samuel Marsden, son of a Yorkshire blacksmith, who was filled with pity for the 'poor benighted heathen people', as he called them. He believed that the only way to save them was with the Cross in one hand and the axe in the other, as symbols of peace and work offered by Christ and his disciples. When the Church Missionary Society agreed to send him to New Zealand he took with him three evangelical laymen ('hardy mechanics') who were to convert the Maori by teaching both the Gospel and the civilised arts and trades of Europe: schoolteacher Thomas Kendall, carpenter William Hall, and cobbler and ropemaker John King – a seemingly excellent trio for his purpose.

Most visitors to the Bay of Islands will have made the pilgrimage, as I have, to the pleasant, lonely landing place where stands a Cross commemorating the spot where Marsden preached the Gospel for the first time in New Zealand, on Christmas Day 1814. His text from St Luke was significant: 'Behold, I bring you tidings of great joy.' His audience under the crimson blossoms of the pohutukawa trees were a few boat and canoe loads of Maori, Pakaha traders and half-caste residents in this first 'civilised' settlement in New Zealand. Then, leaving this community to the inexperienced care of his disciples, Samuel Marsden hastened back to his Australian farm. Although as a priest he revisited New Zealand, he was at heart a farmer, and was early in the field in introducing Merino sheep in Australia, having shrewdly recognised their hardiness and wool-bearing potentialities above those of English breeds.

The three disciples found their fellow-whites, the traders and the riff-raff of the waterside, sunk in lax living, and soon they, too, were unable to resist the plentiful grog and women. As Cook and Banks had found in Tahiti, Polynesian women accepted promiscuous sexual intercourse as natural, and the young Maori women also gave themselves with simple dignity to any man who pleased them and rewarded them with gifts.

Although the scholar Thomas Kendall fell from grace in this respect, he worked hard and fast to learn the native language thoroughly, as the first step in understanding how to apply Christianity to a heathen people. In a very few months he produced the first Maori–English dictionary, *The New Zealanders First Book*, in 1815. Five years later he accompanied the notorious chiefs Hongi and Waikato to England, and engaged with the distinguished linguist Professor Lee in making a full transcription of the Maori language.

It was a fatal trip in one result. The Maori chiefs were dignified, said little, but absorbed much. They observed that the power of the white man ultimately resided not in the Gospel but the gun. They submitted to the admiration and derision of those who stared at the 'savages' during their appearances in London, before royalty, the aristocrats and the vulgar crowds of Georgian England. But on the way home in 1821 Hongi bartered the many presents he had received abroad for muskets and ammunition, at Sydney. He retained only the coat of mail given to him by George IV. Landing at last in the Bay of Islands he gathered his Ngapuhi warriors around him. Many were already armed, having bought weapons from missionaries and traders in return for potatoes, pigs, flax, timber, wahines and even large acreages of land.

With the excuse that as a Christian he must protect the missionaries and the traders from the not infrequent raids of other Maoris, Hongi proceeded to range over the Auckland province, executing the utu of old and present feuds. First there was the existing war with the tribes of the Hauraki or Thames lands. With his fleet of war canoes and three hundred musketeers he sailed south to attack the pa of Totara, where Chief Trembling-Leaf, honourably warned by Hongi that he was to be killed and eaten, awaited him with but one musket and no ammunition. Dishonourably now, Hongi, failing to penetrate the strong fortress, promised peace if he was handed a certain sacred greenstone *mere* (weapon). This was done, the invaders were feasted in the pa, and the surfeited parties fell asleep. Then Hongi arose and set his men to slaughter every warrior in the garrison, sparing not even the high-born captives, whom he killed in cold blood himself.

Nothing could now stop Hongi. His wife Turi, blind but thirsting for human blood, exhorted him to further massacres. Destroying all before him he invaded the Waikato, and there achieved his greatest, most horrible success. Dragging his canoes overland where necessary, or making canals, he reached the Waikato river. His approach was slow, but inexorable; he had to spend weeks removing trees felled over the waterways by the retreating Waikato tribesmen; but at last he invested

the great triple pa of Mataki-taki, where most of the Waikato population were now, as they thought, safe from gunfire. It was said that ten
thousand men, women and children were behind the great palisades
and the system of ditches which defended this pa poised on the edge
of the Waipa river cliffs. It is said that a thousand Waikato spearmen
were arrayed behind the outer ramparts; but they were mown down
by the tremendous firepower of the musketeers. Then came the storming
of the inner defences, causing a panic in which the first to flee were
trampled in the ditches by those following, producing a mass of
smothered humanity into which the Ngapuhi fired until their guns
glowed with heat. Hundreds more leaped or were forced over the cliffs,
to fall to death on the rocks or in the river below.

Dreaming of becoming, like George IV, king of a whole country,
Hongi next ravaged the Bay of Plenty, driving the Arawa tribe into the
interior. He pursued them. They fled to the island of Mokoia in the
great lake of Rotorua. Here for a while Hongi was helpless to attack
them, and they were not slow to mock and ridicule him (from their
lake canoes just out of gunshot) as he lay encamped on the shore
opposite. They knew that his war-canoes were idle upon the shores of
the Bay of Plenty, 25 miles away, over hills rising a thousand feet
between. What they did not know was that Hongi had set in motion
the dragging of his canoes by slaves over this difficult country, and
meanwhile was making sure that none of the Arawa escaped from their
island refuge. Derided for his cowardice in failing to swim to the attack,
Hongi had his ample revenge when his mockers saw with terror the
war canoes launched upon Rotorua. The Arawa on Mokoia Island
were all massacred or enslaved in the battle which followed.

In battle Hongi wore the chain armour given him by the English
king. Neglecting to wear it during a bush-fight, he received a shot in a
lung from which he died fifteen months later. By then many other tribes
had acquired muskets, and his dream of kingship had worn thin with
the increasingly successful resistance. In particular the Waikato tribes
had rallied, and following Hongi's example, had fallen on less well-
armed tribes farther south, the Taranaki. In turn the Taranaki, joined
by the Ngati-toa chief Te Rauparaha, seized lands along Cook Strait

and raided far into South Island, the home of the Ngati-tahu. On first landing in the south Te Rauparaha turned the hospitable welcome of the Ngati-tahu into a blood-bath, and burned down their homes. He then proceeded down the coast to invest their stronghold, the pa of Kaiapoi (near the present Christchurch), but a runner had warned them, and they stood firm. Te Rauparaha, perhaps remembering Hongi's successful ruse, assured the Kaiapoi chief that he only wanted to buy greenstone. Maori chivalry and custom permitted the entry of emissaries into their pas, even in war, and Te Rauparaha was allowed to send his uncle and adviser Te Pehi and seven other leaders to parley further. Suspecting treachery the Kaiapoi closed the gates and, as utu required, killed their enemies, all eight.

This was in 1829. Ten years earlier Te Rauparaha had persuaded his people to make a remarkable migration, from their sandy homeland of Kawhia, in the dreaded shadow of the Waikato tribe, south to Kapiti Island. Like Hongi in the Bay of Islands, he could enjoy there the presence of the whalers and white traders whose ships used the Kapiti anchorage, supplying them with flax and food and timber and buying muskets to arm his warriors. He was joined by his nephew, the bold, skilful Wiremu Kingi with a strong party of warriors from Waitara in Taranaki. Kapiti became a fortress, supported by white interests, from which Te Rauparaha made his sallies of murder and conquest for twenty years, his largess of bloody utu – and non-utu. Now, rebuffed at Kaiapoi, he waited his chance to revenge the death of his uncle Te Pehi, a distinguished Maori chief who had once visited England. It came with the arrival of the infamous Captain Stewart in the trading brig *Elizabeth*. Te Rauparaha bargained with him, in exchange for thirty tons of flax, to carry a war-party secretly to the home of Tamai-hara-nui, head of the Ngai-tahu, who lived at Akaroa, a picturesque inlet on the other side of the Banks peninsula from Kaiapoi. Nothing less than this king should pay for the murder of his uncle. While the warriors lay concealed in the hold, Stewart invited Tamai-hara-nui aboard with talk of trade, and to drink in the cabin. Assured by Stewart that there were no Maoris on the *Elizabeth*, the great chief stepped into the cabin, there to face Te Rauparaha and the son of Te Pehi. The latter advanced upon Tamai

and parted his lips, saying, 'These are the teeth that ate my father!'
Te Rauparaha and his war-party went ashore, slaughtered all they could
find, and burnt the village, returning on board with baskets of human
flesh, and Tamai's wife and daughter. Stewart provided irons to
manacle Tamai, and allowed the ship's galley and pans to be used to
cook the cannibal feast which followed. Tamai managed to warn his
wife to kill his daughter to save her a worse fate, which she did. Stewart
would not allow Tamai and his wife to be killed until the flax was paid
over, at Kapiti. Then Tamai, his flesh already mortified by the irons,
was tortured to death with a red-hot ramrod, and his wife was also
tortured and killed.

News of Stewart's fiendish complicity in this outrage reached Sydney
with the arrival there of the *Elizabeth* with its load of flax. Governor
Darling of New South Wales had him arrested, determined to see him
hanged. It is not surprising however to learn that the prosecution
was eventually abandoned for lack of witnesses; if any appeared they
were quietly spirited away – the white Australian, his own conscience
stained by atrocities practised upon the aborigines, was not willing to
concede justice to cannibals. New Zealand now had the reputation of
being the most dangerous island in the Pacific because of Maori savagery
and cannibalism. Stewart and the brig were set free.

Even so, Te Rauparaha was not satisfied. Determined to destroy the
pa in which Te Pehi had been killed and eaten, he sailed secretly in the
next year to Kaiapoi and surprised the Ngai-tahu working in the potato
fields. Enough escaped into the pa to close the gate and repulse the first
assault, and some fled away to gather reinforcements. Te Rauparaha
dug a trench to the wooden stockade and piled up brushwood to burn
them out. The Kaiapoi relief force managed to slip through the swamp
into the pa at night, and also made an attempt to burn Te Rauparaha's
canoes on the beach, but heavy rain foiled this enterprise. After weeks of
praying to Tawheri, god of the winds, and watching the sky over the
Canterbury plain, both sides got an answer to their prayer; a north-
wester enabled the Kaiapoi to set fire to the brushwood under their
walls, and see it sweep away towards the besiegers; then it suddenly
changed to south-west and the stockade took fire. The men from Kapiti

now began their ferocious, screaming, tongue-protruding war dance, charged through the flaming breaches, and slaughtered the garrison. Thus did Te Rauparaha achieve utu: for each of his eight chiefs killed by the Ngai-tahu within their pa in 1829 (in just utu for Te Rauparaha's first and totally unjust attack) he had killed or enslaved one hundred of the Kaiapoi.

At Kaiapoi I was shown the spot where for many years the piles of human bones lay witness to the cannibal feast of Te Rauparaha and his men. Kaiapoi is a busy South Island farming town today, the beach where Te Rauparaha's war-party landed the resort of Pakeha bathing parties. And on a visit to Kapiti, in the North Island, I wandered round the remains of Te Rauparaha's village and the whaling station, abandoned to the birds; for Kapiti is now utterly peaceful, a national nature reserve where many rare native birds are specially protected and encouraged.

Such are but a few of the many tales of horror and valour of the Maori civil war of the musket, engendered by the white man's introduction of metal, and recorded for posterity by eye-witnesses. In the sudden uprooting of the tribes, complete and unprecedented in a hundred years or more of petty tribal disputes and minor, almost ritual, local wars of a stone-age people, the long-fixed boundaries of the tribal lands were suddenly revised, but the new limits of ownership were never properly defined. This was to lead to much confusion and almost insoluble claims when the war of Maori against Maori subsided after twenty years of self-destruction.

As yet almost no Maori had been converted to the Christian faith, although some had paid lip-service to it at times. So long as they believed in the mana and tapu of tohunga and ariki, their morale remained high and their belief in their native gods and the all-highest Io stood firm. The survivors of the massacres recited their exploits and kept alive and vivid their need for utu, with all the fervour of the mighty warriors they were, or would be. The conquering Maori enjoyed their new dominions; the conquered endured slavery as a better alternative to being eaten – often they were well-treated if they worked well, and sometimes the sons of vanquished chiefs were taken into the house of the

conquering chief and made their sons. But whole provinces were devoid
of human occupants, so huge had been the destruction of Maori population during the massacres. The moment was propitious for accepting the
notion of peace and work advocated by the missionaries eagerly pushing
south from the Pakeha bridgehead at the Bay of Islands. Moreover there
was less need for human flesh as protein; domesticated European cattle,
sheep, goats and pigs were appearing, and a wide variety of farm crops.

Anglican and Wesleyan missions brought the Word, and their
disciples among the tribes carried it ahead of them enthusiastically.
These Pakeha tohunga were straight-laced men who told the Maori
that the nakedness of Eve was shameful, the murder of Cain by Abel
forbidden, and all the Ten Commandments must be obeyed, lest the
hell-fire utu of the Lord, Father of Christ and all men, descend on them.
It was a richly compulsive religion that the Maoris were taught, and it
appealed to their strong love of legend. It spread like wildfire.

When in 1838 the Catholics arrived the Maori had the choice of
three species of salvation. Used to a wide variety of their own tribal
gods, they were not unamused by the undignified competition between
the white tohunga, which at times caused some embarrassing situations
for the latter. On arrival in a new village the missionary might find a
priest of another denomination had already come and gone; and he
might be refused a hearing by the converted Maori, loyal to the pioneer.
In that case his only hope was to avoid declaring the name of his church,
and say simply that his was the *true faith* of Christ, son of God and of the
Virgin Mary. The hospitable Maori would then honour and feast him.

On a visit to the Bay of Islands in 1835 Charles Darwin was pleased
with the orderly and English appearance of the mission station at
Waimate, with its farmlands and crops of barley and wheat, its garden
full of a great variety of vegetables and fruit. He also praised the work
of the Maori carpenter and miller as taught by the missionaries. But
he found the rest of the Maori people were devoid of the charm and
simplicity of their Tahitian forebears; and the greater part of the
English were 'the very refuse of Society'. These beachcombers as we
have seen were largely runaway seamen, escaped convicts, debauched
layabouts and dissolute ne'er-do-wells who existed by preying on the

Maoris and on visiting seamen, procuring wahines, decoying men from one ship to another at an extravagant fee. Another writer considered them 'much greater savages than the natives themselves'.

The atrocities of the tribal wars led at long last to the appointment of a British Resident, James Busby, in 1833, on the recommendation of Governor Darling. But as he was not provided with any bodyguard, and had no legal code, except what he cared to invent, Busby was completely ineffective in reducing the lawlessness. The local traders and settlers were presently obliged to set up their own vigilante committees to protect themselves from both Maori warrior and white beachcomber. They called themselves Temperance Societies, armed themselves, and poured many gallons of grog into sea and river. Finally the British Government, hitherto understandably anxious to avoid the responsibility of policing a remote, profitless land occupied by quarrelling cannibals, convicts and clergy, was forced to consider official annexation. Naval ships had already been sent to the Bay of Islands to protect British lives during the Maori battles of 1837; and the voice of public opinion at home had grown more forceful, backed by that of the settlers and speculators who had begun to pour in from Australia.

The missionaries, watching the corruption and strife of the natives in contact with the unscrupulous white beachcombers and land speculators, were in general opposed to extensive white colonisation of the ravaged and partly deserted tribal lands. These settlers hindered their efforts to raise the natives to the status of a civilised Christian nation, their declared aim. But it was not to be. There was no legal code forbidding the speculators to buy land, and almost no Maori could read or write, but was willing to put his mark to any piece of blank paper in exchange for a musket, axe, blanket, or any other desired Pakaha object. Syndicates were formed in Australia to purchase land in New Zealand. One of these secured, as was thought, the whole of the South Island and Stewart Island for a few hundred pounds. More respectable was the formation of the New Zealand Company, which applied to the Colonial Office for a royal charter to buy land and a licence to manage a proposed new colony. This was the inspiration of the writer and idealist Edward Gibbon Wakefield, a man whose record included a term of three years in prison for a youthful indiscretion, the abduction of an heiress. An intriguing, erratic person, he yet sincerely believed that much of the poverty and hunger of the lower classes at home could be relieved by colonisation of new lands, where self-sufficient Utopias could be set up on practical lines; the sale of land to settlers would provide the initial revenue to finance a firm, just and conservative government by the whites – for the whites.

The harassed Colonial Office, highly suspicious of the plotting of land speculators and their attitude to native occupants, rejected the application. Wakefield and his brothers finally decided to defy the Colonial Office. They prepared a vessel to carry the first load of British emigrants to New Zealand. It is said that the sailing of the *Tory* in May 1839, and the rumours of an intending French annexation, together spurred the British Government to dispatch a Governor-General, Captain Hobson, to treat with the chieftains for land and raise the Union Jack. Another view is that the *Tory* sailed, and the French considered an expedition, because of rumours of British annexation.

Captain Hobson acted swiftly. Both the *Tory* (see print, facing page 64) and the French expedition were *en route* to take up land in New Zealand. With an entourage of civil servants, transferred from New South Wales, Hobson arrived in the Bay of Islands. He summoned the Maori chiefs to meet at Waitangi (Waters of Lamentation). A marquee was prepared on the lawn in front of the Residency, a few yards from the beautiful sheltered bay filled with Maori canoes and Pakeha ships. Hobson invited the assembled chiefs to cede their sovereignty to the Queen, who in return could confirm them in possession of their lands, forests, fisheries and all properties they owned, either individually or collectively. They would become British subjects with all the rights and privileges thereof. To protect them from civil exploitation the tribes would yield to the Queen the sole right of purchasing their lands, if they wished to sell any.

There was a long debate among the chiefs. Some feared slavery, or the terrible fate of the Tasmanian natives – extermination. At last Tamati-waka-nene, prosperous ariki of the Ngapuhi tribe inhabiting the shores of the Bay of Islands, swayed the meeting in a famous speech. He had seen too much of the evil of both Maori and Pakeha lawlessness. He called on his people to forget the past and accept the fact that nothing could turn the Pakeha away. He declared he preferred Christianity, trade and peace to the heathen wars of the past and the present strife. He ended with a direct appeal to Hobson to 'remain for us a father, judge and peace-maker. Do not permit us to become slaves. You must preserve our customs and never permit our lands to be wrested from us . . . Stay then, our friend, our father, and governor.'

Next day, February 6th 1840, some fifty chiefs put signature or mark to the Treaty. A few, such as Tewherowhero, mighty leader of the Waikato, refused to give up their sovereignty, and were to fight the Pakeha for many years to come. But most were happy to acknowledge the Queen as their supreme authority. Secure in the possession of their lands, they felt that the substance was theirs; only the shadow belonged to the distant, unimaginable Throne.

On May 21st Hobson, alarmed at the news that the New Zealand Company was firmly established at Port Nicholson (Wellington), had bought vast acreages of land by direct bargaining with illiterate Maoris, and even operated its own form of government (including a jail), proclaimed British sovereignty over the whole country, the North Island by right of cession by its chiefs, the South Island by right of discovery. At the same time he announced that no land titles were valid that were not given under the Queen's authority.

In July of that fateful year Hobson entertained the captain of the French frigate *L'Aube* which called at the Bay of Islands. Suspicious of the object of the visit, he ascertained that *L'Aube* was to visit Akaroa (scene of Te Rauparaha's treacherous ambush ten years earlier). Hobson ordered a fast boat to Akaroa, which reached there shortly ahead of *L'Aube*, and raised the Union Jack in time to forestall the last attempt of the French to colonise any part of New Zealand.

Ever a strategist, Hobson next year moved the seat of government south, 150 miles nearer the troublesome Wakefield colony, to the splendid bay of Waitemata, a natural harbour large enough to hold the entire British Navy. It was the centre of the most concentrated Maori population in New Zealand, with access to both east and west coasts.

Hobson saw that he must rely on humouring the Maori population in order to obtain the essential food, goods and labour by which alone a white people could prosper in the midst of a warlike people.

Waitemata Harbour was to become the site of Auckland, the largest conurbation in New Zealand, with nearly a quarter million inhabitants today.

Thus, in armed possession of the two finest harbours, Auckland and Wellington, the Pakeha had two main bridgeheads through which in the next hundred years they poured thousands of land-hungry settlers. But until the final peace-making in 1887, certain tribes continued to fight the encroaching settlers, as well as to battle with those tribes which helped the Pakeha by selling land. Regretfully I must omit a whole chapter on the forty years of the Maori-Pakeha war, with its astonishing records of courage in battle of a hopelessly outnumbered people, who were also outmanœuvred and dispossessed with legal argument and legislation by unscrupulous white lawyers and wily law-makers, despite a genuine attempt by a succession of governors to protect the Maori, as promised by the Treaty of Waitangi.

Waitangi and the Bay of Islands today are utterly peaceful, the play-ground of yachtsmen, nature and island lovers, power boats and big game fishermen. Its hundred inlets and winding shores are sparsely dotted with the homes and 'baches' (New Zealand term for chalets) of summer visitors. Somewhat incongruously in its semi-tropical climate, where frost is rare, sheep graze above mangrove swamps. More appro-priately there are citrus orchards thriving behind windbreaks of bamboo and eucalyptus.

The novelist Zane Grey popularised the deep-sea fishing for marlin, swordfish and shark from one of its islands, Urupukapuka. The sport is widespread today in New Zealand waters, but nowhere so good as along this north-east coast of the North Island, where marlin can top 800 lbs, and mako sharks run even heavier.

The skipper of the motor-cruiser in which we explored the Bay of Islands listened over the short-wave radio hour by hour to reports of big fish being sighted, hooked, weighed, or lost – all the way south to

Mustering sheep in high country. The mule team pushes on ahead to make ready the next night's camp

Eroded country in the Tutira district, north of Napier. Overgrazing by sheep destroys pasture cover, then heavy rain washes the soil away

Volcanic activity on White Island, Bay of Plenty. The author watches clouds of sulphurous steam rise from the crater. During an eruption in 1914 a party of workmen were overwhelmed by boiling lava. The island is now inhabited only by gannets and other birds

the Bay of Plenty. But my host Sandy Edgar and I were busy studying the rafts of the seabirds which fish these fertile seas off Cape Brett. Shearwaters (mutton-birds to New Zealanders) abounded – chiefly fluttering, flesh-footed, Buller's and sooty shearwaters; and also red-billed gulls, white-fronted terns, shags and blue penguins.

A new bird had lately colonised this northern peninsular land – the welcome swallow from Australia, whose habit is to nest near water – under bridges, culverts, even on boats. We went ashore under Cape Brett to examine a deserted isolated settlement in Deepwater Cove, in the hope of finding swallow nests. Here was an abandoned farm, post office and wooden homes, an empty but beautiful spot to dream away a summer afternoon, to stroll around gone-wild gardens covered with vines, weeping willow, manuka and kikuyu grass. It was the site of a crawfish cannery; but like so many enterprises in a new country, it had been suddenly abandoned. Under the steep roadless slopes it had no landward approach. So it remained intact, as fair and beautiful to the naturalist as Goldsmith's deserted village of Sweet Auburn, no longer possessed by man, but re-possessed by nature. Reluctantly we departed – without finding any swallows.

Later I saw many swallows with Sandy. Previously known only as a rare vagrant to New Zealand from Australia, the welcome swallow first nested in Northland in 1958. In ten years it has become common all over this northern half of the North Island. Its name is highly appropriate – as the only swallow breeding in New Zealand it is most welcome to Europeans who miss the swallows of home; and besides it is a great devourer of insects, including troublesome mosquitoes and sand-flies. It seems to be spreading slowly into the South Island, where in 1965 I saw two pairs nesting – of all places – in a small motor-boat in regular use on Lake Ellesmere, near Christchurch. In this eighteen-foot launch we were taken out upon this vast lagoon of sixty-odd square miles to see ten thousand (at least) black swans feeding on the lakeweed of this shallow water, a marvellous sight. Like the lemmings, when overtaken by overpopulation and lack of food, the black swans die away in a catastrophic 'crash'. Introduced as an ornament to lakes and ponds, this handsome Australian swan has run amok in numbers – that is to

6

say it has not yet adjusted to its new habitat and ecological niche; but efforts are being made to keep its numbers down by the commercial sale of its eggs.

Our trip upon Lake Ellesmere was a pleasure tempered for me by the thought of those two swallow nests, each containing four eggs, under the cabin roof. Of course the swallows had not dared to stay brooding during our voyage. They left the launch as we got aboard; but when we returned to harbour over an hour later, three swallows came out to meet us while we were still a quarter of a mile offshore. They hovered around, and flew into the cabin and resumed incubation immediately we stepped ashore. Our fisherman host was proud of his swallows, but as he had to use the boat a good deal, I doubt if they succeeded in rearing broods aboard.

To return to the Bay of Islands. Before Cape Brett lighthouse was built at the southern entrance to guide the big steamers coastwise between Auckland and Sydney, the wooden sailing ships of the Pakeha and the war canoes of the Maori were guided by the tall phallic outline of the Ninepin Rock, whitewashed conspicuously with the mutings of seabirds, and pounded by the huge Pacific swell, off the northern cape of Wiwiki. We cruised under the Ninepin, hoping to locate the nests of the gannets which we could see resting there. But it seems that the Ninepin is too steep – the gannets were merely settled there to digest their heavy fish meals. At any rate we could see no nests.

Inside Wiwiki is Whale Bay, yet another abandoned site of those first white fishermen who brought such a doubtful legacy of lawlessness and disease to these shores. Only a few whalebones and the site of the trypots remain – not a human house or soul in sight when we landed and roamed for a while, picking up little bones and coloured pebbles – and a George IV penny.

In the next bay inwards, Marsden's lonely cross symbolised the better side of the white man's intentions. Bees hummed in the stately, ancient, crimson-flowering pohutukawa trees, and sheep nibbled upon the deserted hill above. Vanished are the war canoes and the terror of Hongi of the Musket. This north shore of the Bay of Islands has never recovered from the exploitation of 160 years ago. But there are still many Maori living here, and some part-Maori descended from the first traders and missionaries and settlers, to be found working a ravished land, which is slow to heal.

Vanished too are the great columnar groves of the *Agathis* or kauri forests which provided the ship's spars and building timber of those days. The land was back to scrub, to manuka, to repeated burnings and diggings – in search of the resin or gum of the kauri which could be found in the soil under the original deep forest humus layer. Its collection for the production of varnish had been a minor industry of the impoverished Maori and poor whites here in the north for many years after the forest was gone. There was indeed little else when the seat of government and trade was moved south to Auckland, and the whaling failed. In the process of digging for gum the land became pitted, and overlaid with infertile subsoil, then burnt over yet again, dug again for residual gum, pushed around, spoiled with spoil; until today it is almost worthless, hard to work for farming or forestry.

We had to drive far inland to see kauri forest, to the Puketi Scenic Reserve, for all the coastwise timber had vanished a hundred years ago. Manuka and gorse covered all land not being actively farmed around the Bay of Islands. At Puketi and in the Waipoua Forest still further west a few giants still rise up to 140 feet; these only survived the white man's axe because at the time they were too difficult to extract so far from the sea. Fortunately they are now saved by a wise management of these State forests. From time to time a mature kauri may be felled before it begins to die back, which it may do any time after one to three hundred years. New saplings will fill the gap left by the giant, but because they are so slow to mature kauri are little planted elsewhere. The exotic radiata pine can mature enough to provide plank timber in forty years, and now forms the major product and building material from New Zealand forests and woodlands. If permitted, however, kauri will eventually dominate all other trees in this northern sub-tropical rain forest, rising slowly, majestically above the thick undergrowth of tawa, ponga, and fern, perhaps for a hundred feet without a branch.

Steeped in the history of this Northland, we basked in its glorious sunlight. It was January, the antipodean midsummer, the air sweet after torrents of rain, as we drove north. The lovely hill-girt bay of Whangaroa enticed us, where the massacre of the crew of the *Boyd* had taken place. But the few Maoris we passed all smiled and waved – like every good countryman. On and on, north, by narrowing roads, to the very land's end, much of the land near sea-level, but as yet unsettled, though burnt of all tree cover.

At Houhora we put up at the hostelry which called itself the most northerly hotel in New Zealand. The staff consisted of two handsome Maori girls named Kate and Maggie, who told us that the mullet were fairly leaping at hook or into net. But we stared instead at the welcome swallows, the charming wax-eye warblers in the hibiscus, the stilts and reef herons and black swans in the great empty harbour. I was still obsessed with the Maori legends and more recent history, and wondered at the huge change which had overtaken these golden-skinned people, whose sharp and perfect teeth had not so many generations ago dug appreciatively into human flesh. I remembered the insatiable blind wife of Hongi, Turi the cannibal . . . this was her country!

At Te Hapua, one of the last communities at the end of the peninsula, is a magnificent ornamented Maori meeting house, with a double tower. As we approached, a posse of swarthy Maori shepherds rode down upon us with their dogs, a magnificent sight, and I should not have been surprised if they had thrust out their tongues and uttered the Ngapuhi war-chant. They swept past, intent on their work, ignoring the pale-faced tourists. We gained the next hill, where the road ended, and saw the great strand of Parengarenga, mile after mile of dazzling silver sands, from which the glass-making industry of Auckland derives its raw material.

On now to Cape Reinga, through an open, burnt land of low hills, here and there heavy modern earth-moving machinery carving away slopes, flattening and opening the hummocky land for settlers – not necessarily Maori, for there are many British and European settlers anxious to take up land here. Much of this country is red soil, that which by Maori legend was used to make Hine-ahu-one, the first woman. You cannot do other than think of her and her lover and maker Tane, and

the other highest Maori gods as you approach Cape Reinga, for here
the Dawn-Maid, Daughter of Tane and Hine, retreated to live in the
ocean, and became the Great Lady of Darkness.

Passing through this desert of kanuka (*Leptospermum ericoides*),
close relative of common manuka (*L. scoparium*), and burnt gorse and
bracken, we gazed at last upon Spirits Bay, where the soul of each Maori
takes a last drink at the sacred stream in the cave under the lovely
pohutukawa tree before gliding into the arms of the Great Lady of
Darkness. On to Cape Reinga where the Tasman and the Pacific meet
and strive for mastery. Although it was windless when we arrived,
a strong current rippled over the reefs below the little lighthouse tower,
giving just that impression of confusion. Thirty miles to the north lay
the jagged peaks of the Three Kings Islands, on which rested skeins of
summer mist. In between were black patches of shoaling fish. To the
west of us were the richly glowing golden sands of Cape Maria van
Diemen, so named by Tasman in 1642, a lovely empty land whose slopes
were feathered with the white tufts of toi-toi grass and flowering flax.

I remembered that Tasman had tried to land on the Three Kings, but
had been prevented by hostile Maoris. This land had then been alive
with people, even to those distant barren islands in the fertile sea. Now
it is quite empty, thousands and thousands of acres, exhausted, burned,
waiting – for what?

I had hardly written these words when I heard that 1,687 acres of
this headland have been declared a scenic reserve. An excellent
beginning.

4 South Island Shepherd

Ao-tea-roa, Land of the Long White Cloud. When, like the earliest Maori visitors who named it, I first sailed to New Zealand, I saw the long, high skyline of the South Island Alps, misty-white with distant snow and cloud. The RMS *Rangitoto* was entering Cook Strait on a perfect summer morning. At her rail beside me was a young English family who were going to settle permanently. The awe and excitement of approaching a new promised land after a long sea voyage was mine; and I could see great hope and delight in the sparkling eyes of my fellow voyagers. I could picture the same wonder, mixed with little fears, which must have been in the hearts and minds of those early pioneers: first the Maori wanderers who fortuitously discovered the virgin land over a thousand years ago; then the Pakeha emigrants, who, driven by the same economic urge to find room and prosper, arrived here by design barely one hundred years ago.

The Maoris coveted the North Island, for its better climate and sub-tropical warmth, more in keeping with their tropical Hawaiki. They fought the Pakeha who settled there, bravely with inferior weapons, and killed – and sometimes ate – many whites in the war to possess land before they were defeated and driven to compromise or flee to the interior. Meanwhile the South Island, with a climate very like that of the best of England, was virtually uninhabited save in the north part. A vast plain lay along the south-east coast, covered with coarse grass, from which the moas had but lately vanished and their Maori extermi-nators nearly so. These lands, to be dubbed the Canterbury Plain, were fertile, and called to the genuine farmers among the young men with families who were unable to obtain farms at home, and the young, unmarried, adventurous sons of English and Scottish squires and yeomen whose parents could afford to send them abroad. Thus some of the best British blood sailed out to the South Island when, in 1848, a Canterbury Association was formed to colonise land in the neighbourhood of what was to become Christchurch.

The Canterbury Association was brought into being by a disciple of Edward Gibbon Wakefield, from whose New Zealand Company the 2½ million acres were to be bought at 10 shillings an acre and sold to selected settlers at £3 an acre. The profit was to meet 'the expenses of the Association for emigration, educational and ecclesiastical purposes'. Four ships sailed out of Plymouth, England, in September 1850, carrying the new Canterbury pilgrims in *Charlotte Jane*, *Cressy*, *Randolph* and *Sir George Seymour*. They arrived three months later at Lyttelton, then known as Port Cooper. The emigrants settled down remarkably well; most of them were of stern Puritan stock. They founded a cosy, homely town, with shops, schools and a newspaper. They dressed well; they danced decorously; and established modest farms of fifty to a hundred acres around the future Christchurch, on which they grew wheat and milked cows. Oxen were used to plough and for general draught purposes over the shingly surface of the alluvial plain.

A few years later the discovery of gold in the rivers of the south helped the Association to rapid prosperity. Although the best citizens frowned upon the drunken behaviour of the gold prospectors flowing through the town, they collected high prices for farm produce, horses, oxen and accommodation. Many were Australians who, whether in search of gold or land, or both, saw greater possibilities here in the rich well-watered grasslands of this plain compared with the drought-stricken lands of New South Wales. They saw that Canterbury could support double the number of sheep to the acre, and at the same time yield double the amount of wool per fleece. Moreover the land laws were such that, outside the Association's purchase in the rugged, unexplored hills inland, a settler could lease land for as little as a farthing an acre, with every prospect of buying it himself if sheep proved a sound financial proposition. Agriculture in those hills was not attempted; they were fit only for active sheep.

Samuel Butler was one of the early applicants for the mountain 'waste lands', when he landed in 1860; his story is a fascinating one as told in his book *A First Year in Canterbury Settlement*. In four years he had doubled his capital; then, tired of the eternal talk of sheep, returned to England and wrote his classic *Erewhon*, with scenes provided from his experience of hill country solitudes.

Still more fascinating is the story of some who remained, to found the present flourishing Canterbury families. One such was Charles Tripp, who landed at Lyttelton in 1854. He was the son of the Reverend Tripp, a Devon churchman whose father had married a Welsh woman, an Owen of the great house of Orielton, near Pembroke in Wales. Curiously enough I had myself bought Orielton a hundred years later (1954), and lived in its old manor for eight years, farming its walled demesne. During that time John, great grandson of the Devon parson and farming in New Zealand, came to look over ancestral Orielton, with a vague hope, as Charles had done in a moment of affluence eighty years before, of buying back what was left – 250 acres – of the once large estate of 11,000 acres. He could not afford it, but begged me to sell him the 250-year-old sundial engraved with the Owen name. In a rash moment – but at the time I had no intention of selling the estate – I said that if I ever did give up Orielton, I would present him with this handsome sundial to keep in the family. The mansion with its little park has since become a naturalists' field study centre; and I kept that rash promise – the old sundial now reposes on the lawn of John's home near Outram, South Island.

When Charles Tripp and his friend John Acland arrived in Canterbury they were bitterly disappointed to find that all the flat, ploughable country of the plains had already been taken up, though not necessarily occupied. Told that only wild pigs could survive in the rolling hills beyond, which soared to the snows of the distant Alps, the young men, disbelieving, took horse over the windy treeless plateau. They crossed glacier-fed streams and flooding rivers, and penetrated the rugged country around Mount Peel, Mount Harper, and the lakes which now bear their names. They were looking for a block of 115,000 acres which they had already applied for – blindly on a map – unsurveyed land vaguely but delightfully described in their application as 'Bounded on the north by the snowy mountains, and on the east by the Rangitata river, and on the south by the runs of the nearest settlers.'

As the crow flies this block of 180 square miles was barely fifty miles inland, but the explorers took many days to reach it, and three weeks to examine it sufficiently to plan the location of a homestead. They found it was covered with tough snowgrass tussock, flax, the horrible speargrass, and cabbage trees. They lived meanwhile on wild pig and tame native birds such as quail and weka. With immense enthusiasm they discussed its possibilities, and at night slept by a camp fire under the stars.

Like the aborigine the Maori was expert in burning the forest and scrub carefully, clearing a small plot and firing only as much of the bush as was required for immediate cultivation. He knew that undisciplined fire could dry out the land and cause erosion; it could even, as Samuel Butler reported, dry out swamps and send water, previously trapped by vegetation, rushing towards the sea with valuable topsoil. But Tripp and Acland had decided that, as the weather was dry, they would burn as much as possible of the land they were to farm, in the expectation of new tender grass growth for the flocks they dreamed of possessing. The enormous fires which resulted were such that the explorers could read fine print a mile away at night! All ground life that could not take refuge in damp gullies must have been trapped and burnt alive, including flightless native birds; the feeble winged quail, once abundant, was burnt with her running brood; and many a Captain-Cooker must have been roasted.

The young colonists returned to Christchurch, amended the boundaries on their land claim forms, and gathered the bullock team and dray which were essential to carry stores and equipment over open country. They set out to create a sheep station on the chosen site near Mount Peel. First they built a shack by erecting a palisade of cabbage tree trunks, and filling the interstices with clay. The roof was a thatch of snow grass. The fireplace was modelled with wet clay, which hardened to a stone-like consistency. They still relied on wild pig for meat, hunting these with bulldogs which gripped the pig's ears until the hunter could come up and administer the *coup de grâce*. At least a dozen pigs were killed each week, nearly five thousand in five years.

The first sheep – merinos – were bought and driven about 75 miles from near Christchurch in fourteen days, crossing rivers with difficulty and loss, and requiring day and night vigil to keep them from straying.

The flocks increased with more purchases and natural breeding. Wool was making a good price in London. In 1861, Tripp and Acland, both now married, dissolved partnership by mutual agreement, and divided the holdings by a very fair method: Tripp separated the runs into two parts, allotting good and poor country to each; Acland was then invited to choose one or the other. He decided to keep the original homestead at Mount Peel; Tripp moved to Mount Somers. They were near enough for the new settler, Samuel Butler, at his station called Mesopotamia, to ride down the Rangitata river for a social call, when he would play the piano and try to convert them to his atheistic views. The Tripps enjoyed his visits, he was entertaining and could talk of other things than sheep; he thought for instance that the Maori custom of robbing anyone of their goods if they had had an avoidable misfortune was sound – as it meant that the sufferer would be more careful in future; and from his knowledge of this custom arose the Butlerian concept in *Erewhon* of punishing anyone who became ill. Butler liked to chaff and tease people, and delighted in shocking the prim Victorianism of Mrs Charles Tripp, who was the daughter of the first Bishop of Canterbury, New Zealand.

The sheep were still enjoying virtually virgin country, retreating to the tops in summer, and as yet the mountains were not overstocked. The incessant burning had encouraged much erosion, however. But land values were rising rapidly. Charles, who had trained as a barrister at home, decided to return with the small fortune he had made and buy Orielton. His father had been trying to claim, by right of descent, the title of Baronet bestowed earlier upon the Owen family of his wife. Charles sold his high country sheep run for £30,000 in 1863, to the amazement of his disbelieving old, and now blind, father. But Charles found conditions in England too stifling, the claim to the baronetcy was disallowed, and he failed to buy the Orielton estate. He returned to Christchurch, but life in the budding city there was not to his taste. Restless to be pioneering again, he bought back his run for £35,000, two years after selling it. He settled down happily once more, to improve the station and buy more land on which to place his sons and grandchildren. In one transaction he paid £40,000 for 18,000 acres of freehold. His flock numbered 40,000. He borrowed heavily, paying 8 per cent interest. Always on the look out for the newest methods, forever inventing and pioneering, he overploughed land better left in native grass.

Nevertheless he was a good farmer, as understood at that time. He never allowed gorse, imported and used as hedges elsewhere, to cover his land. He fought it, as he fought the arrival of the rabbit. He was one of the first to use wire to make paddock fences, which were to alter the whole system of sheep farming. Hitherto there had been only a few small wooden-rail fences around the homestead and the woolsheds, to contain sheep and cattle when mustered. He had an eye for a good man and used to go down to the ships as they arrived from England and Scotland and hire the best of the Highland shepherds. Straight from the open moors of Scotland these men were the best musterers of the high country which Tripp occupied. For centuries they had been accustomed to spending days and nights on the unfenced hills, often with only their tartan plaid to keep them warm in cave, hut or by camp fire.

Before the advent of the wire fence the system on Tripp's run was typical of the mid-nineteenth-century era of shepherding. Skilled musterers, each with his own dogs, worked in gangs under the leading shepherd. On every fine day (perhaps one in three in the mountains) they skirmished afoot in long lines across the hills and gulleys, carrying their manuka stick, each in sight of the next and up to a mile apart, their dogs running under strict control between. Sheep could only be gathered with the aid of two classes of highly trained dogs: several 'huntaway' dogs drove the sheep forward with noisy barking; and a few silent 'heading' dogs, released at intervals, would pull back a mob of sheep straying too far ahead. Great care was necessary to prevent mobs funnelling too fast into narrow gulleys, for if one fell along the narrow path others would be forced by those behind against the casualty, and soon the gulley would be piled high with scores of struggling suffocating sheep. Twelve hundred sheep were lost in one day in 1875 in a gulley at Mount Peel.

At night the gathered merinos were brought to a large enclosure close to one of the huts, where the musterers would sleep in their swag bags after a meal prepared by the cook. The latter, known as the packman, had the duty each fine morning of loading food and sleeping gear on pack horses or mules, and moving on to the next rendezvous on the mustering schedule. If no fold existed at any overnight stop the shepherds took turns, biblical fashion, to watch their flocks by night. On many foggy days the musterers would sleep in the hut and yarn away the time, boasting especially about their dogs, aware that until the sheep were all gathered to the woolshed their day's pay was secure, work or no work.

But each year now the new extensive wire fences reduced the demand for free-ranging shepherds. The runs were divided and sub-divided into paddocks, making it so much easier for the sheep-owner to handle his flocks himself. Meanwhile, with the rise in sheep numbers to ten million by 1871, the price of wool fell disastrously. Soon no one wanted to buy sheep, even for stocking new pastures. Lambs became virtually unsaleable in Canterbury. Many were driven to the nearest gorge, their throats slit, and the carcases flung over the cliff. The keas, or mountain parrots, already accused of killing sheep by tearing through the wool of the back and devouring the fat and kidneys, were presented with an unlimited feast of flesh.

After the slump, when prices rose again, the runholders cursed the keas once more and put a bounty on their head.

Now a new hazard appeared to trouble the sheep farmers. Rabbits from Europe had been brought to New Zealand from time to time, from 1838 onwards. In 1864 there were deliberate releases of wild rabbits near Invercargill and elsewhere in the south. The liberations had terrible consequences for New Zealand; but it may be fair to say that those who released them may have thought that the rabbit would be – as in England – no more than a sporting addition to a country notably devoid of small game animals, that it would never rise to pest proportions. This was nevertheless poor reasoning in a country of pastoralists, for already at that time rabbits were giving trouble in Australia; and there were no dingoes, eagles or other predators (save man and the wild pig) to help control numbers in New Zealand.

In twelve years, with no real natural enemies to oppose them, the rabbits had marched far north towards Cook Strait, poisoning the land with their dung and urine as they devoured the grass to the very roots. A Rabbit Nuisance Act was passed in 1876. It had no effect. The burrowing colonists flocked to freshly burned pastures, newly reseeded for sheep, and ate the green blades before they were toughened enough for sheep-grazing. They riddled the dry hills with their burrows, finding ideal shelter under a thatch of tussock clumps. The Government was implored to import stoats, weasels and ferrets; and in a panic obeyed.

Charles Tripp first saw rabbits at his home of Orari Gorge in 1878. In 1881 he killed 400 in one grand hunt. Alarmed for the future of his flock, he advocated rabbit-proof netting fences across the South Island, near his station, to arrest the northward march. Some were built, but they were comparatively ineffective when snow, landslips and river floods breached them. The great Tripp fence across the South Island, 170 miles long and costing £20,400, was never completed. The rabbits were checked but their advance guard had already broken through and in another decade were reported from every dry corner of both South and North Islands.

The Government, supported by the new acclimatisation societies, meanwhile continued blindly, blithely, to introduce all kinds of alien animals. Believing that ferrets, stoats and weasels would ultimately control rabbits, they set about importing, breeding and releasing these on a large scale. Charles Tripp was one of those who argued against the introduction of ferrets and other mustelids, as he wanted to save the flightless weka (a large rail) from their attacks because this tough bird was known to kill young rabbits and grown rats. So he turned out cats instead.

'I do not know,' wrote Samuel Butler in 1860 as he carried a cat on the pommel of his saddle as he rode to his new home of Mesopotamia, far in the 'snowy mountains', up country from Charles Tripp, 'how it is, but men here are much fonder of cats than they are at home.' His cat devoured the little Polynesian rats which scavenged his table crumbs, and helped to exterminate the native quail; and now the quail were quickly finished off by the mustelids, and bush fires. But his cat seems to have avoided the weka (known to him as the woodhen), a bird which he found to be 'an arrant thief, and will steal anything. It is exceedingly bold and will come right into the house . . . one was seen to take up a gold watch and run off with it.'

For thirty years Charles Tripp wrote, and kept copies of, voluminous letters to many correspondents, at the rate of some 1,200 to 1,500 a year, between 1867 and 1897; and it is from these that we gather much valuable information incidental to our story. In 1873 he was writing to a friend about the successful introduction of pheasants, rooks and other birds, and of salmon spawn and 'Thames' trout. Like Butler he found the native wild life of Canterbury mostly rare and vanishing, and wished to surround himself with those creatures and plants which had charmed him in his native England.

In 1895 came a terrible disaster. Snow had been an occasional hazard – as for instance in 1876, and in 1887. After heavy falls the merino sheep had to be extracted from their natural 'camps', where they lay up at night on high ground. They could live for weeks under snow, without food. Shepherds were accustomed to 'snow-rake' sheep, by digging them out of sunless drifts, where a thaw was unlikely, and bring them to sloping, broken, sun-facing ground. A path had to be laboriously cut, or tramped through the snow, to enable them to travel. In 1895 snow fell heavily and repeatedly in June and July, surging over the north-facing (sunwards) ridges and smothering the sheep on the leeward side. The following frost was intense. Rabbits, deer, dogs, birds died by the thousand; and men suffered frostbite. It was estimated that three-quarters of a million sheep were smothered in the South

Island, and twelve thousand of these were Tripp's. It happened to be a year of the lowest prices for wool and lambs.

Already deep in debt, Charles Tripp was now told by his bank that, with his lease having only eight years to run, they must take over the land, as there seemed no prospect of his making a financial recovery. In this desperate hour Charles's son Bernard went to Wellington and boldly entered the Prime Minister's office, having failed to get his own MP to fix an appointment. Taken by surprise, Premier Seddon ('King Dick') listened carefully and promised help. This took the form of a special Pastoral Tenant's Relief Bill which was rushed through Parliament, enabling those who had lost heavily in the Great Snow of 1895 to be given remission of rent or extension of lease. Fortunately, as sheep were down to a shilling or two apiece, the Tripps found restocking an inexpensive operation.

Charles Tripp died in his seventy-second year. His sons carried on the station, but needed to raise capital by selling 27,000 acres to a land-hungry government, which divided the purchase into five pastoral runs and nineteen small farms. But many of these proved to be totally uneconomic to work, so badly was the division made between good and bad ground.

Meanwhile the rabbits had recovered from the snow, and were again devouring the best of the pasture.

Inspired by the high country adventures of his forebears, John Tripp, great nephew of the pioneer Charles, came out from Devon to learn the ways of fine-wool sheep at Orari Gorge. He eventually took a run in partnership with Bernard and Jack Tripp on the north bank of the Waitaki river at Hakataramea. Once again prices were at rock bottom, and the young men learned their shepherding the hard way. How hard it was, I learned, when one day John arrived at Orielton. He wanted to show the ancestral home of the Tripp and Owen families to his charming wife Nan, and young son and daughter. This was for them a holiday with a purpose, like that of their great-uncle Charles, to see Britain, think about living here, possibly at Orielton.

'You see,' said John, 'all our eggs were in one basket – Corriedale wool, which was then, in the slump years of the 1930's, down to a low average price of fourpence a pound. [Today it is nearer four shillings a pound.] We were terribly plagued with rabbits. On my 8,000 acres I killed 82,000 rabbits in one year! As eight rabbits eat or destroy as much grass as one sheep needs, the rabbits were taking the food from more than a thousand sheep! After twenty years of interesting but financially hopeless wool-farming of the high country, Fate had one final blow in store for us. A huge hydro-electric dam was planned – and built – on our land, flooding our only valuable flat of 600 acres, where all our buildings were. As the property was leasehold, very little compensation was payable.'

The four Tripps looked marvellously fit and sunburnt as we talked over a cup of tea on the croquet lawn, where stood the pedestal holding the 250-year-old sundial engraved with the Owen names, a beautiful bronze plaque. (In sunlight this dial also told the hours of noon at a dozen places around the world which in the early 1700's were remote trading posts, before Cook had rediscovered New Zealand. This was the moment when I rashly promised John Tripp he should have this sundial if ever I gave up Orielton, as already mentioned.)

On being forced out of his High Country run by flooding, John Tripp explained, he looked around for some inexpensive land on lower ground, and eventually secured 1,600 acres of undeveloped freehold scrub-covered hill west of Dunedin. It looked poor, it had not been scientifically developed; but ever an experimentalist at heart, and having a wife who loved the outdoor life and rode her own horse and trained her own sheepdogs, he saw its possibilities. About half of it was too steep to plough; but the rest might grow seed crops. He saw that, with the new practice of sowing fertiliser and grass and clover from the air, hill farmers would soon require tons of these seeds. And he wanted to avoid having all his eggs and resources in one basket – wool.

After experimenting with different fertiliser, he found that basic slag was the only one to give rewarding results. The Department of Agriculture considered this must be due to some trace element in the slag; and trial plots of vanadium, molybdenum and tungsten were laid down at the new farm of Dunkery Downs. Molybdenum proved to be the

The attractive whistling frog, an introduction from Australia

The tuatara, with its rudimentary third eye on the forehead this reptile is among the most primitive of living creatures

Three introductions

The opossum, brought in
from Australia

The European hedgehog

The red deer introduced
from Britain. With its lor
reach, this is one of the
most destructive of
browsers and has done
much to strip the high la
of its protective vegetati

miracle worker – at the infinitesimal rate of two ounces per acre.

A very small amount of pure molybdenum was mixed with water and sprinkled on a plot of grass at this low rate (large amounts of trace elements are known to cause serious damage to grazing animals). Before the application the grass had looked yellow and sickly. In a short time the clover appeared, rich emerald green; and for four years afterwards even the footprints of a man who had accidentally walked across untreated ground after watering the molybdenum plot remained clovery green.

The secret of farming this hill country was plain – molybdenum. In scientific terms, the clover John needed to enrich his paddocks cannot live without nitrogen, and the microbes which fix it from the air and live inside the clover nodules cannot complete their normal life cycle without the presence of molybdenum. The Dunkery downland was obviously lacking in this one ingredient, as other soils elsewhere in New Zealand and the world over have since been proved to require this or other trace elements.

These trials of molybdenum were the first really successful ones in New Zealand, and during the next few years John Tripp proved that two ounces mixed with two hundredweight of superphosphate per acre as a top-dressing lasted for four years before the next application was advisable. 'To have had even a little toe in this pie has given us a great kick,' concluded John, 'especially as much of New Zealand's second and third class land has also benefited.'

Turning to his wife he waved his hand towards the massive Georgian front of Orielton House and said, 'Nan, how would you like it if we bought back the ancestral home? Could you live in it?'

'Could we afford it? Ronald Lockley says he can't, but somehow does, with early potatoes and a Jersey milking herd – concentrated farming. I think you'd like that, John,' was her reply. 'It's very beautiful here, these tall trees and old parkland, and ancient woods. These huge beeches shut you in . . . we'd miss the rolling hills and the wide open country. But I'd swap homes for one year – just for the fun of it.'

I saw why Nan Tripp would not change when I stayed at Dunkery Downs years later. After seventeen years of making a home John and

7

Nan had one as gracious, if not as vast and mouldering, as Orielton. A house carefully built of native timber, with wide picture windows framed with wisteria and clematis. In the garden a lily pool, rose walk and fruit orchard. The children had both lately married, and now John worked the whole 1,600 acres alone with one man; while Nan still rode after the sheep. 150 acres of Montgomery clover seed bring in a useful revenue, and have paid for a special header (combine harvester) costing £3,500, as well as £500 spent annually on dividing up paddocks with new fences. But main revenue continues to be from sheep. The original 800 have grown to about 4,000, the wool per sheep has doubled from 5½ to 11 lbs a fleece, and lambing success has crept up to 115 per cent. So the farm output has increased about tenfold; all due, John declared modestly – forgetting their own labour of love – to a few ounces of a trace element.

Here and there on the farm only a few pockets of the original forest have been left. Nostalgically, New Zealanders love their 'bush', their native trees, now that many of these have been reduced to vanishing point through intensive farming, burning and overstocking. In the early summer mornings at Dunkery Downs we went out over the dew-wet paddocks to listen to the liquid songs of the bell-birds, far-off, from thinly wooded gulleys. 'When we first came,' said John, 'we could hear a tremendous chorus: a dozen of them would be singing in a row, each ringing its own peal of seven bells. Like Captain Cook heard it in the Marlborough Sounds. It was marvellous – but today you don't get anything like the effect. I'm saving that bit of bush there, just for the sake of the remaining bellbirds.'

The man who for much of his life has managed one of the largest and highest sheep stations, Mount Possession, happens to be my wife's cousin. His son Rob has recently taken over the station, so enabling his parents to retire. We found the father Sam Chaffey and his wife Lesley at home at Aotea, a lowland farm in kindlier country, inland from Blenheim, in the north of the South Island. Singlehanded, sixtyish, the Chaffeys content themselves with a mere 7,000 acres and 'just a handful of stock' – 2,500 merinos and 100 cross-Angus cattle. This left them, Sam added cheerfully, characteristically, but quite without boasting, a lot of spare time in which to enjoy sailing in Queen Charlotte Sound.

Sam is typical of all that is finest in New Zealanders who have been brought up to earn a living in the tough conditions of shepherding the high country: long days in the saddle, sleeping rough at nights, physically poised to enjoy both work and play to the full. I soon saw why he was content to leave the edge of the snows for this delightful new home in the foothills by the canyon of the Awatere river. As we drove across the green meadow to Aotea House, quails and hares ran over the track, and oystercatchers piped overhead, their young chicks feeding near the river bed. Tuis and bellbirds were rifling the nectar from the abundant fuchsias and other flowers around the verandah. Goldfinches, chaffinches and greenfinches sang in the spring sunshine, and there were many blackbirds, thrushes and starlings (one pair had a nest in the large post-box at the entrance gate). In the whole of New Zealand I never saw a place I liked more than Aotea, to live in forever.

Perhaps because of the fine weather and the springtime, this 'little' station seemed bursting with wildlife. A falcon, now scarce in New Zealand, swooped with lightning speed upon a starling which had been in chuckling song on the roof of the house. Cuckoos whistled in the pines which shielded the house, planted by a former owner. Fantail warblers and bush robins entered the rooms, to hunt for flies and moths. All around the tumbled hill country is well supplied with red deer, wild pig, goat, opossum; animals which the shepherds hunted for food and fur. And on the high ground, under the distant snows of the Spenser and Kaikoura Ranges, there are chamois in plenty.

'Big game country,' commented Sam, 'but life at Aotea is soft. We ride less, drive the car instead.' As we bumped over winding bulldozed tracks, to examine pockets of ground reclaimed from manuka by tractor discing, after burning, and now newly sown with phosphate, grass and clover mixture from the air, he compared his former hard but exhilarating life at Mount Possession with his present smooth existence.

'It's summer here. But I heard from Rob today that there's been a heavy fall of snow at Mount Possession. These November snows soon melt away, and anyway the sheep haven't yet got to the tops – they're safe on the lower slopes. It's the July and August snows are the killers.'

I ventured to remark on the huge erosion cracks and bleeding soil we had seen yesterday on passing the naked brown Seaward Kaikoura Ranges.

'People,' said Sam with that compassionate smile for which he is well known, 'are erosion mad. Got it on the brain. Geologists love it – it's just what they adore to see. Stones and soil visibly on the move, talking aloud, talking point by which the soil conservation boys justify their salaries. Writers like you are stimulated into lyrical papers by it. Farmers curse it. You must read Guthrie-Smith – he wrote a book about it. I've lived with it all my life. Taking the long view, it's been the farmer's best friend. Without erosion there'd be no Canterbury Plain, only a steep volcanic cliff going plumb down into the deep blue Pacific, down to the haunts of cod and snapper and crawfish. Yet people talk as if there'd never been erosion before white men arrived. Why, it's been going on every day, every hour, every minute for a hundred million years. It's the law of gravity – same as enables me to lie flat in bed while my bath water runs down the pipe, or this car to coast downhill. As a runholder all my life, mustering sheep over the 200,000 acres of Mount Possession high country, I've seen some grand examples of erosion – avalanches, moving mountains, vast surges of gravel to the sea when the great rains come. But I'm not denying that man hasn't accelerated the process by introducing deer, goat, chamois and thar to eat the high tops bare. And some shepherds will overstock their runs.'

Mount Possession today is somewhat smaller than when Sam first managed it. His son Rob has control of nearly 140 square miles of this toughest of stations around the headquarters of the South Ashburton river – not so far from Butler's Mesopotamia. Due to the rapid denudation of the alpine chain this river has become more and more violently destructive, in spate sweeping eastwards masses of shingle and loess, overwhelming the lower richer pastures, smashing bridges, smothering roads, even toppling houses.

At a conference of experts attending a field demonstration at Mount Possession there were fierce arguments as to what might be done to reclothe the naked mountains with vegetation which might arrest further slips. One of the problems of high country is that the merinos, like their cousins the chamois, thar and goat, are seasonal conservators of their hill grazing. They dislike the coarse feed of the lower land. They move up in spring to nibble the sweet new growth released by the melting of the snows, until they reach, by midsummer, the limits of vegetation. Far below them the ungrazed grass grows into a foggy state in the valleys, forming a natural hay *in situ*. To this the merinos will return only when winter forces them to descend for shelter and sustenance. The merinos of these high solitudes are almost as wild as the deer, chamois and thar, fleeing in panic at the sight of man. The only difference in fact is in a degree of inherited domestication which enables them to be rounded up by a good team of dogs – and it has to be a good team – directed by a skilled musterer. A proportion may never be rounded up, remaining unshorn for another year, or for life, as 'woollies', quite wild and free.

At the conference, then, the traditionalists argued that to secure young growth it was essential to burn old tussock; and that fencing mountain country, even if subsidized by the government, was futile, far too costly in materials, labour and maintenance; and, besides, snow damage was severe each winter, and sheep simply walked over fences when snowdrifts covered them.

The Catchment Officers wished to fence newly eroded country, subsidising the cost to the runholder on a two to three basis. Until the vegetative cover has regrown, slopes would not be grazed, and then only lightly. The development of a thick sward of natural reseeded turf is a proved check to severe runoff and erosion. (I have seen this in Wales where a strip of mountainside had been burned bare of its peaty carpet and had slipped away downhill after one violent rainstorm. But each side of the slip the thick unburned carpet of natural vegetation had retained its firm grip on the stone and rock beneath. Later the sun burned the bared surface bone dry, but the natural turf each side still remained green and moist, collecting the night dews like a sponge.)

It was argued that the 23,000 sheep on the 108,100 acres of Mount

Possession worked out at only one sheep to five acres. But could this thin, cold, high country support anything more profitable? Someone at the conference mentioned deer-farming; but there were tolerant smiles at this, for one deer needs (so someone declared) fifty mountain acres to maintain itself. Merinos are the most economical of grazers, if properly managed. They do not breed fast, are not allowed to lamb until they are four-toothed (two to three years old), and then only enough ewes go to the rams – for $4\frac{1}{2}$ weeks – to provide replacements. Ram lambs are castrated at one month old at Mount Possession. A number of strong wethers are saved which, living on for as long as their wool yield is profitable, become the natural flock leaders, knowing the ranges and wise to guide the ewes to shelter in storm and snow.

What about reafforestation? A government forester to whom I spoke after leaving Aotea said forcefully: 'Clear the tops of all stock. Let the natural flora regrow. It should not ever be grazed again – for it never was grazed by mammal until the Pakeha arrived. Lower down, where trees will grow, plant this sick, naked land with economic species, chiefly the exotic pines. They grow rapidly in New Zealand. They produce pulp, paper and plank within thirty years – an industry with a tremendous potential – far more lucrative in the end than the merino. But we in the Forest Service have to fight the men in the Lands Department, who are dunned by the sheep men demanding more pastoral leases. It's a desperate struggle between those who believe that the high country must be saved by reafforestation, and as the playground of the hunter and tourist, and those who prefer overstocking and erosion by the cloven hoof!'

And meanwhile what of the shepherds in possession, whose livelihood is no less important? Rob Chaffey's remarks at the conference at Mount Possession were as sound and as practical as any. He proposed, on behalf of the New Zealand and Australian Land Company, for whom he manages the station, to continue his father's policy of planting shelter belts across the bare valley floors, where trees are most likely to survive and thrive. This has checked erosion and allowed grass and clover to grow, and fix nitrogen. In due course full-scale cultivations can take place on what are now unpalatable, coarse valleys. There would be a strong programme of sweetening the run with aerially sown super-phosphates containing the necessary trace elements. In short, begin at base, improving the mountain from the bottom upwards, rather than from the top downwards.

5 North Island Pioneers

Now that the excitements of the tribal (stone-age period) and racial (Pakeha musket period) wars were over, the depleted exhausted Maori people settled down to an uninspiring life of peace on the land. They now had a wonderful new selection of European vegetable and animal foods, which could be grown at home, or bought at the price of their labour. Some started livestock breeding in a small way, but far more took up jobs on Pakeha sheep and cattle farms, rode horses for the first time, and gained experience of European methods of land management. But very few were able to expand their individual farming efforts, even with the requisite knowledge gained. Any development of Maori land required the consent of all the members of the tribe, owing to collective family or tribal ownership.

The endless discussions at the marae usually resulted in stalemate. Some of the shareholders would be sure to object, often because of an old feud or unsatisfied utu, to the applicant who wanted to use some of the land to farm for himself. Even if a majority consented, the Maori who farmed the land would be expected to pay its profits over to each shareholder in proportion to his inherited interest in the property. There was absolutely no incentive to farm on the scale of the Pakeha, and every reason why the landholding Maori should continue to subsist thinly on the produce of long established smallholdings and tillage gardens, leaving the rest of the ancestral land in bush for the hunting of birds and introduced wild animals, such as wild pig, rabbit, opossum.

Yet money was needed to buy the guns which were so much more efficient than the stone-age snares and lances for hunting; to buy cloth of wool and cotton instead of laboriously weaving garments from flax and wild bird feathers; to buy European food, and enjoy beer and spirits which were new pleasures to enliven the dull life of peace. Such money could only be acquired by selling labour, timber, flax (rapidly falling in value), and land. The individual could benefit himself by working for a wage; but if he sold land, or timber from that land, the money had to be shared equally between the numerous tribal owners, and therefore usually in small amounts. None of the recipients had any thought of joining together to invest the proceeds in buying more land, or in replanting the forest. Such a plan was beyond their experience: hitherto land and forests could only be gained by right of inheritance, or by might of war. Crushed by the steam-rollering onset of the Pakeha civilisation, which had finally outlawed their reliance on war, the vigorous culture of the Maori now lay in ruins. It is not surprising that many had sold or leased land invalidly – by individual contracts later repudiated by the tribe. To live they had to sell something, anything; to survive as a nation they needed to keep and work the land.

The Pakeha settler in the warmer North Island had borne the brunt of the fighting, and casualties in the land wars, as well as much responsibility for them, because, as we have seen, the Maori people were more numerous here than in the cooler South Island, and had closely occupied all the land or, if not physically in possession, claimed all as tribal property. This was the main stumbling block to the white settlers' progress; even when he thought he had bought or leased land he discovered all too often that his title was suspect. But nothing seemed to dampen the ardour of those early colonists. In his full and fascinating account of his sheep station *Tutira*, in Hawke's Bay, H. Guthrie-Smith writes of 'the glories, the delights, the ecstasies of improvements, for there is no fascination in life like that of the amelioration of the surface of the earth. For a young man what an ideal existence! – to make a fortune by the delightful labour of your hands – to drain your swamps, to cut tracks over your hills, to fence, to split, to build, to sow seed, to watch your flock increase – to note a countryside change under your hands from a wilderness, to read history in your merino's eyes. How pastoral! How Arcadian! I declare that in those times to think of an improvement to the station was to be in love. It was a joy to wake, to spring out of your bunk half dressed already – there wasn't a nightshirt north of Napier then – to glance through the whare's open door at the clear innumerable hosts of stars, in the huge fireplace to open up the warm cone of soft grey ash piled carefully overnight, to push into its heart of glowing red the dry kindling, to see the brief smoke ascend, to hear the crackle of the rapid flames. Oh, those were happy days, with no cares, no fears for the future, no burden of personal possession, when every thought was for the run, when every penny that could be scraped together was to be spent on the adornment of that heavenly mistress.'

When he expressed so articulately the joyful thoughts of young farming pioneers the world over, Guthrie-Smith was taking over in 1882 some 61,140 acres of 'derelict' fern and bush from two brothers who owed to a Loan Company £9,750 – the price paid by Guthrie-Smith and his partner A. M. Cunningham to get the brothers sufficiently out of debt to obtain possession themselves. We may follow the development of this typical North Island sheep station, where the terrain was so stubborn to accommodate the white man's dream, to yield to his furious energy, misapplied in ignorance of the requirements of its aeolian (wind-borne) pumice soils, in total inexperience of stock management. Tutira was part of a vast territory purchased about 1860 by the Government, but subsequently by a rough justice much of it restored to native block ownership. Tutira itself was claimed by forty of the Ngai-tatera tribe, who leased it in the first place for 21 years at £150 per annum, that is to say £3.15.0. was to be paid annually to each of the forty Maori signatories.

The first lessee, Newton, stocked it with 4,000 merino wethers in 1873. These were hastily mustered and driven towards Napier on news of the murdering raid of the outlaw Te Kooti upon Mohaka, a dozen miles or so away; thus, as Guthrie-Smith notes, saving them temporarily from the worse fate of the total mismanagement which followed. For Newton was to lose half his flock in two or three years: many died, trapped in bush or swamp; many went wild; many were chased to a standstill by

Maoris who, if they did not kill and eat them, sheared and carried off their wool. In 1875 Newton gave up; the Tutira lease was sold to Ed. Towgood for £5 – a fee meant to cover also any abandoned and wild sheep left on the run.

Tutira was again stocked with 4,000 merinos, and in 1877 was sold, complete with sheep and one hundred cattle to G. J. Merritt for £2,500, about the value of the stock. Almost immediately, in March 1878, Merritt sold to the Stuart brothers a one-half share in Tutira and 3,600 sheep for the same amount – £2,500; and later in the same year they took over the remaining half, probably by way of an existing mortgage, for no money is mentioned. During the enthusiastic care of the Stuarts and another partner Kiernan, who kept a diary, the first homestead was built, a weatherboard hut fifteen feet by twelve feet, for the bachelors.

Four years later the improvements made by the trio had cost them £9,000 in borrowed money. The merinos were totally unsuited to this low warm, barren, burnt-over country of soft hills thick, not with grass, but with fern and scrub. They died of lack of feed, of eating poisonous tutu berries when no other food was available, and many ran away forever. Prices and credit were very low. Kiernan's diary ends dismally with the words: 'Very miserable on account of bad news – no heart to do anything.'

But Guthrie-Smith and his partner, having paid £9,750 to purchase the lease and allegedly 10,500 sheep, and so clear the Stuarts of debt, fared little better at first. Only 7,000 sheep were mustered for shearing in the first season. Lungworm, footrot, poison weeds, brambles, and mysterious diseases (lack of certain trace elements, unknown at the time, was probably the main cause) took a heavy toll. When expensive rams from lush South Island pastures were brought in to improve the Tutira ewes they too sickened and died. The station was already sheep-sick, and the new pastures, laboriously sown after incorrect burning had devoured the humus layer, reverted almost at once to fern. Wool had slumped on the world market. Guthrie-Smith's partner was unable to stand the financial strain and was obliged to buy himself out of debt. He paid £100 into the Tutira account, and accepted a nominal five shillings from Guthrie-Smith for his half share of the derelict station.

Tutira was at rock bottom – 'things could not possibly be worse'. But there was enough patrimony available to save Guthrie-Smith from abandoning this stubborn land which he had grown to love. There was, however, no money to replace stock losses – fortunately as it turned out, since this meant that the surviving merinos, with lower stocking, had better grazing, and more time to grow into a station-bred acclimatised flock. When in 1886 wool rose by 2d a lb, a profit of £500 actually appeared on the books! T. J. Stuart, who had remained all along as a shepherd attached to Tutira, as to a wayward mistress, now bought back a half share. For the next twenty years Guthrie-Smith and the faithful Stuart lived 'a hard but glorious life on wild pig, wild beef, and gone-wild mutton, shot, dressed on the spot and packed into the homestead.'

During this time the lease was not allowed to expire: long before the end of its term it was twice exchanged for a new 21 years lease, in order to make improvements worthwhile. The rent to the Maori owners was of course doubled each time; and there were now, by sub-division of inherited shares, a couple of hundred cheerful Maori beneficiaries, many of whom were by nature impecunious, and would write in quaint English asking for cash advances from Guthrie-Smith. He thought the Maoris a fine race – 'I can find nothing but good to say of them. The [lease] system, however, was wrong – one party doing the work, the other holding power to evict without compensation for improvements.' At the end of 21 years, nevertheless, Guthrie-Smith renewed the lease a third time, having in 1903 bought out his partner's share, together with 32,000 sheep.

There had been many reverses, through mismanagement and times of slump. 'Lord, how delighted we were!' wrote Guthrie-Smith when, after a bitter slump, the price of lambs rose to 4 shillings a head. But more and more paddocks were created by fencing, each usually a hundred acres in extent, burned, stocked to crush the fern, then sown with grass. Often it was only the sweepings of local stores that were sown – better seed could not be afforded: grasses today despised by graziers, such as fog (*Holcus lanatus*), goose-grass (*Bromus mollis*), fescues and innumerable adventitious weeds, foxglove, vetch, suckling clover. Guthrie-Smith had a botanist's delight in watching the success or failure of every plant that germinated, even the thistles. The smiling Maoris were paid to march up and down the burned ground, throwing the indifferent seed with ancestral skill upon the promised land – which still belonged to their tribe.

In his book *Tutira*, Guthrie-Smith describes how the tremendous heavy rainfall at intervals over the heavily stocked, treeless run caused terrifying erosion, when the saturated sub and surface soils slipped downhill like snow sliding off a roof. After a violent 'buster' the edges of former slips ooze with clay, new red-raw wounds smear the green slopes, scalp-shaped patches detach themselves. Huge corrugations wrinkle and slide, smothering and smashing sheep struggling in mud. When the rains subside the waters still run under the porous soil, hidden rills which suck the soil and humus, and even rock, away downhill. There are no trees, no tree roots to bind the land any more. Yet at one time the land, the whole coast, was under forest. Present fires revealed the outlines of whole trees fallen to the ground and burned; and of deep roots charred to dust – and dangerous to man and horse as forming pits to trap the unwary foot and break it. Some of this ancient forest was still standing when Guthrie-Smith took over in 1882; a thousand acres of tall boles blackened by the fires of the Pakeha who had preceded him at Tutira. He believed that the North Island from hill-top to foreshore was once under forest, but that the Maoris, in their gradual assault on the bush from the time of their arrival, had steadily pushed the great trees farther inland each year.

Over a hundred years earlier Cook and Banks record seeing (October 1769) in Hawke's Bay '3 or 4 prodigiously pretty groves of tall trees;' also Banks notes that at night 'we were off Hawks bay and saw two monstrous fires inland on the hills: we are now inclined to think that these and most if not all the great smoaks and fires we have seen are made for the convenience of clearing land for tillage.' October was the time for planting the kumara.

Fire, destruction of humus, cutting away of river banks by the sharp hooves of hungry sheep, carrying away of topsoil; to these were added the occasional earthquake, and particularly the severe one of 1931, which did no more than throw Guthrie-Smith to the ground, but tore up his fences, overwhelmed a few sheep and cattle, and caused the death of 251 people in the near-by town of Napier.

The merinos were ultimately supplanted by the fine-woolled, dual purpose Romney Marsh sheep so popular in New Zealand today. The profit from these helped to clear Tutira of its debts, and enabled the purchase of two adjoining runs. A new homestead was built. But once again improvements had to be held up, because of leases running down past the half-way mark. And once more the Maori owners, now in their hundreds, were in dispute as to what course to take, and how much new rent could be demanded. The improved land was theirs by Government decree and could be had for the taking if the lessee refused to pay a quadrupled rent; the title, lease or freehold, had never been beyond dispute for the simple reason that some of the owners had consistently refused to sign any documents out of sheer 'wait-and-see' tactics. In reality the Maori freeholders had no intention of taking over and farming the land, even if they could all have agreed on such a plan; but they had taken to debate and litigation and paper battles as the next best amusement to the now forbidden war and cannibalism, and they could hardly lose. It was good sport. They were delighted when, with much difficulty and anxiety, Guthrie-Smith won a new lease of thirty years, after a Royal Commission enquiry.

Then came the first world war and service overseas for Guthrie-Smith. On his return to Tutira, a world slump. To gain capital, division of the land into sub-leases was necessary. Out of the original run he retained only 6,940 acres to live on 'in retirement' with his daughter. Botanising, bird-watching, writing, the sage of Tutira ended his days happily overseeing the beloved land around the Lake, watching his young neighbours make those same mistakes on that same land which he and earlier settlers had made, seeing them enjoy tough, long hours of work and want, which has built the character of New Zealanders.

Such was and still is the way of life of the New Zealand farmer, who may taste to the full the bleak sorrows and the sweet abiding joy of pioneering on the land.

As a memorial to the shepherd, naturalist, and writer, Lake Tutira is now a permanent nature reserve.

In *Tutira* Guthrie-Smith correctly forecast the continued division and sub-division of the great sheep stations of the last century, whose ranges seem vast today. In New Zealand there are only a few five- and very few six-figure acreage runs left, and these are chiefly in the least accessible parts and tougher conditions of the South Island high country. He envisaged the growing competition for land which would force prices up, and demand a much higher production per acre to meet both the higher rents and the better standard of living. Twenty years after his death the inevitable process is well advanced. The stripping of the last areas of native forest, outside the present Forest Reserves, in every area suitable for sheep or agriculture is being completed. He wrote, 'No farming, happily, can plane away cliffs or fill up gorges.' So far he has been right: these have remained the last stronghold of native birds. And, fortunately, many New Zealanders are beginning to understand the importance of these oases, and to cherish them for both economic and aesthetic reasons.

The Bay of Plenty farm at Te Ranga, where my daughter and her husband live, is a good example of the development from bush of a small North Island sheep run, having the characteristics of rolling hill land, rising to a thousand feet above sea level on light pumice soil (Kaharoa Ash Shower), and intersected, like Tutira, by deep gorges and shallower gulleys. Every one of its 350 acres has been won from well-grown North Island primary and secondary forest. Some of it, the homestead portion, is freehold; the rest is under the usual complicated Maori leasehold.

The Te Ranga story is worth telling here, as it is typical of how the young New Zealander or other settler can make his way to owning his own farm. To raise capital, John worked on his father's farm for wages, and later as a share-milker for five years. John also took over a distant block of partly improved bushland from his father, who had used his spare time and money (from dairying) in clearing and fencing a portion year by year, and putting down enough sheep to master the new-sown pasture. A keen share-milker, under the usual form of contract with the owner of the milking herd, receives 29 to 50 per cent of the milk cheque, a rent-free cottage and other perquisites, according to agreement, which enable him to save up to £750 a year – if he is thrifty and capable. He needs a hard-working partner, one who can take over singlehanded the fifty to a hundred milking cows if he is ill, who can drive a tractor and lorry, and yet keep the home and his meals under control. The happiest and least expensive way (at first) to do this is to marry the right girl!

In due course, some years after they had married, the opportunity came to buy a small farm next to the already mentioned bushland at Te Ranga. The price of land had already risen considerably in the area, but the State is able to help with long-term mortgage loans. They gave up the exacting work of the 'cow-cocky' for the present easier life of stock raising, and concentrated on breaking more bush each year.

In felling his selected acreage, where the contour allows, the bushman makes what is called a 'drive'. He chooses his line of doomed trees and chain-saws each nearly through, so as to fall in the one direction. Then the last tree at the top of the slope is sawn right through; it topples, striking the next, and the whole 'drive' goes down like a row of nine-pins. This saves both time and danger from trees kicking back. For convenience (of clearance later) sawing height is about two to three feet from the ground, except in the case of valuable timber, which is felled close to the ground, and extracted beforehand for sale to timber merchants. All else is burned.

Certain trees such as puketea *laurelia novae-zelandiae* will not burn easily. They are killed by the subsequent fire or left as they stand; they provide shade as long as they may – many will gradually die from exposure and windblast. These isolated sentinels are favourite look-out perches for kingfishers, which love to haunt the new clearings and dart down upon their prey – lizard, worm, frog, grasshopper, and insect. When making a nest-hole in the rotting wood of such a tree the New Zealand kingfisher does an amusing strip-cartoon act: it repeatedly flies like a dart at the selected spot, forcing its bill deep into the soft wood until it has cleared a hole large enough to sit in and work without the aid of its wings.

Sheep are New Zealand's wealth, but overgrazing has been, and is, a dangerous threat to the whole ecology

A Kaka perches on Robert Falla's he
on the island sanctuary of Kapiti

The Kea, or mountain parrot, displayi
the brilliant underwi

When thoroughly dry, the felled area is fired – at Te Ranga usually in February – it is hoped just before gentle rain. Grass and clover seeds, superphosphate with trace minerals, are sown immediately on the first calm day, aerially (since the use of a ground drill is impossible), the careful farmer following up with a bag or two of seed to scatter under logs where the plane-sown seed failed to penetrate.

Granted sufficient rain the seeds take well in the warm fertilised ashes; and so do numerous weeds, especially fireweed, inkweed, thistles, and blackberry. The new paddock is grazed lightly as soon as the clover is in its second trifoliate leaf, and judiciously at intervals later; control of fast-growing clover is desirable and the tillering of the grass encouraged. When, in a year or two, the tree stumps are beginning to decay, and the ground is not too steep, a bulldozer is called in to lever them out of the soil (hence the height of the cut above ground) and shovel the logs and rubbish into heaps for burning. By a system of hard grazing, alternating with periods of complete rest, the paddock gradually looks 'respectable' at last; that is to say the tall weeds disappear, and the green curves of the pastures please the shepherd's eye with their smooth fertile appearance; this stage usually takes five years, from bush.

Intensive management of reclaimed bush is annually putting up yields. The hill farms of the Bay of Plenty can now support five breeding ewes to the acre, producing 100 per cent lambs, and 10–11 lbs wool each. Thus a modest living for a young family can now be earned by proper management of about 1,100 breeding ewes and replacements, to which should be added the revenue from a certain number (say one beast to ten ewes) of cattle raised as stores. As grazers the two animals are complimentary. For these farmers the eggs are in two baskets: sales of wool, lambs and old ewes; and beef. The market may fluctuate, but in a world getting hungrier every day New Zealand stock farmers are more secure than most of us.

There is an abiding satisfaction in pioneering, as Guthrie-Smith so graphically described, a noble delight in trying to force two blades of grass to grow in place of one. It is not in man's nature to stand and stare too often – until he is too old to work any longer: then he may pause and ask himself if it was all worthwhile. But the young farmer

8

must be up and doing, scorning the old-fashioned ways of his parents, learning by their mistakes, eager to adopt new methods, intelligent to save labour, to prevent disease, to cure it when it comes. It is all part of the fascinating struggle which keeps him on his toes, alert to weather, rising early (if not too weary with the previous day's labours or last night's television), tackling the day's problems, joys, disasters. For farming is made up of avoiding a series of imminent disasters in order to achieve a major triumph.

This liveliness and enthusiasm of the young people at Te Ranga was a principal joy to the author (now grandfather of two small boys) who, as student of animal, including human, behaviour, saw that this pioneering life, though full of problems, was happy, full and rewarding. As a temporarily retired farmer, he found it much to his taste to watch awhile, and study an almost Arcadian scene. It humbled him, as he stood on the verandah, looking out over the landscape to the distant Bay of Plenty, to the pale blue horizon of the sea, where a tall plume of steam rose from the far volcano of White Island, to think of what the settlers had achieved in these hills. Instead of a vast forest of tall evergreen trees and tree-ferns in which, less than two hundred years ago, strikingly beautiful native birds were hunted by stone-age Maori living in small clearings here, the scene was almost English. A tar-sealed road wound up the ridge, with gates each side leading to sheep and dairy farms of between a hundred and five hundred acres, to woolshed and cowshed. Each house nestled against a grove of mixed native and exotic trees and shrubs, each with a highly productive flower and vegetable garden. In between the farm homes, which were mostly out of sight of each other, were rolling paddocks of bright green dotted with a few clumps of bush or isolated trees, and fenced with the usual seven-strand wire and concrete and wood posts. Excepting the deep river gorge, with its sheer walls hung with native trees and vegetation, and some still uncleared patches of bush on steeper land, most of the hills in sight were under pasture, and rotationally grazed with Romney sheep and Angus cattle, with here and there a herd of milking Jerseys.

Instead of news of tribal warfare, brought by a Maori scout on foot through the bush-tracks, or tidings of a cannibalistic feast such as the early Bay of Plenty missionaries would hear of only 120 years ago, the mail van would zigzag up the road, past singing yellowhammers and goldfinches, past kingfishers upon the telephone and electricity wires; it would stop at the post-box beside each farm gate, to deposit letters, parcels, bread, milk and everything else each farm family required and the mailman had agreed to deliver. His service is a far more vital and useful one than in the UK. But he is always busy and never delivers to the house door; except in an emergency he never gets out of the van!

Yes, it could be an English scene, or one from the border hills of Wales or Scotland, except for those interminable wire fences, except for the stronger sunshine, the bluer sky, and the structure of the farmhouses. In a land of frequent earthquake and ground tremor, these are mainly of wood, with one floor, and with a roof of galvanised sheeting which will not cascade in pieces as slate and tile do when shaken. Fortunately, although native timber for building is now rare and expensive, there is plenty of pine available from the fast-growing New Zealand exotic forests. The Bay of Plenty is one of the most thermally active districts of New Zealand, and its settlers are quite accustomed to having their homes shaken (rarely with violence); usually no more damage is caused than a book falling from a shelf, or the swaying of curtains and other hangings, or a crack appearing in the wall of the chimney, the only masonry part of the home.

As far as the resemblance to the United Kingdom goes it is deliberate, fostered by generations of British settlers, who brought with them their customs and habits, and their preferences for certain plants and animals, to influence their environment. They were helped in this by a climate which, although warmer and much more pleasant to live in, otherwise closely resembled that of home as to temperature and rainfall – and therefore its faunal and floral potential. I could enjoy finding English habits in the people, English flowers in the gardens, English birds everywhere – a nostalgic enjoyment, heightened by seeing so many of these imported delights flourishing; and on the other hand there were the surviving native species to be studied and identified – with a new wonder and curiosity.

But even as I watched New Zealand pipits, English starlings and

Indian mynas – three species thriving since the forest was destroyed –
all hunting the green turf for the too numerous grass grubs, my gaze
strayed often to the nearby gorge, where the river ran deep through
cave and arch, crayfish- and eel-haunted pool, and debris-filled gulch.

Here I could find some of the vanishing plants and birds of the pre-
European epoch: rare, confiding native robins sang there, and still the
strange prehistoric kiwi probed the soft ground and rotten timber, and
shrilled its name loudly at night, defying change.

Thanks to the pioneering of these pumice soils by the first farmers (those
unfortunates who mostly passed through a phase of bankruptcy, from
which some never returned to the land), the present generation has
learned from past misfortunes. In this area near Rotorua hundreds of
early twentieth century farmers watched their animals waste away from
a mysterious, terrifying disease called 'bush sickness'. The lands they
occupied were found to be unfit for stock farming, so were planted with
conifers, or reverted to bush. This failure was proved to be due to a trace
element deficiency: that is to say, ruminants will thrive only if cobalt
is added to the pumice soil, in the same way as molybdenum is essential
on certain pastures elsewhere.

We have described in the last chapter how fortunes were made – and
lost – on the larger sheep runs; and in the analysis of the accounts of
these it can be seen that for those who stayed the ultimate profit was
made less on the improvement of the run than on the rising value of land
for settlement. While so much of the natural fertility of the run was lost
by burning the humus, and run-off of topsoil, the farmer was often able
to make enough in the end, and retire in comfort, by dividing up his
land and then selling on a rising market. Land bought at 10s an
acre by one generation has been sold for £200 an acre by their children,
in certain favoured districts. But for the occupying farmer of today and
the future it is not so much a question of sheer acreage as of what the
land yields.

The increasingly intense meat and wool production drains much
calcium and other nutrients from the soil. Ideally, the robbed land
needs to be fed annually with what has been lost; but man is not yet

expert at working out the correct formulae and application, although he makes a brave attempt through the paid scientists of those revered places, in the eyes of the worried New Zealand pastoralists, the agricultural research stations. At present there is an almost fanatical belief in the efficacy of superphosphate. At all costs, he is told, he must apply superphosphate, and after that – or rather with it – whatever the scientists declare is necessary to correct the mineral trace element deficiency, a few ounces per acre of cobalt sulphate, molybdenum, copper or sulphur. But at least three and preferably five hundredweight per acre of superphosphate. To the super can also be added DDT or other chemical killer of grass grub and caterpillar.

Too much trace element of one kind or another will actually cause its own 'disease' and kill what it is meant to save. Not enough is yet known about surpluses and residues, and more particularly of the persistent residues of insecticide sprays, herbicides, DDT and other killers of life. What is also disturbing is the high incidence of parasitical worm infection of pastures, making frequent dosing of lambs, sheep and cattle necessary. It is said that the sheep's worst enemy is another sheep. But in order to keep up with rising costs and to boost production the New Zealand farmer has to stock more and more heavily. As a direct result of this high animal population internal parasites, salmonella, staggers, twin-lamb disease (pregnancy toxemia) and the nutritional diseases are more prevalent. The expedient answer to many, and some apparently new, ailments, is yet more chemical dosage for animals and land, and each application results in an addition to the residual poisons already present. Certainly it is impossible to believe that these chemical compounds, which often contain highly toxic elements such as arsenic and strychnine, leave no residues – as some manufacturers freely assert. It is already believed that their cumulative effect is reducing natural levels of fertility and health of both stock and land.

Much stricter control of chemicals used in agriculture is essential. Fortunately both the New Zealand and the UK governments have at last begun to ban the use of the most virulent of them, causing known mortality in wild animals, including fish and aquatic life.

6 The Exterminations

In the middle of the last century, while the Maori were still fighting the settlers in the North Island, the Pakeha were occupying the South Island without serious challenge. Land-hungry British immigrants had discovered that the most profitable export venture was wool, the demand for which was steadily rising on the London market. And now came the discovery of gold, west of Dunedin. Settlers and prospectors flooded into the Otago district from the North Island, from England and Scotland; and miners poured in from the worked-out Australian goldfields. Carrying a swag of food, sleeping-tent and panning tools, they landed at Dunedin and fanned out along the river beds from the original big strike, quickly pre-occupied, at Tuapeka. They penetrated deep into the forests, wading through torrents, surmounting gorges. They reached the west coast. Here towns sprang up overnight, with populations of several thousand, where a boat could put in with supplies and take away the ore. These shanty towns died almost as quickly as they had come, as diggers worked out the slender surface gold. But for a few years conditions were wild as any Western film of today, complete with stage-coach robbery and murder.

The tougher gold seekers toiled far into the mountains and fiordland ravines, oppressed by the sticky heat, sandflies and summer rains, shivering in the harsh frost and snows of winter. Often these solitary pioneers had only dog and gun left with which to pick up food from the country; their hard tack eaten, they depended on shooting or dogging a bird or wild pig. The dogs were most useful, almost essential; for they could scent a pig and grab it by the ear; and they could easily run down many flightless or weak-winged native birds. The latter were so tame that they could sometimes be knocked on the head with a stick.

We have already described how Samuel Butler and other pioneers lived off the land in the foothills of the 'snowy mountains'. The first of the native birds to be exterminated was the native quail *Coturnix novaezealandiae*, of which Butler wrote in 1863, 'It is exactly like a small partridge, and is most excellent eating. Ten years ago it was very abundant, but now is very rarely seen. The poor little thing is entirely defenceless; it cannot take more than three flights, and then it is done up. Some say the fires have destroyed them; some say the sheep have trod on their eggs; some that they have all been hunted down: my own opinion is that the wild cats, which have increased so as to be very numerous, have driven the little creatures nearly off the face of the earth.' All the adverse factors described by Butler combined to do so, finally, by 1870.

Those cats! Butler carried one on horseback, laboriously, affectionately, to live with him at Mesopotamia, and so accelerate the process he described. Thirty years later a unique little bird, the Stephens Island wren *Xenicus lyalli*, was found living on the small island of that name in Cook Strait, an island noted today for its population of tuataras. For centuries tuatara and wren had been living together without the larger reptile destroying all the tiny wrens, one of which would have been – and probably often was – a comfortable meal for a full-grown tuatara. In 1894 a lighthouse was built on the island, and Lyall, the keeper, reported this minute brown-yellow bird, new to science: 'it ran like a mouse and did not fly at all.' At that time a forest of kohekohe and nikau palm covered much of the island. The lighthouse-keeper introduced cattle and sheep, but it was his cat which wiped out the last wren almost as soon as it was reported.

The native quail has been replaced by imported quail. The Californian quail (1865) has done well and is locally common in both islands. The Australian brown (1866) and the Virginian bobwhite (1894) quails are found only in the North Island.

Next on the list for extermination was a much larger bird, much sought after long before European settlement. Unique to New Zealand, it was strikingly handsome. Its long glossy black iridescent plumage, and especially the white-tipped tail feathers, were prized by the Maori. The huia *Heteralocha acutirostris* lingered into the present century, in the shadows of the great forests of the North Island. It was as large as a magpie (about eighteen inches long), and a useful item of food. Each side of the long bill was a round orange-coloured wattle. But the unique feature was the ivory white bill: in the male this was stout and slightly arched, for digging open the tunnels of grubs living in rotten wood and forest litter; in the female the bill was much longer, slender and curved downwards like a scimitar. Her part was to extract the grubs after the male had opened up the holes.

The long female bill did not develop until she had left the nest as a fledgeling; but once mated the huia pair were inseparable and complementary partners for life, according to Buller and other early naturalists who were fortunate to observe them alive. In no other bird in the world does the bill size and shape differ in the sexes in so distinct a manner.

It was the prerogative of the chief or tohunga of the Maori tribe to wear the white-tipped huia tail feather in the hair as sign of exalted rank. The skin, with the wings and feet removed, was sometimes hung from the ear lobe as an ornament, conferring yet more mana upon the high-ranking Maori. With his few stone-age weapons of wood, stone and bone, his fine long bone-tipped bird lance and flaxen snare, the Maori lived with the huia, rather than ruthlessly exterminating it. The dense, uninhabited forest was its safe retreat. Here it was regularly hunted, traced by the appearance of rotten wood split open by the male, or by the loud whistling note from which the Maori name is derived.

The Maori hunter would imitate this note to draw the huia within range of trap or spear. And not seldom since has the ornithologist, seeking the huia still in remote New Zealand forest, in the Ruahine, Kaimanawa and other North Island jungles, also called its name in vain hope of success. I myself have been guilty of wandering in the beautiful wooded mountains above Waikaremoana and calling its name in that same vain quest, in those uninhabited jagged mountains and ravines named after the bird – the Huiarau Range. But the only response was the crashing of wild pig and deer in alarm. Remembering the astonishing re-discovery of the takahe after forty years of presumed extinction, some naturalists have persevered to this day in seeking the huia. It was last seen alive in the bush about 1907.

Like so many native birds the huia was an indifferent flier, progressing by hopping and bounding from branch to branch, or along the ground, frequently flirting and fanning its handsome tail. Only rarely would it make a short flight in the sunlight above the forest canopy. Its favourite food was the huhu grub, the large succulent larva – also eaten by the Maori – of the longworn beetle *Prionopus recticularis*, that huge, alarming-looking insect which I encountered on my pillow on my first night in camp in New Zealand. (It had been attracted by my bedside lamp.) The huia would drag forth the grub from its lair, then, holding it under one foot, would rip away the hard foreparts, toss it into the air, catch and swallow it head-first. Occasionally the Maori hunter would take young huia from the nest, cage them and rear them on grubs. But few white people ever saw the nest, and there appears to be only one egg in existence – in the Dominium Museum.

As soon as the Maori learned to use a musket he began to kill large numbers of huia, principally because Pakeha collectors paid good prices for the skins. During the disruption of the Maori civil wars and the struggles against the Pakeha there was deep penetration of the interior forests; the unsettled tribes hunted freely in the territory of other tribes, seeking what they might take – from the heads of their enemies to the birds of their hunting grounds. The huias disappeared fast, the flesh into the pot, the skins saved for trade. Huia, tui, native thrush and other sizeable birds would be cooked and preserved in their own fat for future consumption; a method of preparation much esteemed by the Maori. For the feast at any ceremonial gathering a wild pig, roast and stuffed with birds, was a special delicacy. But now it was every man for himself – and Pakeha money.

Yet the Maori cannot be blamed for the extinction of the huia. This was begun by the greed of the Pakeha, bartering muskets and metal for huia skins; and completed by his introduction of cats, ferrets, stoats and weasels.

The New Zealand thrush *Turnagra capensis*, or piopio, is, or was, not a thrush at all, although thrush-like in appearance, with mottled brown and white breast, olive-brown back and a tail as long as a blackbird's. This beautiful bird was last seen as late as 1955, in the forest above Lake Waikaremoana which I explored briefly ten years later. But I did not hear that flutelike call of the piopio, or the varied and sustained song which Buller describes in his manual of New Zealand Birds. I heard only the pretty notes of the European song-thrush, a far more wary, alert bird well used to avoiding the mammal predators which have destroyed the piopio.

The piopio was already rare in Butler's day. It was so tame that in the early gold-rush days in the fiordland rain-forest numbers pecked around the camps like chickens. They were rapidly exterminated by hungry prospectors and their dogs and cats. They were not flightless, but flew, or hopped through the foliage, omnivorously taking fruit and insects. They nested in trees, but close to the ground where cats could climb to devour the nestlings.

Perhaps a few still survive in the last inaccessible, unexplored forest? If so, I fear they are doomed.

The extermination of the laughing owl *Sceloglaux albifacies* is less understandable – but once again it is safe to blame man, and cats. It was once numerous in both islands, during the first decades of colonisation. Considering that the harrier has been one of the most successful of New Zealand's birds, it is a puzzle why this large owl, feeding on similar small animal life, failed so quickly. In colour it was a warm golden brown, with white stripes on the back, partly white face and with white-barred tail and wings. It was successfully bred in captivity – and the notes made then, (W. W. Smith and W. L. Buller), are about all that is known of its breeding habits. It laid two white eggs, usually in a hole in the rocks, and the female incubated. Smith analysed its pellets and found they included beetles, rats and mice; in captivity it ate these, also lizards and raw meat.

There are many Maori stories of the strange cries of night-birds, which evidently spring from the yelps, hoots and weird shrieks which this native owl made. Like the laughter of the yaffle or green wood-pecker of England, the laughing notes of this owl were regarded as foretelling rain, and with about as much verisimilitude. But heard at night its 'loud cry made up of a series of dismal shrieks' was terrifying to nervous and superstitious persons.

Naturalists are still hoping to find a colony surviving in some remote South Island fastness. It was last seen in July 1914 at Blue Cliffs, Canterbury. Only two specimens are known from the North Island, the last is dated 1868.

In the frenzied introduction of alien species early in the present century the European little owl *Athene noctua* was freed (1906–10) in Otago, and later in those very districts from whence the laughing owl had virtually vanished. This partly diurnal owl has since spread over most of the South Island. It has an undeserved reputation for killing game chicks; in fact this very pretty owl with the soft mournful call is probably more beneficial than harmful to man, living largely on small rodents, beetles, insects, worms and only occasionally birds – I have seen it take starlings and sparrows at the nest. Nor does it seriously compete with the native morepork owl *Ninox novaeseelandiae*, which is a forest bird. The robust morepork has adapted excellently to modern settlements, and remains common, but is essentially a cover-loving owl. The smaller little owl likes open country, with few scattered trees. The history of its introduction in New Zealand seems to be following that of its release (some twenty years earlier) in the British Isles: a slow, steady spread, initially numerous locally, then becoming more thinly distributed in the colonised areas. It has been released also in the North Island, where its success is uncertain as yet.

Huia, native thrush and quail, laughing owl. So far then, four once numerous birds unique to New Zealand exterminated since the European 'civilisation' settled the North, South and Stewart Islands. There were other extinctions, more inevitable, on the smaller outlying islands far from the main three, which need not concern us here – the Kermadec, Chatham, Auckland, Campbell, Macquarie, Bounty and Antipodes islands, which are under the sovereignty of New Zealand. The Chatham

Islands, for a while a penal settlement, and scene of the extinction of a race or 'subspecies' of Maori man, have been frequently mentioned in this book. The extermination of much of their subspecifically distinct plant and bird life is an example in miniature of what has happened, and is still in process of taking place, in New Zealand proper.

Had this book been written only twenty years ago, I would have included in the list of extinctions a fifth bird, a kind of giant moorhen – the notornis (*Notornis mantelli*) or, as it is more generally known in New Zealand, by its Maori name, the takahe. But, dramatically, fifty years after the last live takahe was recorded, Dr W. R. B. Orbell stumbled upon a colony in a valley high above Lake Te Anau during a search for deer in 1948. Quite by chance, too, I met Dr Orbell one lunch hour beside Lake Te Anau, in 1962; and learned from this keen mountain tramper some of the details of the re-discovery. At that moment I was waiting for the amphibian to take me from Lake Te Anau up into the country of the takahe.

The Wildlife Branch of the Department of Internal Affairs has, since 1952, studied the takahe colony where Orbell first found it, beside the mountain lake now named after him, making an annual visit to count and mark the individual birds of 'Takahe Valley'. I was specially fortunate in being able to join the 1962 party under the leadership of Ken Miers.

A fresh breeze lifted the three-seater seaplane from Te Anau up towards the snow-covered Alps. Flying at 4,000 feet, above the forest of evergreen nothofagus beech, we steered into the valleys of the Murchison Mountains. In twelve minutes the 80-mile long windings of Lake Te Anau had disappeared as we glided down upon Lake Orbell, at 3,000 feet above sea level. In two more flights the hard-worked plane brought up the rest of the party and stores, then skimmed away between the limestone bluffs of Takahe Valley, leaving us to the marvellous peace of the uninhabited wilderness.

Looking up hopefully to the white crags, I half-expected we might see, in such a highland setting, an eagle or two – though I was well aware that the New Zealand eagle was long extinct (page 29). There were some medium-sized birds high up there, soaring on broad pinions.

'Keas!' smiled Ken Miers. 'I'll call them down presently, if you'd like to see them really close. But don't look up in the sky. Keep your nose to the ground for New Zealand birds. You never know. We still hope to find the last little moa, huia, laughing owl. And I'll show you the trails of a very rare parrot, the flightless kakapo.'

As we waded ashore towards the little hut which was to be our head-quarters I could hear the prattle of lesser redpoll and chaffinch, two introduced finches which are the most conspicuous and numerous small birds of the New Zealand highland forest and sub-alpine tree line. A handsome paradise drake was flying low over the lake where his duck had already hatched her summer brood; he whistled a warning to his family.

Evidently some passing deer-hunter had used the hut in the winter; we found the door open and everything movable had been dragged out into the open, and lay in confusion around. Food tins were broken into, or dented as if by a blunt tin-opener. Boxes of sugar and flour were ripped wide and spilled. After an exchange of suitable expletives about deer-men and their habits, the little group of scientists began to laugh. As they restored order in the little 10 foot × 8 foot hut, organising their equipment and sleeping bunks, the merriment grew. At last I was enlightened by one word from Ken Miers: 'Keas!'

'Tea-time!' announced botanist Colin Burrows.

There was great enthusiasm to see how the takahe had fared over the last winter. As soon as we had drunk the billy of tea, we were organised by Ken to form a line abreast to walk the knee-high spongy tussock grass along the side of the lake. 'Sing out if you see any fresh cigarette-shaped droppings, or torn tussock roots. Or a red beak gliding through the grass tips.'

In a few moments we had seen just that – a brief scarlet flash – and, signalling us to form a wide pincer movement, Ken was away like a deer, making great leaping strides over the clumps of tussock. Then with a faultless tackle he rolled on the ground, his arms cradling a full-grown takahe. Rushing up to him I nearly trod on a scrawny black chick half-hidden under long grass. I plucked it forth. Adult and chick were photographed, measured, and each banded with a serially numbered metal ring around one leg; then released.

Now we could admire this rare creature in all the glory of its breeding plumage. Not that it is rapturously handsome – in fact it has a top-heavy, clumsy appearance because of the massive bill – but a bird close to extinction does have a special quality (merely of being rare). Its silky plumage was gleaming with iridescent blues and greens, the long narrow feathers resembling those of a cockerel's shining hackles. Bill and legs were bright red, the frontal shield of the male has an especially rich tone – a real scarlet. But the sexes are closely alike, the male perhaps a little heavier. In my arms I could feel its plumpness – it weighs over five pounds – and thought, maybe a little sacrilegiously, that it must have made a good meal to a hungry Maori, or gold-seeking Pakeha, or a dog hunting for food in its haunts. It looked strong enough to defy and escape from harrier, cat, pig, ferret, stoat and weasel; but obviously the tender black nestling I had caught would be vulnerable to every kind of predator which its parents could not drive away. This chick still carried on the upper mandible the little spike (egg-tooth) with which it cracks its way out of the egg.

The clutch of one or two cream-coloured, mauve-blotched eggs is laid in a nest or bower between the *danthonia* tussocks. Both sexes incubate, and the period is about one month. However, as far as possible, the takahe, a very strictly protected bird today, is left alone, even by the investigating scientists, until the eggs have hatched. Then a limited programme of counting and marking the birds in one study area (Takahe and the adjacent Point Burn valleys) is carried out. This wise conservational policy seems to be paying good dividends: first know your bird without destroying it, and you can then plan its protection. To know a species properly it is necessary to mark the individual; and in most cases birds are more easily caught while they still have seasonal allegiance to territory and young. Takahe adults skulk close to, and thus betray the whereabouts of, their crouching chicks; hence the one opportunity to catch both. It is of course essential to a life-study to mark the young, in order to find out when they breed and how long they live.

Each day we followed the same routine, fortunately in perfect sunlit weather (I was thanked for providing this: too often these expeditions are spoiled by heavy mountain mist and rain!). The days fled all too fast. We would tramp through the golden brown meadows of tussock clothing the floor of this valley, which is an old glacial moraine, examining the wide stretch of territory claimed by each pair of takahe. Many were already ringed. When we had counted (and caught most of) the valley population we moved 500 feet up through the nothofagus beech clothing the slopes, to reach more tussock above the tree-line, in search of more takahe. The red deer had already migrated to the cooler open tops, rising to 6,000 feet. Much hunted today as noxious animals because of the erosion they cause (as well as for venison, now in demand), the deer fled at sight or scent of us. These were the only mammals we saw in this high country. Birds, too, were generally scarce here, where the brown native pipits piped inconspicuously, and no skylarks sang. But in the forest below, the long-tailed cuckoo shrilled its piercing note as it flew through the beeches, an elegant mottled brown bird. And we saw its victims: the brown creeper and the canary-coloured yellowhead, in whose nests it deposits its eggs. Although these two lively tree warblers are totally unalike in plumage colour their calls are so similar, I could not distinguish them by ear alone. In the mossy branches along the upper edge of the forest the tiny rifleman flitted elusively, mouse-like, a veritable tree-creeper in miniature.

As the sun glided westwards, below the jagged screes, we descended to the still warm valley and our hut. Here an old friend of Samuel Butler and every other early settler awaited us: the woodhen or weka prowled around, as tame as a farm hen, seeking our scraps, a brown, inconspicuous, bantam-sized bird, as flightless as the takahe. By all the factors which exterminated the vanished huia and quail and thrush, it should not have been there. It is however morally a very tough, courageous bird and, as one of our party put it, 'would eat its grandmother if hungry enough'. It is an expert rat-killer, but inquisitive to a degree, a 'busybody', a thief, respected, but loved by no one. Other birds about the hut were grey warblers and fantails, and a tomtit which perched by the door and helped to rid us of two nuisances – bluebottles and sandflies.

The sandflies were the worst, but fortunately kept regular hours, enjoying their blood meals and raising bumps upon our skin mostly by day, abandoning us in the cool of night. It was stuffy in the overcrowded hut; I would wake to the songs of birds, including song-thrush, black-bird and dunnock; then my morning joy was to escape from my hot sleeping-bag and dive naked into a pool in the ice-cold burn below. Here a pair of whio or blue duck, rare except on remote mountain streams, would watch me from a boulder, almost within touching distance, so tame is this pretty dove-grey duck which loves the high country torrents.

Tamest of all were the kea parrots. All day they had been soaring about the limestone bluffs which shut in the valley. At dusk one evening Ken Miers called one down with a loud whistling 'Kee-ya!' In a few minutes it arrived with a scrabbling upon the corrugated iron roof of the hut as we sat inside at supper. Presently the kea, which is quite a large bird, a foot and a half long, richly olive-green with a scarlet underwing and rump, and blue-margined quill feathers, strolled in through the open door. It walked up to the sizzling camp fire and pulled out some of the burning sticks. With its powerful bill, which has a top mandible with a long hook (like a secateur blade), it would have seized my proffered finger if I had not withdrawn it cowardly at the last moment. It tried to pull my handkerchief away instead. It grabbed the loose end of my sock which I had pulled forward to protect my slipper-less foot. Thirstily it drank cold tea from the billy. It carried hot tins (thrown into the fire to burn the labels in preparation for rusting and destruction) out of doors, evidently with a plan to investigate these amusing items in a safer environment. It ate a little of most foods we threw upon the floor – sugar, oatmeal, meat. Then it flew off into the semi-darkness, in response to the call of another kea.

When it returned it seemed shyer. There was a dispute among us as to it being the same bird. 'It ought to be ringed,' I suggested, 'then you'd know.'

'See if you can catch it! I've never been able to.'

I made a grab, at what I thought was a favourable moment, when it was deeply investigating a discarded boot. As if it had eyes in the back of its head the kea flipped clear, and walked indignantly to the door. It was lured back with a tiny lump of butter thrown on the floor.

Beautiful tree ferns are
characteristic of New Zealand
native forest . . .

. . . as are these giant Kauri in
Waipoua State Forest,
Northland

Two flightless birds. The Kiwi, national bird of New Zealand, capable of defending itself with its powerful clawed feet, is not yet rare

The Weka is as large as a small pheasant, and strong enough to kill rats. Tame and inquisitive, it was easily killed by man, but still survives in certain districts

'Can't ever resist butter!' Ken assured me.

I flung my coat upon it suddenly. In vain. The kea leaped clear, and began tearing at the coat. Revenge is sweet. Everyone was laughing, mocking.

'You'll never do it!' was the challenge.

I eased my mountain stick into position, so that it touched the foot of the open door. I laid a trail of butter from the door to the middle of the hut. The kea hesitated only for a moment, then, cocking its head comically, it began to mop up, industriously licking its way towards the centre of the room.

One violent shove with my stick and the door slammed. The kea ran to the crack beneath it in vain. My coat was dropped upon it. The first kea was caught – and ringed. My mana, and later the kea, soared into the sky.

One kea came back, long after dark, and slithered around the metal roof of the hut, making a rumpus all through the night, as if determined to punish us by keeping us awake. Was it the ringed one? The kea hid in the shadows every time we went out to see. It appeared to be listening, cunningly, to us. All we could hear was the call of the morepork owl, and the two notes of prowling kiwis, the female's hoarse, asthmatic gasp and the male's more melodious 'ki-wi' call. The kea seemed to need no sleep. It did not leave the roof of the hut until first light.

Takahe valley is a glorious wild place, the world shut out from its pristine lake, tussock meadows and woods, where flightless rare birds roam. The lake was alive with dragonflies, which helpfully hunted and devoured the sandflies, where paradise duck and the bright-eyed black scaup or teal had their young. Some of the flowers were charming: white gentian, pale blue harebell, senechio, mountain daisies and violets; but the tussock dominates all in the open. The alpine meadows of New Zealand lack the brilliant display of their European counterparts.

The takahe study has revealed that this giant moorhen is holding its numbers better than was expected: about eighteen pairs in the two valleys of the study area; and since my visit more pairs have been located over the two hundred square miles of the Murchison Mountains.

9

Probably there are at least 150 pairs still breeding in this sub-alpine country.

It is evidently long-lived. We caught two which had been banded seven years earlier as adults; and the record so far is of one bird twelve years banded, which means, as the takahe does not breed until two (or more likely three) years of age, an unfinished longevity of fourteen years.

There was not much time to sit and study the pairs, as we were tramping all day on the census and banding exercise; but there were one or two hours off duty when I caught glimpses of the takahe off guard. One old bird was quite oblivious of my crouching presence as it browsed the succulent danthonia tussock, holding down the stems with its powerful feet. It then ripped away the dead bark with an upward sweep of the bill, and devoured the soft core complacently. It seems to be a vegetarian by force of circumstances, but in captivity it has been seen to kill and eat rats, mice, guinea pigs and small birds. The downy chick is fed assiduously by the adults, but is also an opportunist: through the glasses I watched one chasing the blowflies, and the slender red dragon-flies which were engrossed in conducting their nuptials by the stream.

Helped by the surveys of previous seasons, especially the summary by Dr Gordon Williams, it was fascinating to comprehend takahe behaviour in its natural environment, and compare it with that of other birds I had studied. For example, there is a sound rule that where the sexes are alike in external characters and colours, monogamy is practised – as in gannets, gulls, puffins, takahe and many others; but not where the sexes are unalike, as in jungle fowl, pheasants, blackcock, ruff and reeve. In these last the males compete for females by fighting and display. (But there is one bird in which the female is more gaudy than the male: in the phalaropes the handsome females do nothing but lay the eggs and flirt with several males, which, far less splendid in appearance, take on the incubation of the eggs and rearing of the chicks unaided.)

It seems from the ringing records that the takahe, once it has established a territory in the tussock feeding area, remains in possession for the rest of its life, forever mated to the same partner 'as long as both shall live'. When one of the pair dies another, usually a young bird, takes its place. Senior birds remain firmly on established territories, but tolerate their own chicks well into maturity, even far into the next breeding season. This friendly association of young birds of the late year with the nest and eggs and youngsters of the new season is typical of the gallinule or moorhen family.

Falla observed other moorhen-like behaviour at the nest: 'The sitting bird was called off by its mate. The bird responding darted with a crouching run to the caller and straightened up, facing it with the two bill tips almost touching and both necks upstretched. After some seconds one bird, I think the original caller, crouched and moved round the other with a gyratory movement which presented the spread white under-tail coverts to the other's view. Drooped wings and fluffed-out flank feathers gave the general impression of a round target ringed with blue.'

The calls we heard as we searched for chicks were the explosive alarm notes of the parents, a loud *oomph*, a warning heeded by the young one, which crouched down. But if we waited patiently it would presently get up and betray its position by a plaintive piping note to attract its parents.

So long as the weather is fine and the ground free of snow the takahe live their family lives in the open tussock, feeding predominantly on the tussock and other mountain grasses, but they also eat the flowers and leaves of other low-growing plants; we found mountain daisy and violet cut down beside the fresh cigarette-sized droppings. In captivity the takahe will wash vegetable food in water; and eat grit freely. In hard winter weather they move into the shelter of the beech, where they feed principally on the fronds and stalks of the plentiful ferns. Several nests may be constructed, one for the actual incubation, others to accommodate non-breeders or to sleep in: another moorhen-like habit.

Predators seemed scarce in this upland country, which may be why the takahe has managed to survive here. The harrier is rare – it could not kill an adult, but might be able to snatch up a young chick takahe. But could even the adult takahe defy a wild pig, stoat or ferret which found its nest? A bird is sometimes found sitting on an empty nest as if the eggs had been taken. Nevertheless ground predators are few, Ken

Miers said: an occasional stoat or ferret, but no cats or pigs. The reason for the takahe surviving only in high, remote country must be sought elsewhere.

The general opinion among the experts who have studied the bird in the field is that the takahe has been driven to the mountains by that change of climate which had caused the decline and extinction of most of the grass-eating moas even before man arrived in New Zealand; that as a bird of the cool tussock lands of the late ice age it retreated before the advance of the forests over the lower ground during the warming of the climate. It vanished from the warmer North Island so long ago that it cannot be satisfactorily identified in the Maori legends of the north; nor has it been recorded there except as sub-fossil bones. In the South Island, according to that expert, Gordon Williams, 'only in Western Otago are there reliable records of sightings in European and pre-European times, and acceptable records of Maori traditions which tell of hunting birds in the mountains between Lake Monowai and Te Anau'. He considers that any part played by man and natural and introduced predators in hunting the takahe or unfavourably altering their habitat has probably only accelerated a natural trend towards extinction.

For once it seems we can exonerate man, and relegate the approaching extinction of this plump, edible-looking creature to causes primarily beyond his control. Enisled in the cold, inhospitable mountains not yet coveted by man except as a summer tramping and deer-shooting range, where at present even sheep are banned, the takahe awaits the fate of the moa, the dodo and the great auk. Its greatest enemy is itself, its failure to adapt to the warming climate and less austere diet. Minor foes are the deer which overgraze the tussock, and an occasional carnivorous ground predator. Man is no longer an enemy, but a firm ally; even to the extent of trying to breed the takahe in captivity, but without success so far.

Extinction of this plump, edible-looking creature? These words bring to mind the sensation I had of holding that large, round, fat body of the live takahe in my arms. If ever it is bred in captivity successfully, I envisage takahe farms springing up in a big way!

Kakapo *Strigops habroptilus*. The kakapo I saw at the Mount Bruce Native Bird Reserve, in roomy captivity, was a beautiful creature, a delicate moss-green and yellow, lighter on the breast, and streaked and barred above. Its whiskered face, sharply arched bill, and rosette of feathers around the eyes gave it an owl-like countenance; and in fact the first settlers called it the owl-parrot. I was struck by its size, more than two feet from head to the tip of the long tail, and the big, broad wings. Yet it is a flightless ground parrot.

I studied kakapo trails through the bush in Takahe Valley, but although we looked out for signs of the birds themselves, they have not been seen for some years in this vicinity. Their old trails are kept open by the deer: the deer jump over the low branches and roots, the kakapo walked *under* them. And man finds it convenient to use these old kakapo trails also; the deer have provided walking height along routes which the kakapo liked to make along dry ridges. Paths used only by birds were well-marked tunnels under the bush, rather like European badger trails between burrow and feeding grounds. No doubt the weka and the kiwi also use and keep open these kakapo routes; the three flightless birds are not competitors, for the weka picks up animal food from the surface, the kiwi probes for worms and grubs in ground and rotten wood, but the kakapo is principally vegetarian. A sure indicator of the presence of the kakapo is the ball of chewed material left hanging on tussock clumps after the parrot has extracted the nourishing pith.

One day we climbed up to the bluffs which hang over Takahe Valley, and explored along their foot. There are many holes in the limestone here where formerly kakapo rested by day, and sometimes nested. We found the dry balls of kakapo dung, well-preserved by the limestone dust. In the debris of one larger cave we poked around in search of moa bones. Ken Miers had found here, in 1949, the evidence of a Maori hunting party. With Robert Falla he had examined the tussock beds, a flaxen snare, fire-rubbing stick, a used flax sandal, and other signs of temporary occupation. Exploring the hunter's midden Falla had recovered some bones and the yellow-bronze double-shafted feathers of a Megalapteryx moa which the Maoris had eaten. One bone had a series of deeply sliced knife cuts, possibly the work of a party of fugitive

Ngati-mamoe Maori, who could not have obtained a metal knife much earlier than the date of the European explorers, whalers and sealers frequenting the Foveaux Straits at the end of the eighteenth century.

Hope of the survival of this small forest-living moa were raised by this discovery; but although it had come at the moment of the re-discovery of the takahe and triggered off a new keen combing of the beech forests of the alpine and fiordland valleys, no moas have ever been seen alive by white men. Captain Cook does not mention them, nor do his gentlemen biologists; but it is significant – in view of the 1949 discovery – that Cook presented the few natives of Dusky Bay (lying to the west of Lake Te Anau) with hatchets, spike-nails and probably knives when he landed and stayed for six weeks there in 1773.

At that time, although Cook does not mention the kakapo either, but refers only to the abundant wild fowl and an immense number of woodhens (wekas), kakapo must have been numerous around these sounds under the mountainous fiordland coast. From the earlier accounts of the explorers and surveyors, such as Arthur Harper and Douglas, the owl-parrot was found in hundreds everywhere in this western terrain, from Nelson to Stewart Island. The white explorers and prospectors practically lived on kakapo, weka and kiwi, caught by their dogs. It is said that when the 'gold' track was made over the Haast Pass, the roadmakers' gangs relied on the abundant kakapo to provide a welcome change from the interminable salt mutton. But in Samuel Butler's time the 'green ground parrot, the kakapo, a night bird', was 'hardly ever found on the eastern side of the island.'

When I met Major Robert Wilson, an old correspondent of mine, for the first time at his home at Bulls, in 1961, he told me that about 1890 Henry, a ranger of the west coast sounds, had collected – an astonishing feat in itself – up to five hundred kakapo and placed them on Resolution Island, which is a large island above Dusky Sound. Stoats and cats had begun to kill them on the mainland; and it was hoped to build up a strong colony on this island. A vain hope, since by 1940 the stoats, which probably swam across to Resolution Island, were swarming there, and there was not a kakapo left. Wilson had seen one of Henry's kakapos, in a cage on the Government steamer *Hinemoa*, when on one of his island-going expeditions. 'I used to feed it with raw potatoes which it would accept with one claw, and eat with a gentlemanly air.' He never saw one wild and free, but in 1915, when exploring the high Kaimanawa Range, he heard its bittern-like boom from his camp in the bush under Makorako. This must have been its last stronghold in the North Island, for it was never recorded again; and indeed was apparently scarce there a century earlier.

Nesting and living by day in holes the kakapo is particularly vulnerable to introduced dogs, cats, ferrets, stoats, weasels and even rats, although probably it could defy the last but not save its eggs or small chicks from them. But the evidence of rangers and others show that after the feral cats had taken heavy toll, its chief enemy has been the stoat. The mustelid had only to follow the well-worn trail of the kakapo from its nocturnal feeding ground to its diurnal burrow to obtain a substantial meal at any time – so long as the supply lasted. During the period of its spread into fiordland the stoat lived almost luxuriously upon the tame native birds. It multiplied excessively in a very few years. Wilson thought it would not be able to overcome a weka, which might even kill it; and that a kiwi could repulse a stoat with savage kicks of its clawed feet: hence, he thought, the continued survival of both. But the native thrush and the kakapo were easy victims; and even as late as 1936 the stoat was killing kakapo just for the sake of killing. The owl parrots were often found freshly killed but not otherwise touched; and at times were taken home and eaten by hungry human finders.

So the final decline of the kakapo has been very rapid, and due almost entirely to introduced mammals. Like the takahe, it is a bird of the sub-alpine forest and tussock (which reaches to sea-level in cool fiordland), living almost entirely on vegetable matter, fungi, and possibly a few insects and the occasional lizard; and this habitat preference limited its range, which has evidently been steadily shrinking since the melting of the last glacier.

We found no fresh signs of kakapo, and it seems it has vanished forever from Takahe Valley. Rightly the Wildlife Branch is far more worried about the kakapo than the takahe today. But what can be done? Can the owl parrot be reintroduced to Takahe Valley and the Murchison

Range which is a bird reserve where ground predators have become scarce today, not so much because of human control but chiefly because their food-prey is hard to find?

But first catch your kakapo. Numbers are now so low that it will be hard to collect a breeding nucleus. As it would be risky to release adult birds in a territory strange to them, where their first reaction would undoubtedly be to set off in search of home, it seems necessary to try to breed them in captivity. And this is being, or will be, attempted at Mount Bruce (page 214). Colin Roderick, in charge of this Native Bird Reserve, told me of his adventures in a recent expedition to capture such a nucleus in the only area where they are obviously present today – the Milford Sound-Cleddau watershed.

Colin considers that the kakapo, despite its owl-like face, and long, stiff, kiwi-like bristles around the base of the bill which indicate a habit of moving through confined spaces at night, is less nocturnal than is generally reported. After heavy rain they may come out on to dry ridges to bask in the sun. He found several special dusting places where they indulge a thorough dry-cleaning of their soft, loose plumage. He was able to track one kakapo from such a dust-bath or 'bowl' as he called it; and captured it, and brought it to Mount Bruce. Also, it is not by any means flightless. If necessary it can take off from a height and glide or flap downwards for a considerable distance; but normally when hunted it runs through the undergrowth, or climbs over and up fallen trees. Apart from the danger from mustelids, it seems to suffer from competition with deer, and possibly the increasing herds of chamois; these frequent the trackways, disturb the system of dust 'bowls', and devour the grasses and plants of the kakapo gardens, along its established feeding trails and ridges.

When these cloven hooves appear the kakapo vanish.

There are other birds on the danger list, which it may be increasingly difficult to save if New Zealand permits more wild country to be overrun and native forests to be cut down. All the native parrots are suffering from the impact of European settlement. Here are some notes about these and others in considerable peril of extinction, today or tomorrow.

Kea, *Nestor notabilis*. It is curious that the kea, so impudent and fearless towards man, should be a comparatively successful bird; like the vanishing kakapo it nests in vulnerable places, in holes and crevices at ground level. Its ability to fly well, and its habitat of high country, has evidently saved it so far. Tourists visiting the Hermitage under Mount Cook will be amused, as I was, by watching the keas. At this hotel they sit about the roof, admire their reflections in the window glass, and seize opportunities to grab food from the kitchens, or steal objects – as they did in the Takahe Hut.

Thanks to today's more enlightened policy towards this and other scarce birds the kea is actually spreading north from the Southland districts to which it had been confined in the period of intense persecution, often with a bounty on its head, for the alleged sheep-killing by certain rogue individual keas. At Mount Aspiring 1,500 keas were killed for bounty from 1942 to 1958. However, it is very far from being numerous, and needs protection to maintain a strong breeding stock.

Kaka, *Nestor meredionalis*. About the same size as the kea, with the same scarlet patches, and similar, but darker, body colour. I photographed this forest parrot on Kapiti – perched on Robert Falla's head, so tame are some individuals in this sanctuary, thanks to feeding by the Warden and his wife. With Robert Traill on Stewart Island, I watched gregarious kakas feeding on tree fruits and the nectar of rata, and heard their satisfied hoarse chucklings, and then ringing musical cries as they flew to their roosting places in the tall trees above Paterson Inlet. A decreasing species, it is rapidly vanishing from the main islands with the felling of its habitat, the native forest, unable to adapt to commercial conifer plantations or settled areas. Its habit of nesting high up in hollow trees has helped to protect it from ground predators; but not from opossums which, even if they do not take its eggs, eat up its main food supply of leaves and tree fruits.

Parakeets, *Cyanoramphus* spp. Less than a foot long, including the long tail, yellow-green birds with blue wing flashes. The red-crowned parakeet *novaezelandiae*, once abundant, is now very rare in mainland forests, and more or less confined to the island sanctuaries offshore, from Stewart Island to the Three Kings.

The yellow-crowned parakeet *auriceps* still survives in the mountain forests of both North and South Islands, barely holding its own. It enjoys complete protection, and remains in good numbers in the island sanctuaries. The orange-fronted parakeet *malherbi* is confined to the South Island, from Nelson to Fiordland; this little known, smaller, alpine species is now very rare and must be close to extinction.

Stitchbird, *Notiomystis cincta*. The cock bird is most handsome, with velvet black head and throat, a tuft of white 'ear' feathers (which can be erected), golden-yellow waistcoat, and white wing bar; the hen is generally duller, without any black or conspicuous yellow. Like the tui and bellbird, it is a nectar eater, with brush-tipped tongue. About the size of a robin, it haunted the deep forests of North Island, and was once numerous near Wellington. It must now be one of the world's rarest birds, only surviving on Little Barrier Island. Here for the moment it is safe. The Wildlife Branch plans to reintroduce the stitchbird to other island sanctuaries if all goes well with their study results.

Saddleback *Philesturnus carunculatus*. Like a large starling, glossy black with bright chestnut back-saddle, and orange wattle. A relative of the huia, and like that bird it hunts much on the forest floor, but it has also recently been shown that saddlebacks exploit more than any other bird the insects that live under bark and in holes and cracks. Wherever cats and/or European rats have landed on small islands the saddleback has disappeared. At the present time the North Island subspecies survives only on Hen Island, Auckland, where only the harmless native rat lives. The South Island subspecies is found only on three small islands off Stewart Island; on one of these the recent irruption of black rats has started a rapid decline of saddlebacks and other endemic species. By 1890 it had become very scarce in both North and South Islands, due to cats, rats and mustelids Fortunately it has taken kindly to breeding in captivity in spacious conditions at Mount Bruce, and already surplus young birds have become available for restocking island sanctuaries.

Kokako, *Callaeas cinerea*. Resembles a small rook superficially. Plumage generally dark grey-blue, with large wattles which are rich orange (South Island subspecies) or deep blue (North Island subspecies). It is a vegetarian living largely on the leaves, flowers and fruit of native trees and plants. Unusually shy for a New Zealand bird, it is forever on the move and difficult to study. It has practically vanished from the South Island, and in the North Island is but thinly scattered in native forest, with one colony on Great Barrier Island. Very much on the danger list.

Bush Wren, *Xenicus longipes*. Of the three little New Zealand *Xenicus* wrens, the Stephens Island species *lyalli* has been exterminated by cats (page 119). The rock wren *gilviventris* is confined strictly to the alpine zone of the South Island, descending to the sub-alpine scrub in winter; it is not rare as yet. But the bush wren, unlike its relative the rifleman, seems to have been unable to adapt to settled areas or conifer woods, and is now very rare, apparently confined to the Urewera native forest in the North Island, in Fiordland, and on islets off Stewart Island.

(For the status of other scarce species, see the full list of birds, native and introduced, breeding in New Zealand: Appendix, page 218.)

7 Acclimatisation Madness

Man must ever meddle with nature. That most humane of men, Captain Cook, thought he was benefiting the Maori people and future settlers when he put ashore geese, chickens, sheep, goat and pig – for Banks records that the only quadrupeds were dogs and rats. When the *Endeavour* was heeled (careened) ashore in New Zealand on both islands during the first voyage, 1769–70, Cook does not mention the possibility of rats, known to infest most of the sea-going vessels of his day, going ashore too – a splendid opportunity for them. However, it is possible that Cook, who paid great attention to health and sanitation, had kept his ship rat-free from the start of the voyage; he could not afford to waste any provisions. Banks never saw the native rat he mentions; it was the small Polynesian rat, *Rattus exulans*, known to the Maori as kiore, and freely eaten for food. As it closely resembles a European black rat, but is only half the size when full-grown, it could easily have been mistaken for one.

Two months before the *Endeavour* departed from New Zealand shores, the French Explorer Surville landed in 1769 and sowed vegetable and other seeds in the Bay of Islands. At the turn of the century came the whaling ships, at that time notoriously infested with black rats *Rattus rattus*, known to this day as the ship rat. We can begin our melancholy tale of the acclimatisation of alien mammals in New Zealand, other than man, with the rats.

Rats. It is safe to say that this ship rat was the second rat to land in New Zealand, the first being the above-mentioned kiore. The brown rat *Rattus norvegicus* came later. It had not arrived in Britain before 1730 and had not increased to the extent of supplanting the black rat as it now has. But it still frequented the ships which had brought it overseas from its Asian homeland, and accompanied man, with the black rat, in his nineteenth-century exploration of the world.

Among reliable early references to the brown rat in New Zealand is one by Charles Darwin, who found it well established in the Bay of Islands in 1835. In *The Origin of Species* he writes, 'How frequently we hear of one species of rat taking the place of another under the most different climates!' This is what is happening in New Zealand today. The native kiore rat was found on most Polynesian islands and was once common throughout the main islands of New Zealand, although much hunted and eaten by the protein-hungry Maori, in whose canoes it arrived as a stowaway (or accepted passenger) during those early voyages of colonisation. Today it is probably extinct in the North and South Islands, although there may be a few relict colonies in remote Southland forests. To study it one must visit the few offshore islets where the European cats and rats have not yet landed; and here it thrives.

The kiore is the sole mammal permanently inhabiting the volcanic White Island in the Bay of Plenty. While camping there I had a good opportunity to observe it, for it came tamely to scavenge for the scraps from our meals. It seemed to be a thorough-going opportunist, eating bread and bacon rind, and chewing industriously at any raw fish we left about. Its main diet must be vegetarian. It can climb trees and eat the tender leaves and buds in the tops; but on White Island it was most numerous near the gannet colonies, where at night it could move around close to the sleepy gannets and devour the abundant fish offal lying near the nests. It is probably too small to be able to harm the burrow-nesting petrels, whose powerful beaks can draw blood from a hand incautiously inserted.

In general coloration the kiore is halfway between the two European species, perhaps more like the black (Figure 5). The brown-black pelt is overlaid with longer hairs of black and white, the whitish underparts tinged with yellow, and the tail long in proportion to size. Those we caught on White Island averaged under 4 ounces (950 grammes); a

Norway rat   **Ship rat**   **Kiore**

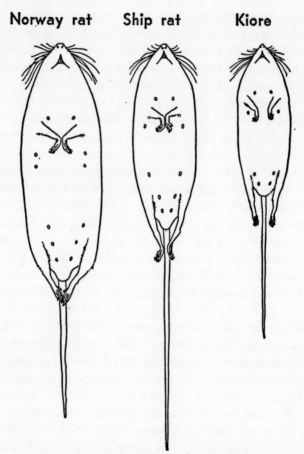

Figure 5. The number and arrangement of teats and
differences in tail length in females of three rat species
(*after J. S. Watson*)

ship rat weighs twice as much, and a brown rat up to four or five times that weight.

It is believed that the black or ship rat arrived in Britain about eight hundred years ago in the ships carrying the returning Crusaders from the Holy Wars in Palestine, for there is no earlier record of rats in Britain. As it is a vector of the bubonic virus it is believed to have been responsible for the plagues which subsequently ravaged Europe. On arrival in New Zealand it found food abundantly along the shore at whaling stations, then moved inland, partly to occupy the empty habitat of, and partly to compete with, the kiore. Like that species, it is a natural climber, even to the extent of nesting in trees.

It is a simplification to believe that the black rat, and subsequently the brown rat, were responsible for the disappearance of the kiore on the mainland. There were other powerful agents of extermination. It is interesting to read of Samuel Butler's exploration of the South Island high country in 1860. He was a hardy character, and even slept in the snow; but at times 'the rats used to come and take the meat from off our very plates by our side.' Only kiore rats were impudent enough to do this, for they were fearless of man in those wilderness regions. And to reduce their numbers Butler carried a cat, as so many other settlers did at that early stage of setting up homesteads. Cats, and later ferrets, stoats and weasels, all attacked and exterminated the kiore, whose only serious pre-European enemies had been certain bird predators; the Maoris had regarded it as a valuable protein food, caught it in specially constructed traps, and even protected a breeding stock.

On the evidence of the history of the two European rats in Britain, one would expect the heavier, tougher brown rat to supplant the black rat over much of New Zealand. It may yet do so, but at present the two rats seem able to co-exist in the same areas, even in the same buildings and on the same farms, in every part of the main islands. It seems, however, that the black rat in New Zealand has largely reverted to its original habit of nesting well up in trees, thick bush, haystacks and – in buildings – in the walls and upper floors; in this way it avoids territorial disputes with its more powerful cousin. Although the brown will climb, especially to avoid ground predators (I have pulled brown rats out by their tails from the middle of a hedge into which they had climbed to escape ferrets exploring their burrows below; they were too busy watching the ferrets to see my arm approaching), it is normally a ground feeder and nester. The black rat will hunt for food (fruit, berries and the eggs and chicks of birds) in its tree haunts.

The brown rat is hardier, able to thrive in conditions of severe cold where the black rat cannot, as in Arctic and Antarctic settlements, in cold stores and freezing works at a constant temperature of 20° F, as well as in the humid conditions of sewers, drains, rivers and swamps, wherever it can find food. It will live on small rocky islands virtually bare of vegetation, existing on a diet of shellfish and the droppings of seabirds. But it will also thrive in tropical climates.

On one island nature reserve, Kapiti, all three rats exist. Here severe control measures against the rats and their feline and mustelid enemies, while not successful in achieving the desired extermination of the 'foreign' rats, have possibly kept the populations of all three at a level well below the natural climax, and thus ensured the survival of the weakest, the kiore. All three species have been trapped on the heavily bushed Stewart Island and some of its off-islets, where control measures are too difficult to carry out effectively; here the three are competing for territory and food at the expense of the native birds and plants – and the winner is likely to be the brown rat.

The European house mouse, *Mus musculus*, found a niche for itself ready and waiting when it arrived – an unwanted stowaway – in those same ships which brought the rats, early in the nineteenth century. There was no other small mammal able to compete for the terrain it inhabits: crevices, burrows, cracks and holes too small even for the kiore, whether in man-made buildings or in field or forest. It spread rapidly over the whole of the North, South and Stewart Islands, colonising the land from sea-level to above the tree-line, able to survive and breed successfully on a wide range of diet – vegetarian and insectivorous. Like the rats, for a while it was explosively numerous locally, as is so often the case with an animal placed in a new and favourable ecological niche. It has since settled down to a level of population much like that of the house mouse in Europe. But as there are no field mice or voles to compete for food and territory the house mouse may be relatively more numerous in New Zealand. Instead of the intermittent vole plagues suffered in Europe, local plagues of house mice are experienced, chiefly in the country. There is a popular and quite erroneous belief that two species of mice exist in New Zealand – a field and a house mouse. The difference is one of situation only. Given sufficient food the house mouse

The harrier, New Zealand's largest surviving bird of prey

Introduced browsing animals have become a serious pest, causing erosion of mountain-sides and degradation of native plants and forests. This hunter has shot one of the fine thar which, with chamois, overgraze the high tops

The elegant sooty tern is a rare visitor to New Zealand proper, but nests on the Kermadec and other sub-tropical islands to the north

The black-winged petrel, like other members of its family is singularly ill-equipped for life on land, in this case it is climbing a tree to gain height for take-off

will thrive on a meat diet in a freezing works as well as it does on a mixed diet in wood and farm land.

The introductions of the European rats and the house mouse were accidental. Alone, these rodents cannot be proved to have had any calamitous effect sufficient to cause the extermination of any single indigenous bird or plant species in so large an area as the North or South Islands. Only on some small offshore islands have the black and brown rats managed to wipe out whole populations of birds, especially burrow-nesting species. Of such exterminations by rats on small islands there are plenty of examples in every hemisphere the world over.

It is with the deliberate introductions that we come to the conscious folly of man, born to sin. Yet as folly is often more fascinating than wisdom, we follow the effects of these acclimatisations with the deepest interest.

Pig, *Sus scrofa*. Joseph Banks notes in his *Endeavour* journal, 1769, that the Tahitians 'have Hogs, fowls and doggs. Their pork is certainly most excellent tho sometimes too fat.' After leaving Tahiti in August the *Endeavour* sighted New Zealand for the first time on 6th October 1769; about a fortnight earlier Banks had noted that their livestock on board consisted of '17 Sheep, 4 or 5 fowls, as many S.Sea hogs, 4 or 5 Muscovy ducks, an English boar and sow with a litter of piggs; in the use of these we are rather sparing as the time of our Getting a supply is rather precarious.' Certainly there was none to spare on this voyage, but Cook and others in subsequent voyages landed European, and probably South Sea, pigs. Jean de Surville, who actually landed in New Zealand in December 1769, just as Cook was leaving, narrowly missing sight of the *Endeavour*, gave the Maori of Doubtless Bay pigs, fowls and seeds in return for their helping his men ill with scurvy.

The gone-wild pig undoubtedly caused some loss to native ground-nesting birds, as it multiplied throughout the islands. With its considerable sense of smell, and its powerful snout, it could scent and plough out shallow burrows, dens and runs occupied by kiwi, kakapo, kiore and other ground dwelling animals, and devour old and young and eggs. But its main diet is known to be fern roots, insects, grubs and fruits. As it increased in numbers it was eagerly hunted for meat by

10

settlers. It is doubtful if it has ever been so numerous as to constitute a serious threat to any one endemic bird, or to be more than a contributory factor in the considerable damage to plant communities caused mainly by deer, goat, rabbit, opossum and man.

More serious has been the introduction of the goat, *Capra hircus*, that curse of so large an area of the world when permitted to increase beyond the capacity of the environment to feed it without degradation of the flora. Unchecked the goat will reduce forest to grassland, by eating all the leaves it can reach and stripping the bark of tree and bush. Flocks of goats and sheep are said to have created the present Sahara; and today can be seen reducing to desert large regions of the dry Near East countries. On some small islands off New Zealand they have practically denuded the soil of plant cover; and a campaign of extermination is now waged upon goats which inhabit island nature reserves. For the reason that it is an omnivorous vegetarian it was kept – and is still kept– by many flockmasters to eat down weeds and tall plants unpalatable and even poisonous to sheep and cattle. Goats will eat tutu, hemlock and even stinging nettles with relish, a little at a time, without any dire effects.

Usually these goats on large sheep stations live ferally, resisting dogs, which are sent to round them up, by retreating to cliffs and gullies; their numbers can only be controlled by shooting. But many have escaped from these weed-control duties, arbitrarily imposed by man, on the grazing runs, and vanished into forest and high country. They have multiplied vastly in certain terrain, such as bare sea cliffs, mountain tops and screes, appropriate to their origin as rock dwellers. In the Hawaiian Islands I saw large flocks of feral goats decimating the landscape of the high lava flows of Mauna Loa National Park, when searching for the rare ne-ne or Hawaiian goose which haunts this 5–8,000-foot volcanic country. During my stay there the National Park rangers, in one drive, using horsemen, dogs and helicopters, forced 1,500 feral goats into a corral (these were sold at three dollars apiece to the protein-hungry half-caste peoples of the island). Several feral dogs were encountered and shot on this drive; these normally live close to the goats in a curious one-sided partnership. They are quite savage and capable of attacking man; and for this reason the rangers never penetrate their haunts unless armed. To the extent that they are feared by man the dogs act as bodyguards to the goats. When hungry the dogs pull a goat down and devour it. The goats, which are not fast enough to escape the dogs, have perforce to live with their guards which in turn only kill what they require to satisfy hunger.

These highlands of Hawaii are occupied by cattle ranches where wild dogs are tolerated in the lava flows because of their appetite for the useless goat. But feral dogs, when they are reported in New Zealand from time to time, are ruthlessly hunted and shot because of their attacks on the sacrosanct sheep. So far feral dogs in New Zealand have never been allowed to become numerous enough to form tribute-taking bodyguards to the numerous feral goats and sheep.

The gone-wild cat is a major problem. The true wild cat, *Felis catus*, is unknown in New Zealand. The first settlers in the early nineteenth century brought with them domesticated cats of all colours and breeds as part of their household chattels, partly as pets, partly because New Zealand already had the reputation of being infested with rats – although few knew that it was the virtually harmless kiore rat which had earned the new country this notoriety.

The cat arrived about the same time as the house mouse. There is a reprehensible trait in many men which permits them to escape responsibility for killing those inedible domestic animals which can no longer be housed or cared for, by setting them free. In the case of cats it is argued that they are fully able to hunt and feed for themselves; and some people heed the superstition that it is bad luck to kill a cat, especially if it is black in colour. No doubt when the first whalers, earliest of white settlers in New Zealand, set up their shore stations they carried the ships' cats ashore, to deal with the abundant rats which fed on the offal of their trade. The argument was that the more cats there were, the less rats there would be; and so the cats were allowed to breed freely, taking to the bush to nest for preference. There was then a comfortable living for the cats, not so much on the native and ship rats but upon the stupidly tame birds. Without doubt the feral cat killed thousands of quail, kakapo, parakeets, saddleback, native thrush, wrens and other birds, now rare or extinct, which were abundant 150 years ago. At that time the cat had only to stroll towards a native bird, which had no foreknowledge of a small four-footed enemy which could leap suddenly; and indeed, like the fantail, robin and tomtit today, may even have been curious enough to hop or fly to meet a cat – and its doom!

In New Zealand, as in many places the world over, cats have been introduced upon small islands, often for no valid economic reason, but with disastrous results for bird life. Nor have the cats succeeded in wiping out the rats, be they kiore, brown or black species, or all three. Thus, on Little Barrier Island – 7,544 acres of native bush – the kiore exists today in fair numbers yet, although preyed upon by feral house-cats introduced and escaped about eighty years ago. The warden of this nature reserve endeavours to kill as many cats as possible, for this is the last breeding place of the beautiful honey-eating stitchbird (page 138) in the world. It seems impossible to get the last cat in such a large area of bush, but their numbers are kept low; and fortunately for the stitch-bird the surviving cats have plenty to eat without hunting strenuously through the trees for the nectar-seekers. Examination of feral cat faeces on this island shows that the main summer diet is the abundant burrow-ing petrel; and in winter the summer's increase of the kiore rat is available.

Most native birds have not yet learned to be shy of man, and they are even less wary of cats. But introduced birds, from Europe in particu-lar, have an inherited fear of biped and quadruped predators which gives them an alertness to watch for, and to flee, or at least to keep a safe distance, from mortal danger of this sort.

Supreme example of the stupidity of man due to ignorance of the ecological factors involved, and of the selfishness of sportsmen without regard for the livelihood of other land users, was the introduction of the rabbit, *Oryctolagus cuniculus*. However, it must be remembered that the early nineteenth-century settlers were tough adventurous outdoor men, who were accustomed to carrying a gun for two reasons: self-defence against the Maori, whose lands they occupied either by agreement or by force; and to shoot animals for food or as pests. These men found New

Zealand strangely deficient in supplies of game birds and mammals. Saving that worthy fighting character, the wild pig, there was no other exciting sporting game, and hardly anything to shoot except sitting targets like the little native quail, soon exterminated. In Australia trigger-happy settlers were enjoying a considerable sporting chase after kangaroos and wallabies, and other marsupials, as well as the wild dogs or dingoes. Rabbits, too, had lately been introduced for sport, but were as yet scarce, in Australia. It was not long before they arrived in New Zealand.

The first liberations, from New South Wales stock, occurred in 1838. Between that date and the 1860's many more importations occurred, chiefly in the South Island, where the sheep and cattle men were becoming established on the broad Canterbury plains and inland hills as a new prosperous yeoman class. Of mostly British parentage, they longed to re-create for themselves the best of the homeland environment, so nostalgically remembered in exile. This was the era of acclimatisation societies and sporting clubs, spread not only by the farmers but just as enthusiastically by business interests in the towns. The support of the provincial governments was thus assured. Regardless, or perhaps we should say ignorant, of the consequences, there were liberations of game of all kinds: pheasants (1842), peafowl (1843), rock-dove (1850), white and black swans (1864–68), guinea fowl (1864), sundry quail species (1865 onwards), mallard (1867); and others, such as grouse and partridges, which failed. Even while the Maori wars continued there were introductions of red deer (1851), opossum (1858), fallow deer (1864) and hare (1867), which must have surprised fugitive brown-skinned warriors chancing upon these new exotic Pakeha creatures which had joined them in the fastnesses of the bush. Cage loads of British singing birds were imported from 1862 onwards in the determined and not unsuccessful effort of the acclimatisation societies to re-create the sounds and atmosphere of the land from which their members had emigrated voluntarily and the birds compulsorily.

By the time the Australians had begun to realise that the rabbit was not behaving as it did in Britain, but was instead multiplying beyond reasonable sporting numbers and destroying pasture as fast as the farmers tried to create it, it was too late to stay the flood. In Australia, a few years after poachers had been fined for shooting rabbits, the 'grey tide spread at a staggering speed of seventy miles each year' (Serventy). A new industry sprang up, at the expense of farming, an export trade in skins and dried carcases which later reached six figures sterling annually within the century.

In New Zealand the rabbit did not become firmly established until about 1870. It then exploded in all directions, as described in Chapter Four. By 1876 it was necessary to introduce legislation to control the pest. All things were in its favour, however.

Old tussock is hardly palatable to sheep until spring has come to allow the tender, vigorous new shoots to grow from the old roots. But too often the inexperienced settler burned the country when it was excessively dry; and so destroyed the very roots of the vegetation. While this was recovering the rabbits ate every fresh blade as it appeared, being closer grazers than the sheep and cattle; they starved these out, leaving only the bracken and the unpalatable weeds. Cloven hooves trod and cut the bared soil in the search for green blades. The first dry weather, accompanied by the strong prevalent winds, set the loosened earth in motion. The settlers of the Canterbury lands were often to complain bitterly of increasing dust storms which choked them day after day and smothered everything with moving soil. Then when the sudden violent rains came the streams and rivers emptied the land of the dust in the form of mud and moving, slipping silt. Whole hillsides slumped into the valleys, down towards the sea.

The rabbit was a leading accomplice in this tremendous erosion initiated by man in his foolish policy of untimely burning, and persistent overstocking of the land with both domesticated and wild animals.

Looking around for relief from the curse they had laid upon the promised land, those runholders who were not actually engaged in the export of rabbit skins and carcases (which rose to £1 million in wages and sales by 1939) now saw a simple remedy in the introduction of the rabbit's natural enemies. They believed that certain predators, in the settled conditions of the rabbit's European home, had for centuries effectively controlled rodent pests. The introduction of the rabbit without its enemies had disturbed 'the balance of nature' – much talked of at this moment. A concerted effort must be made to restore that balance, by introducing the mustelids, which would also keep the abundant rats and mice in check.

From 1882 onwards, for some thirty years, consignments of ferrets, stoats and weasels from Britain were liberated in New Zealand with the full approval and financial backing of the government. Most of these shipments in fact were arranged by the New Zealand Agent-General in London, to the joy and profit of gamekeepers in Britain, who were thus paid twice over to catch 'vermin' on the estates of their masters. They even offered to send foxes; luckily for posterity this was vetoed. The fox had already been introduced in Australia for sporting purposes from 1845 to 1864: at the latter date the Melbourne Hunt Club had released foxes in order to hunt them with foxhounds in proper Jorrocks style and not – as might have been supposed – to keep down the rabbits which were by that date already a nuisance to farmers and a profit to skin dealers. The fox is now abundant in Australia, and extremely unpopular (Serventy writes, 'There is some evidence linking the disappearance of native animals not with the appearance of the rabbit but with the appearance of the fox'). Among those who vetoed the liberation of the fox in New Zealand were shepherds who had emigrated from the mountains of Scotland, Wales and the borders; they declared that foxes were lamb-killers.

All three mustelids were widespread in New Zealand by the early 1900's, but to the bitter disappointment of the runholders they had virtually no effect on the rabbit population. Instead the ferret *Mustela putorius*, and the stoat *Mustela erminea*, were busily occupied in exterminating the absurdly tame native birds. The stoat was particularly successful in its bird hunts: it caught the smallest birds; one stoat's nest in 1926 at Doubtful Sound was lined with the feathers of tomtit and fantail. The stoat has moments when it indulges in extremely playful behaviour, leaping about, wrestling with another stoat, boxing, turning somersaults, rolling on the ground. It has often been reported as using these antics to entice birds within leaping distance. One can well imagine how close native birds would come to examine this behaviour,

from their tameness and curiosity in approaching man: then one leap –
and the stoat can leap at least six feet in one bound – and the victim is
captured, and rapidly killed with bites at the base of the skull.

Least successful numerically since its liberation has been the weasel
Mustela nivalis, but perhaps not surprisingly, since its main food in it
Eurasian home is small mammals, which abound there: mice, voles,
moles, and immature rats and rabbits. In New Zealand only the kiore
rat (easily killed at any age by the weasel) and the introduced house
mouse were available, although in summer there would be the nests of
European rats and rabbits to exploit, and the eggs, young, and sitting
birds of ground-nesting species. The weasel also climbs freely, like the
stoat, in search of birds when ground food may be scarce. Probably
the introduction of the weasel did more harm than good by destroying
the eggs and young of native birds; and assisting the extinction of
the harmless kiore rat on the main islands.

All three mustelids appear to have most numerous in the peak period
of rabbit farming and abundance, 1924–36, as shown by figures of
rabbits exported. This was a slump time for New Zealand; and the
rabbit-devastated land was a disheartening sight. I quote from *Rabbits
Galore*, by W. H. McLean, who records the following inscription which
he found scribbled on a milestone in the North Island in 1934:

> Land of gullies and valleys deep,
> Full of rabbits and lousy sheep,
> Rich man's paradise, poor man's hell,
> Land of B—, fare ye well!
>
> (signed) Aussie.

At last it was realised that the mustelids were worse than uselesss
and in 1936 the protection they had been given since liberation was
removed entirely. This was another peak year of 17,372,000 rabbit skins
exported. It is interesting to note that a fall in rabbit numbers occurred
as soon as it became legal to kill mustelids anywhere, anytime; but one
cannot reliably correlate the two facts as cause and effect. The rabbit
population seemed to be undergoing an irregular cycle. From 20,776,000
exported in 1924 there had been a gradual fall to 6,825,000 in 1931,

similar to an earlier seven-year cycle of 12,254,000 in 1910 falling to 5,768,000 in 1917. This periodicity was investigated by the mathematician Whittle; but events made further cyclic studies unprofitable. When, by 1945, exports had again risen – to 17,673,000, it was necessary to revise drastically the old Rabbit Nuisance Acts, the first of which had been passed in 1876 (page 93). In 1947 the government established a Rabbit Destruction Council and declared total war on the rabbit by every means of extermination, foul or fair. But not until the export of rabbits and their sale for fur or food was totally prohibited in 1954 did success follow.

Rabbit dealers were very angry, but the prohibition has had striking results. At the present time the rabbit in New Zealand has been so reduced by poisoning, fumigation, shooting and other control methods that it is no longer a major hazard to farming. The Rabbit Boards set up in each district of many square miles send teams 'on safari' to work the runs, block by block, concentrating on each reported re-infestation. In *Rabbits Galore* McLean states that his aim is to keep the rabbit population at not more than five per thousand acres. To do this over the hundreds of square miles of the Wairarapa district which he supervised required a staff of twenty trained men, ten Landrovers, two utility vehicles, two Landscout cycles, and a central office (where some research is carried out). His success has been astonishing, considering the vast and rugged terrain, but it was only achieved at the cost of vigilance – and ratepayers' money.

The stock farmers are delighted. While they help by sniping off the odd rabbit at leisure, chiefly at night by shooting under lights from a Landrover, the responsibility is the Board's. Ratepayers meet the cost out of levies, and the government makes a pro rata grant. It is at last recognised that it is easier, and less expensive in the long run, to control five rather than five hundred rabbits per thousand acres.

Incidentally the virus of myxomatosis, introduced in 1951–52 after its spectacular success in the humid areas of Australia, and its subsequent, even more spectacular, success in Europe, was a complete failure in New Zealand. Neither the New Zealand mosquitoes nor sandflies act as effective vectors of the virus. During the long voyages in sailing ships which brought the rabbit first to Australia and then to New Zealand in the last century, the rabbit's own flea *Spillopsyllus cuniculi* (which in field research for the British Nature Conservancy in 1953–54 I proved to be the principal carrier of the virus in Britain) died out. For this reason: it is now known that the eggs of this flea do not hatch unless dropped in the warm earth nest of a doe rabbit; nor can the female flea lay fertile eggs unless she has had a meal of blood (containing vital hormones) from a pregnant doe. So, unable to reproduce in the hutches on board ship, the fleas died out during the long voyages. However, in Australia the kangaroo flea sometimes attaches to the rabbit, and it is a moderately effective vector of the virus, but not sufficiently so to cause a major epidemic. Certain Australian mosquitoes alone were responsible for spreading the disease along the river systems in Australia.

Despite world publicity given to the success of introduced myxomatosis in Australia, it is there confined to damp, mosquito-ridden districts. In the dry regions it is quite ineffective. Australia still has a rabbit problem, aggravated by the fact that some States foolishly permit the sale and export of skins and carcases, and so rabbit-farming goes on. The pest is likely to become even more serious as the myxoma virus continues to weaken, and more and more individuals become immune.

To return to the mustelids; and their present numbers in New Zealand now that the rabbit is firmly under control. A questionnaire in 1961 resulted in replies from ninety people. All three mustelids were scarcer. Stoats were the most numerous of the three, with weasels very local. Ferrets seem to have retired to live in a habitat typical of the European polecats, from which they were originally domesticated: open paddocks, tussock, and riverside swamps.

The stoat is universally widespread in North and South Islands, reaching into the sub-alpine areas and rain forest, where the ferret and weasel are rare. The stoat has been trapped in the haunts of the takahe. An examination of the stomachs and intestines of 52 stoats, showed that 23 of the stomachs and 14 of the intestines were empty. In the remainder were traces of 2 mice, 2 rats, 5 rabbits, 2 opossums; mammals bulked largest of any other group. There were also 22 traces of birds, 5 of fish, 18 of insects – chiefly wetas (crickets), and some traces of spiders and mites. Stoat droppings indicate that they will take crayfish, and they have been seen feeding on spent salmon.

Both stoats and ferrets are reported as feeding on carrion – of fish, deer, rabbit and garbage. In addition stoats were seen at bird, opossum, hare and sheep carcases; and the ferret at goat and hedgehog also. In both rabbit was the predominant food.

The brown hare *Lepus europaeus* was introduced from Britain in 1851 and 1867, again for sporting purposes. On the whole it has not been a serious menace. Unlike the mountain hare – fortunately not introduced – the brown hare is solitary except at the mating period. It likes a wide territory in which to roam. It is found at all levels from the shore to the alpine tussock country, most numerously in rich open grassland. Females average well above eight pounds, males nearly a pound less; there is a tendency for the hare in the South Island to weigh heavier than that in the North Island. It is not much persecuted; and there is a curious prejudice against eating hare in some persons, which may have helped its survival. Its principal enemies, apart from man, seen to be harrier, ferret and stoat; yet there are few reports of the mustelids taking hares. Guthrie-Smith describes how the hare, on its first appearance at Tutira about 1893, was ceaselessly persecuted by the harrier: 'Prior to the day when hares became inured to persecution and had discovered how to escape their relentless enemies, they not infrequently could be noticed hirpling about the run half-plucked with two or more birds in hot pursuit.' Hares are frequently killed on the road, and their carcases are then eaten by harriers, which also take young leverets.

Locally hares can cause damage to young orchards, garden and crops, but on the whole control by shooting is not difficult. Hares have certainly increased since rabbits declined under the control exercised by the Rabbit Boards. More are shot from Landrovers than during the height of the rabbit plague. Yet the rate of reproduction is only about half that of the rabbit, averaging 4·8 litters of 2·14 leverets each, or just over ten young annually per adult jill. In New Zealand, however, the female born early in the spring may breed in her first year, at six months, producing one or two leverets (early breeding is rare or un-known in Europe and Canada; in New Zealand it is probably due to the longer growing season). Possibly, too, the lack of competition from rabbits has resulted in less pre-natal reabsorption of embryos, which occurs in both these lagomorphs under conditions of overcrowding, malnutrition and psychological stress, and is a useful form of birth control. Again, while hares are shot at night along with rabbits the hare is immune from the effects of fumigation and ferreting of burrows, which it never enters at any time.

There is hope of increasing respectability for Jack and Jill Hare. Regarded as a game animal the hare in New Zealand has lately become an article of export, along with venison, in the expanding overseas market for wild meat.

Although a late introduction in New Zealand the hedgehog *Erinaceus europaeus* has had an astounding success. It was first liberated in the South Island in the 1870's and the North Island about 1910, evidently for sentimental reasons: the settler forever trying to re-create the environment of the country he had abandoned for the wide open colonial spaces, where he found no native mammals but only disappearing native birds to solace his lonely life. It was kept at first as a pet to grace gardens and orchards, especially in suburbs where, as in England, it thrives on semi-protection due to man's interest in the 'harmless hedgepig'.

Soon, however, the hedgehog had strolled far into the bush on its nocturnal adventures. It was no longer regarded as harmless. Discovering hedgehogs close to the despoiled nests of introduced pheasant, quail and duck, members of acclimatisation societies raised a howl of rage; and in no time a bounty was offered for its snout. But it was no use. The hedgehog continued its march through the land at an astonishing rate. Thousands were accidentally, and some deliberately, killed on the road daily – a process still going on. The hedgehog had come to stay, as permanent as the settlers themselves.

It is surprising that, in view of the accusations of damage to other wildlife hurled at this little animal so loved by children and many adults for its gentle movements, interesting coat of prickles, tameness and appetite for worms, slugs, snails, bread and milk, little scientific work was done on its natural food in New Zealand until Robert Brockie's study published in 1959.

From the contents of ten stomachs and ninety droppings of hedge-hogs, mainly from Wellington province, Brockie records that the main food items on pastureland were slugs and moth caterpillars; and in the sand dunes, snails, millipedes and (introduced green) frogs. Traces of worms, beetles, earwigs, spiders, flies, woodlice, ants, wetas, cicadas and various insect larvae were also found. There was no sign of the remains of the eggs or chicks of ground-nesting birds, although skylarks, pipits and pheasants were nesting in the area at the time that some of the droppings were collected for analysis. On tests, hedgehogs in capti-vity made no attempt to break open or eat hens' eggs offered to them, although they greedily ate the contents when the eggs were broken before their eyes. The hedgehog in Europe is known to smash open and eat the eggs of smaller birds; and Warden Herbert Axell told me that he had to protect terns' nests at the Dungeness Reserve in Kent, from the night raids of hedgehogs, by fencing them in. The hedgehog ingests some of the shell in devouring the egg, and this is passed in the faeces – a sure sign of a meal of eggs.

But in New Zealand it is no egg thief, finding abundant food in the (mostly objectionable) slugs, grubs, etc. On balance the hedgehog is a highly respectable settler, and ought to be fully accepted as such by the biped who liberated it so carelessly, and who now kills it by the thousand, albeit unintentionally, on the road at night.

In a count of 570 animals (mammals and birds) killed by traffic on the road between Taupo and Wellington, made by members of the Animal Ecology Section of the DSIR, in driving over twelve months, hedgehogs formed 54·5 per cent, and opossums 6·3 per cent of the total. The mortality on these roads was highest in the summer, January to March, when it averaged 60 dead hedgehogs per 100 miles, falling to 5 per 100 miles in August and September, but rising sharply again to 50 in October. These are conservative figures. In some counts I carried out in the summer on fast roads in both South and North Islands I could average more than one hedgehog per mile. Brockie himself reported 132 bodies counted on 135 miles of road between Waikanae and Taihape.

Despite this high mortality, chiefly on fast main roads outside towns, the hedgehog in New Zealand shows no sign of a fall in numbers. Although it was supposed that most of the hedgehogs run over might be juveniles wandering in search of new homes, it was found that they were in fact nearly all adults. Any species that can afford to lose mature individuals at this rate must have a very high reproductive rate, evidently much higher than in its European home, where the toll on roads of the same category is comparatively insignificant (under one per hundred miles in Hampshire, England, according to J. L. Davies). This high reproductive capacity is evidently associated with a shorter hibernation or resting period in winter – only three months compared with six months in northern Europe.

As to the hedgehog's natural enemies, too little is known of these, even in its European home. Foxes and badgers are said to be able to unroll and tear apart the hedgehog in Britain, but neither of these animals exists in New Zealand. Polecats (and therefore presumably feral ferrets) are said to open their scent glands upon a hedgehog, overpowering the victim with so foul a stench as to compel it to unroll, helpless, as if anaesthetised.

But who has seen this – in New Zealand?

8 The Ravished Forest

The last chapter recorded only the beginning of the acclimatisation madness; we have yet to describe the liberation of more and larger mammals – the browsers whose impact on the New Zealand forest and bush has been catastrophic. The individuals and societies clamouring for these liberations left unheeded the warnings of a few thoughtful scientists and others who pointed out that woodlands in New Zealand had evolved in the total absence of large browsing mammals, that if the unique indigenous avifauna and flora, already suffering from the early introductions of the pig, goat and rabbit, were to be saved from further deterioration, all further importations of wild animals must be prohibited. Such a law was to be passed only when the degradation of the forest was complete.

Rabbit, goat and pig were devastating the forest from the ground up. Not satisfied with these enemies, the acclimatisators introduced deer, accelerating the process, and brought in opossums, thus completing the degradation from the tops of the trees downwards.

With what impatience did the sportsmen settlers, especially the large communities of Scottish origin, await the arrival of the red deer *Cervus elaphus* from their native land! The first liberations were in the South Island in 1851, at a time when there still remained some 25 million acres of forest out of New Zealand's land area of 66 million acres. More releases followed, in North, South and Stewart Islands, but the increase seemed slow, little shooting was possible, the deer tended to be sedentary; and for fifty years the disappointed acclimatisation societies carted red deer zealously in all directions, including the almost inaccessible Fiordland glens, such as the Lillburn Valley and Dusky Sound.

It was assumed that as the finest red deer of Europe had developed in a temperate woodland environment, the species would thrive in the temperate virgin forests of New Zealand. This proved to be the case at first, in most areas of release. By the turn of the century some spectacular prime heads were shot, exceeding in size any recorded in Scotland.

Not content with this success, the acclimatisation zealots imported other kinds of deer: fallow deer in 1864, sambar deer in 1875, Japanese deer in 1885. Still later, long after the red deer had become a nuisance, there were more deer species liberated: moose in 1900, Virginia deer in 1901, wapiti in 1905, and Javan rusa deer in 1907. None of these, however, has succeeded so well as the red deer; they have remained limited to a few isolated localities. The fallow deer has had a limited success in both North and South Islands, and has even modified the bush where numerous. The moose, liberated in south-west Fiordland, has not significantly increased and seems to be dying out. On Stewart Island the Virginia deer eats its way through the bush, acting as a kind of trail-maker for the heavier, taller red deer. Wapiti from North America mingle with red deer west of Lake Te Anau, and may interbreed with them, producing very fine heads.

Meanwhile the red deer has colonised all major native as well as exotic forests, excepting the sub-tropical Northland kauri forest. It has climbed all the higher mountain ranges where bush and tussock are found in conjunction. Its success lies in its versatile grazing and browsing habits. It grazes grass and forbs in the open, especially on fine days in summer, retiring much to the shelter of trees in strong snow and wintry conditions, when it browses its favourite evergreen leaves and foliage. It is not a lover of closed canopy woodland; it needs grass more than it needs foliage.

Most of the native trees and shrubs of New Zealand are evergreen, their leaves providing deer with an unfailing reservoir of palatable browsing throughout the year – very different from the predominantly deciduous woods of Europe leafless in winter. Virtually undisturbed in the mountain forests uncoveted by man, red deer populations have

The rare notornis
(Maori takahe)
at the nest

One of the young
notornis captured
during the ringing
expedition

Notornis in breeding
plumage

The kakapo, or owl-parrot, is flightless and close to extinction

increased to pest proportions, leading to selective grazing and reduction
of the more palatable native trees and shrubs, such as mountain beech
Nothofagus, coprosmas, notopanax, olearia. Reduction and modification
of the bush is partly achieved by browsing the palatable tender shoots of
seedling trees growing from seed fallen from tree-tops out of reach of the
deer; thus forest regeneration is checked and ultimately, if the deer
persist, the bush becomes rough pasture dominated by unpalatable plants.

Like the merino sheep, red deer move up to the mountain tops in
summer, away from the biting flies of the forest and the valleys. Like
sheep they seek the tender young mountain plants and grasses which
shoot forth as the snows melt and the sun warms the thin soil. Their
sharp hooves cut the ground, sometimes deliberately if they scrape
stones away in the search. After heavy rain the loosened soil and scree
slips away downhill.

In due course these surface slips which have settled on the mountain
slopes after such an avalanche become stabilised and healed by regrowth
from seeds – provided the deer do not immediately browse there. Unfortunately this tender new growth is much sought after by the deer and
sheep, and often, before it can form a spongy protective mat of vegetation, it is devoured and the mixture of stone, rubble and soil, as before,
is swept further downhill with the next torrential downpour. The chain
reaction – familiar to readers of this book by now – goes on so long as
these mammals feed in numbers on the mountain tops and steep slopes.
Ultimately the succession of slips engulf the long-established plant cover
of bog and lakeside on the valley floor.

Once the deer have become established in a suitable terrain the
adults, as in many species of animal, settle to a routine and a territory
which they will not easily abandon. From the sub-alpine zone and
mountain tussock country they move down into the valleys for shelter in
winter, when they may venture upon the sheep and cattle runs. The
autumn rut is over, the stags have ceased to roar; the younger stags, if
they have not been driven away altogether, are now accepted as part
of the community of old stags, breeding hinds and young females which
will inhabit the range for another year, moving within prescribed limits
seasonally, altitudinally.

II

Studies of red deer populations in New Zealand have indicated that after colonising a new area, a peak of numbers is reached in from twenty to thirty years. This first peak usually coincides with the destruction of the accessible palatable plants – which are, incidentally, also richer in nutrients than the unpalatable plants. The deer are now forced to be less discriminating, hunger compelling them to attack what is left: unpalatable plants and the tougher parts of already browsed and degenerated vegetation. So begins the stage of semi-starvation and poor condition which may last for several years, with a few individuals escaping to new areas of colonisation and food before the privations of winter cause the death of the weakest of the stay-at-homes, especially the adults which become sedentary with age.

Through overgrazing and erosion the indigenous plant community has suffered a change in composition, which is irreversible so long as deer (plus sheep, goat and opossum) haunt these solitudes. Winter has searched out the weak deer, and, with the decline in population over the years after the peak, those plants which could not resist the browsing pressure are gradually replaced by still tougher woody, herbaceous vegetation which will begin to cover up the slips and ground eaten bare earlier, thus permitting a partial return of the plant-soil partnership which resists erosion. But the land can never support again the first-peak numbers of deer. The more edible virgin or pre-mammal climax native plant community has been replaced by a coarse permanent vegetation. It will be browsed by the resident deer likely to remain generally in indifferent health and low numbers in balance with this unpalatable food supply.

An example of this sequence of events was recorded by five ecologists who made a summer expedition in 1957 to the wild, uninhabited, bleak Cameron Mountain country around Lake Monk in southern Fiordland. They showed that the initial colonisation by deer, begun in 1901, and preceded by opossums a few years earlier, reached a peak in the mild winters of 1936–38, but at the time of the expedition the red deer, feeding on degraded plant cover, were down to a very low subsistence level and so poor in condition that it was doubtful if they had enough body fat to survive the winter. Opossums were not seen at all.

Peak red deer populations were widely reported during the first world war, when so many active deer-hunters were serving in the forces. Afterwards, in response to public agitation over deer-damage to forests, a bounty was offered by the government on every deer tail. Thus, yet again, a deliberately introduced species had become a serious pest, had been classified as a 'Noxious Animal', and hunters were paid to go forth and destroy them. From 1931 to 1962 government hunters shot 867,220 deer; private deerstalkers shot many more. Most of the resulting venison was left where it was shot; it was too difficult to extract from the bush and there was little demand for it.

This heavy 'predation' by man has had the interesting effect of improving the condition of the deer – as reduction of numbers of red deer in Scotland has. Extermination of red deer in New Zealand forests, however, seems impossible, and the task now facing the conservators is how best to manage and improve both the trees and the deer, by modern techniques of game management. As I write this, New Zealand has arrived at a third stage in the cycle of public emotion over introduced deer. First the wild enthusiasm of the acclimatisation decades; then the bitter disappointment at the degradation of forest with erosion of soil caused by overpopulation which led to the bounty payments for each deer tail; and now the realisation that a new equilibrium may be possible – between the deer and the degenerate forest, which can be turned to advantage by keeping deer numbers at this lower level by judicious hunting; and not without profit.

Improved transport technique has assisted in commercialising the comparatively new trade in venison by enabling deer meat to be lifted out of remote rugged roadless country by helicopter, direct to road transport and so to the freezing works. The biggest demand for venison comes from West Germany and the Netherlands at present, and the price per pound is better than that for lamb. The antlers fetch a very high price; even the unborn fawns (slinks) are saleable, if dried, for export to the Orient. Looking several years ahead, there is no doubt that an increasingly protein-hungry world will stimulate further this demand for deer-meat. Already deer are becoming scarce near the towns, where they are hunted for both venison and sport. Wealthy 'big game' shooters from the USA and elsewhere are encouraged to visit New Zealand, where the finest red stags in the world can still be shot, as well as the noblest of wapiti. The foreign exchange resulting from both the venison and the hunting is welcomed by the government. One can even forecast the imposition of hunting licences and a close season supplanting the present licence-free hunting of deer the year round!

Just as the red deer and the opossum worked at the destruction of the trees from below and above respectively, the liberation of snow-line grazing mammals precipitated the degradation of the alpine vegetation. Sheep and feral goats had long visited the cool mountain-tops, but only in small numbers in summer, moving away, or being moved, from the storms and snows of winter, to lower altitudes.

The early signs of denudation and erosion they produced were ignored, however, and in 1904 thar *Hemitragus jemlahicus* from Asia, and in 1907 chamois *Rupicapra rupicapra* from Europe, were liberated in the sub-alpine zone near Mount Cook. Thus two more alien species were encouraged to attack the last accessible native flora – that of the highest peaks – which had never known a pressure greater than the beaks of native birds cropping the alpine berries and fruits in autumn.

The thar is a splendid-looking caprine beast with wide-spreading sickle-shaped horns, a picturesque figure outlined against the mountain-scape. It is agile and difficult to hunt because of its ability to scale steep rocks. But as many as five thousand have been shot in a single season of late years, since protection has been removed. It continues to spread slowly along the higher central alpine backbone of the South Island, forming dense herds which eat a locality quite bare before moving on.

The chamois, lighter, with small horns, but an even more active climber, has spread much further, working its way from alpine summit to alpine summit below the permanent snow-line, south to Mount Anau and the Franklins; and as far north as the Tasman Mountains which gaze down towards Cape Farewell. It has also spread east to the bare heights of the Kaikouras, (where Tapuenuka raises its naked head 9,465 feet above sea-level), the only known nesting place of Hutton's shear-water. In the first year of large-scale destruction of this new 'Noxious Animal', 1936, nearly three thousand were killed by government hunters; in 1959 over seven thousand were officially booked as slain by the same hunters; and the total of all chamois killed by both official and private hunters continues to rise annually.

No enemies save man trouble these masters of the alpine scene; there are no mountain lions or pumas to strike down the adults, or bears to take the fawns, or eagles to sweep the little ones to death. When summer comes the chamois and thar move upwards to take the last plants of the rock-crevices and screes which hold together the frost-cracked surface; then move on. Their light treading is not light enough to prevent minor slips of stone which may develop into great shingle avalanches when the rain-torrents fall.

There are many full species of opossum in Australasia, but only one in America. The species liberated in New Zealand was the Australian brush-tailed opossum *Trichosurus vulpecula*, so called because its strong prehensile furry tail is bare along the lower side. It is roughly the size of a domestic cat, but varies considerably in both size and colour in New Zealand; many of the subspecies which range over Australia and Tasmania were imported during the early liberations which began in 1858. In Australia this 'possum' (as it is called there) is considered useful, or at least harmless, feeding largely on gum leaves, and it has a taste for the objectionable mistletoe, a parasite of forest trees. In balance with its predators and food supply it occupies its ecological niche without causing devastation of the environment. It is known to raid orchards in Australia, but not seriously enough to merit all-out persecution. It is shot for its fur; and generally regarded with affection for its attractive appearance.

This opossum is easily killed at night once it has been located by spotlight, for it has the habit of remaining perfectly still when surprised. It also enters a baited trap with ease. These two traits suggest that it is unintelligent, if not downright stupid. Yet it is not without charm, and its family habits are sound – judged by human standards. Looking at an opossum treed in the torchlight one night I could not help but admire the wise-looking puppy face, with wide, alert ears, and huge black eyes which stared with the gentle patience of the Cheshire cat in *Alice in Wonderland*, waiting for us to go away and leave it in peace to devour more apricots. But it was no grinning matter for this individual; or my host, who said angrily, 'I hate the little beast! I'll have to kill it.'

He fired two revolver bullets at a range of eight feet. The opossum, mortally wounded at the first shot, seemed not even to blink. It remained in the same posture, staring at us from a crotch of the apricot tree five feet above our heads, its tail tightly coiled around a small branch, so that I could not believe it was dead. Its eyes still seemed to look at us reproachfully. Five minutes passed. My host fetched a pole and prised the opossum's rigid clinging claws away from the tree. Slowly it was levered backwards, its tail still gripping the branch, its eyes still wide open. It was quite unconscious, although its heart was beating tenaciously, when at last it fell to the grass.

This habit of 'freezing' when surprised by its only real enemy in New Zealand, man, is the cause of the destruction of thousands of opossums on every road in New Zealand. In the beams of the car's headlights you will see the reflection of the large eyes as the animal crouches, seldom making any attempt to avoid being run down; occasionally it may make a confused amble straight to death in a late reaction to the increasing intensity of the light. New Zealanders whose orchards and woods have suffered – and few have not – from the ravages of opossums can hardly be blamed for a sigh of satisfaction when the wheel crushes the life of this 'noxious animal'.

'Every road in New Zealand' is not yet quite accurate. Its present range covers Stewart Island, South Island and most of North Island, as far as the Bay of Islands. From the last it is slowly moving north towards Kaitaia and the land's end of Cape Reinga. But in motoring that way the evidence was plain to me in 1966: no more squashed opossums on the roads north of Kaikohe.

In the frenzy of acclimatisation in the last half of the nineteenth century, the opossum had been introduced as a welcome settler, a handsome marsupial which was also likely to be very profitable, by producing fur from the empty forest and unproductive bush lands of New Zealand. Opossum had become a fashionable fur on the world market, and fortunes, it was predicted, might be made if only the animal would take kindly to a new land and climate. Nearly a dozen

types of colour and size were recognised for classification by skin
dealers; but scientists could find no clear evidence of even sub-specific
continuity in the colour phases, and it is now considered that all types
interbreed freely. Meanwhile, as soon as it was seen that the opossum
had indeed taken kindly to New Zealand, and was increasing in the
latter half of the last century, hundreds were line-trapped in the
districts of the first liberations, by private individuals, by acclimatisation
societies, as well as by the government (which both sanctioned the
importations and protected them by Acts in 1861 and 1880), and
liberated in new districts.

During the first world war doubts arose about the value of the
opossum to the economy. The first scientific investigation into the effects
of this 'asset' to the bush (forest) was presented to Parliament in 1920.
Professor H. B. Kirk reported no real damage to wildlife, plant or bird,
and recommended further liberations in all forests 'away from orchards
and exotic plantations'. The State Forest Service confirmed his recommendations by a special report in favour of the opossum in 1928.

This virtual protection enabled the opossum to consolidate at the site
of the new liberations, and by 1940 it had covered the whole of the
South Island and two-thirds of the North Island. Importations and
further liberations ceased – they were hardly necessary, and in fact
many conservationists were complaining forcefully of the widespread
damage and erosion following the grazing and browsing partnership of
rabbit, deer and opossum. A further annoyance lay in the opossum's
habit of climbing any sort of wooden post, and short-circuiting high
tension wires, resulting in wide areas of blackout and cessation of
essential farm and town electricity services. The electric power boards
throughout New Zealand have been forced to fix a sheet of metal around
all wire-carrying wooden posts as a standard practice, to prevent these
unorthodox suicides disrupting supplies of current.

All protection for the opossum was removed in 1947 when uncontrolled shooting and trapping was permitted. One more deliberate
acclimatisation had become a 'Noxious Animal'.

Recent studies show that some opossums in New Zealand breed all
the year round, but because of the size of her marsupial pouch the

mother can only nurse one young one over the twenty-two weeks of lactation. However, there is soon another embryo in the uterus, for the female mates at once after parturition, immediately the tiny kitten – a mere half-inch long – has crawled by its forelegs along the track of wet fur which its mother has licked from the genital opening to the pouch. Should one kitten be lost, another is born only seventeen days after mating. But if milk still flows to feed a pouched kitten the fertilised egg or eggs remain free and detached in the uterus, in the form of a minute undeveloped blastocyst. This delay in implantation of the fertile egg occurs in several mammals, both marsupial and placental, and is an interesting form of insurance, securing fertile mating in a wandering species at the one time when male is certain to find female 'at home' in the nursery; but the female is unable to support an immediate pregnancy while feeding the young resulting from the earlier copulation. Attracted to the female while her genitals are in an enlarged condition from parturition, the male is able both to mate and remain to protect the female at a critical moment for her.

Generally the male opossum attends the female during late pregnancy, parturition and lactation, even giving the kitten rides on his back when it is old enough to leave the pouch. The family group is close-knit. Later the male may leave the female for a while, but the kitten remains close to its mother until the approach of the next mating time, when the male rejoins his mate. He is expert at building a weatherproof nest, which may be in a hollow tree, in thick vegetation, or in a hole in a dry bank. Here the family will sleep together all day, and if the night be cold and wet most of the night too. Feeding is restricted in rough weather, but bellies are filled to bursting on fine nights, when great quantities of leaves, fruit, berries, twigs, etc., are consumed.

Food preferences are such that high numbers of opossums in forest areas result in progressive elimination of tree and plant species in order of palatability. Pracy and Kean show that the foliage of these, where available, is preferred roughly in this order: kononi, rata, titoki, clover, five-finger, kamahi, kohekohe, tutu, hinua, wineberry, broadleaf, kanuka, lacebark, lawyer, leatherwood, totara, rangiora, toro, maire, ngaio and lancewood. The flowers of rata and clover are favourites.

Almost any native and orchard fruits are devoured, as well as roses and cultivated flowers, their leaves and fruit. Opossums gobble vegetables, polyanthus, carnation, cyclamen, gladiolus, godetia, eucalyptus, etc, etc. In one night a family party can clean up many rows of gardener's cuttings; as well as young trees newly planted to arrest that same soil erosion which this marsupial has caused by devouring the foliage of and killing native plants and trees.

In thick forest opossum damage can be overlooked, since browsing invariable begins on the tender foliage in the crown of the tree; and unless driven by shortage of upper leaves, the opossum does not attack the tough middle and lower foliage which hides the denuded top from the ground. When the loss by eating exceeds the gain by new growth the tree becomes skeletal, but has more the appearance of disease than of overbrowsing by opossums, which deceives the inexpert observer.

One characteristic sign of opossum trouble is bark-biting and stripping, which can kill a tree either directly or through the exposure of the cambion to insect and fungoid attacks. Opossums will eat bark close to the nest during wet weather especially, and bark-biting is more frequent in wet than in dry climates.

The opossum does in fact prefer dry, warm conditions, and in New Zealand has become most numerous in the east of the North Island, where it breeds twice a year in a climate closer to that of its native Australia. In the wet Southland forests it breeds once a year only.

The favourite browsing tree konini thrives in the open North Island eastern lands. Here the opossum does severe damage to the surviving bush, aided by the attacks of rabbits and goats at ground level, on the steeper slopes of the dry ranges. Where these are insufficiently patrolled by vermin hunters the result is complete defoliation of konini, rata, kamahi, five-finger, rangiora, etc. The ravished slopes will cover up, after spring rains, with temporary annual vegetation such as the water fern *Histiopteris incisa*, in summer, but this dies completely in winter, when violent rainstorms and wind cause the denuded hillsides to slide into the valleys. Everywhere the dismal sequence was obvious to me in wandering through these eastern North Island hills and dales where man had established vast sheep runs he could not adequately patrol for the reduction of noxious animals. Here and there the groups of trees and native bush which had been left to provide shade for stock were dying from above and below, the valleys were choked with gravel, the streams and rivers buried under lifeless shingle. And this eastern land is already too thirsty, too short of water to supply its growing town populations.

Will the opossum go on increasing? In the wet rain-forests of the south it seems to have stabilised at a medium level of numbers following the first successful liberations. But in the North Island it seems to be still on the crest of a wave of expansion, and far above the low level of population man hopes to see. Some I saw in the east of the North Island were moving about in daylight, afflicted, I was told, with a kind of fatal distemper. The nature of this is now being investigated in the hope of finding a fresh approach to the campaign against the opossum, by adding perhaps a virus disease to aid extermination. Anything – even a Pied Piper who could charm the gentle vegetarian opossum – would be welcomed by a government which has angrily outlawed yet another animal it so eagerly imported. Lately, trade in opossum skins has been booming. Instructions have been issued to Rabbit Boards to include it in future control and eradication operations.

Hatred for the opossum is partly responsible for the accusation that it eats the eggs and nestling of birds. The evidence for this is not reliable. It is consistently vegetarian, but it harms birds in other ways. It devours the flowers, leaves and seeds of native trees from which many native birds derive their nourishment, particularly the kaka parrot, the para-keets, kokako and native pigeon. These and the tuis, bellbirds and other honey-eaters are decreasing rapidly where opossums abound.

Finally there is some considerable risk of catching valuable native birds, including kiwis and wekas, in the break-back traps and wire snares set for opossums, despite regulations as to how and where these devices may be laid. Various poisons doped with aromatic lures have been tried, but again with too little regard for their selectiveness; harmless animals die as well.

Last of the grazing animals to be considered is a group which have, because limited in numbers and area occupied, had the least overall effect. Six species of Australian wallaby (small kangaroo) were introduced in New Zealand in the period of furious acclimatisation, late in the nineteenth century. Prime Minister Sir George Grey, familiar with wallabies from his former residence in South Australia, first stocked Kawau Island in the Hauraki Gulf, with five of the six species introduced to New Zealand in the 1870's.

At the present time the red-necked wallaby *Macropus rufogrisea* survives mainly in the Hunter Hills of South Canterbury. The Dama or silver-grey *M. eugenii* is confined to Kawau and the Rotorua district. Both these are common in Australia and in zoos all over the world. The brush-tailed rock wallaby *M. penicillata* is found on Kawau and Rangitoto Islands only; it happens to have become rare in Australia, and in fact is among the rarest animals in the world. But it dominates Rangitoto, which is an island reserve at the entrance to Auckland Harbour, and has to be kept under control so that it does not outgraze its food supply. Two hundred were shot in 1966.

The other three wallabies are found only on Kawau, which is not a large island. Here, along with the two mentioned above, they became so numerous as to destroy the ground vegetation as well as forest, farm and garden crops. They have been hunted and shot in vigorous eradication campaigns during the present century. It is not surprising that one if not more species had to go to the wall in the struggle to survive interspecific and human competition in such a limited terrain. The black-striped *M. dorsalis* has become the rarest; but fortunately it is still not uncommon in Australia; it was last recorded on Kawau in 1954, and may still be there. The swamp or black-tailed species *M. bicolor* flourishes on the island.

It was thought that the Parma or white-throated wallaby *M. parma* had become extinct. It had not been identified in Australia since 1926, and specimens were sought for by biologists who visited zoos and museums all over the world. It happened to be an ironical situation that during this time, when the Australians were writing the obituary of this little kangaroo, the owners of property on Kawau were killing indiscriminately hundreds of this species and throwing the carcases away as just 'vermin wallaby' without bothering to identify them specifically.

The campaign, largely of poisoning, culminated when about three thousand wallabies of all species were slain on Kawau in a single year in 1965; and later it was estimated that about two hundred of these were the rare Parma wallaby! Then the Director of the Western Australia Museum identified specimens from Kawau, and ordered a pair of Parma for breeding purposes. At the cost of damage to the pine plantations of Kawau, the Parma has survived after all, to return to colonise its native Australian haunts, where today wallabies are strictly protected. (There have been only a few instances of a similar rescue of a species approaching extinction. The Duke of Bedford bred in spacious captivity at his home, Woburn Park, England, the Pere David's deer, since exterminated in China, but now re-established there from Woburn. The Arabian oryx, believed to be virtually extinct as a wild animal, is breeding, somewhat tenuously, in enclosures in a comparable desert climate in America. And the Hawaiian or ne-ne goose has been saved in captivity by breeding at the Wildfowl Trust in England, the surplus young birds being sent to re-colonise the volcanic mountains of their island home.)

This rare Parma wallaby has evidently fitted successfully into an ecological niche on Kawau Island, where its numbers are sufficient for limited export of breeding stock. But it is essential to give it adequate protection, if not as a permanent resident at least until it is fully rehabilitated in Australia. Wallabies are hard grazers of young, new and secondary forest shrubs and trees. One can understand the rage of foresters on Kawau whose plantations have been cut down by these attractive leaping creatures. In Australia wallabies have many natural enemies, including dingoes, foxes and eagles, but virtually none in New Zealand, where they tend to increase rapidly and change bush to coarse pasture, a habit at first not unacceptable to the pioneer settler. But when the wallabies continue to spread over the newly sown grassland and compete seriously with farm stock, as is happening in the South Canterbury Hills today (where the red-necked wallaby was so enthusiastically liberated in the last century), they are listed as noxious animals, to be shot and poisoned at every opportunity.

Altogether, out of some fifty species of mammal, excluding domestic stock imported, thirty have become established in New Zealand (list, page 230). All but four of these were deliberately introduced and – excepting perhaps the moose, doubtfully surviving today – have become officially blacklisted as Noxious Animals, or are regarded by the majority of land-holders as pests!

One would have supposed that this experience would have taught the Islanders a severe lesson; yet still from time to time one hears or reads of demands to introduce yet more alien species. A law now prohibits such imports except under special licence, which may be granted to educational and research institutions, including zoos, but not for acclimatisation in the wild.

As to birds, if settlers had had their way in the last century nightingales and many other soft-billed singing birds would inhabit the Arcadia they proposed to create. But none of the long-distance migratory birds imported from Europe at that time survived. Doubtless, on liberation, their ineradicable instinct was to fly south in winter (the New Zealand summer) which would have sent them to the South Pole; and north in their European summer (the New Zealand winter) to be lost in the Pacific Ocean.

It is calculated that some 130 species of foreign, chiefly European, species of birds have been liberated in New Zealand in the last 150 years. But only 33 species have become established (page 227). Fortunately only a few of these have been classed as unmitigated pests. Those enthusiasts who introduced the sparrow, starling, myna, rook and magpie would find themselves unpopular today, and these birds being shot as 'vermin' by many landholders. But the singing birds – skylark, song thrush, blackbird, dunnock, greenfinch, goldfinch, chaffinch and yellowhammer – are generally an accepted and pleasing feature of the country. In fruit-growing areas and orchards some of these are unwelcome, and the abundant lesser redpoll, which attacks fruit buds and young fruit, is rigorously trapped and netted.

The Canada goose is a successful introduction in the South Island, where it has taken to nesting in the fastnesses of high country, moving down to lakes and rivers in the winter. Even more successful has been the Australian black swan *Cynus atratus*, now dominating all large shallow lakes throughout New Zealand, with fantastic numbers on Lake Ellesmere (page 81). Mallard, introduced as early as 1867 from Britain, and in this century from the United States, has increased so much as soon to outnumber the common grey duck of New Zealand *Anas superciliosa*, with which it readily hybridises.

9 River, Lake and Sea

English and Scottish settlers who had enjoyed fishing the rivers and lochs of home were disappointed that the fresh waters of New Zealand were singularly empty of sporting fish. The Maoris hunted the large eels, and caught them, with lampreys, in traps and weirs. They also enjoyed the numerous freshwater crayfish, and used to dry the tail-ends in the sun as a winter store food. But other edible fish were few; a small one which they called inanga (the 'mountain trout', but not a trout at all), a smelt, a grayling and a few other scarce and insignificant species which they needed all their traditional skill with green flax nets to capture.

The Pakeha saw that the rivers were ideal for stocking with trout and salmon, as good as the famous Norwegian fishing streams, flowing swiftly over boulder-strewn shingle. The problem was how to get the ova of the best European trout and salmon to survive the long sea voyage of twelve thousand miles. There were several attempts to transport salmonid ova and some were total or partial failures. It was not easy to keep the eggs cool as the clipper ships dawdled through the tropics on their three months' voyages. But by 1860 some ships carried auxiliary steam, and in the next ten years faster communications led to the first consignments of ova arriving in viable condition.

As far as I can trace from the literature it was in 1864 that some 120,000 ova arrived safely in Tasmania, whose cool mountain streams were considered to be perfect for a salmon and trout hatchery. Salmon had indeed been the prime interest, and only three thousand of the eggs in this consignment were brown trout – put in almost as an after-thought.

These trout ova had been stripped from carefully selected mature fish. Some 1,200 were presented by Admiral Keppel who fished the famous Itchen river in Hampshire; and about 1,500 were sent out by that distinguished angler and writer Francis Francis. The latter batch were from fish netted at Thirlow's Mill on the river Wye at High Wycombe, Bucks. The parent fish were prime seven, eight, even ten, pounders. James Englefield wrote of this stretch of the Wye that it had been 'for centuries deservedly celebrated as one of the purest and best of the small streams in England, not only for sport with the fly rod, but for the edible qualities of the trout so freely produced, for their perfect form, beautiful markings and sheen of silver shading to gold.'

What good fortune for generations of trout and trout-fishermen 'down under' that it was the progeny of these noble fish, thriving so well in Tasmania, which provided the first class stock to colonise suitable waters. The first consignment reached New Zealand in 1868. Growing rapidly to giant sizes in the South Island rivers, they were true to Englefield's lyrical description, and more. The clean waters abounded in trout food. Five years later Charles Tripp was boasting in a letter dated 29th May 1873 that 'the Acclimatisation Gardens [of Christ-church] have lately imported some salmon spawn and we have fifty young fish and lots of trout; not the brook trout, but the heavy Thames trout.'

The brown trout were not only very successful, but were to become natural colonisers themselves. They made their way unaided by man out of the stocked rivers and entered unstocked rivers, including those of the warm North Island.

Understandably the salmon were not so successful. When they made their annual migration to the sea, most of them disappeared forever – their European kith and kin at this age were swimming twelve thousand miles away in the chilly North Atlantic and Arctic deeps! Interestingly, the few survivors, chiefly in South Island waters, seem to have adapted their habits and become lakebound, avoiding the sea, perhaps like the European huchen (*Hucho hucho*) or land-locked salmon.

Land of the Settler: the native forest departs

Little blue penguins coming ashore at night

A yellow-eyed penguin on the nest

Pacific salmon, which live shorter lives and normally only migrate once to the sea and back, then die after spawning, were also introduced, but with no greater success.

Not satisfied with the success of the brown trout, and the slow progress in salmon numbers, anglers, moved by the sight of great rainbow trout on their visits to North America, imported ova from California. The first lot arrived in Auckland in 1887. They found good feeding and the right temperatures in the warmer waters of North Island lakes. In a few years the great thermal lakes of Taupo, Rotorua and Rotoiti were stocked. There followed a period of forty years of sensational records of trout: brown to 24 lb., rainbow to 15 lb. The largest of the North Island lakes, Taupo, 1,211 feet above sea level, is still the mecca of rainbow trout devotees, not only of local but of overseas anglers. A whole township of 'baches' (shacks), and places of accommodation for fishermen sprang up almost overnight. Today there are many hotels, and it has become fashionable to spend the Christmas (summer) holiday at Lake Taupo, which also has fine bathing beaches, hot springs and many square miles of blue water for sailing, water ski-ing, and cruising. But the beautiful glowing trout – now perhaps overfished – reign over all.

Brown and rainbow trout are two of the very few introduced species which have not become noxious animals. They have provided both sport and a welcome addition to the food supply. As fast as they multiplied and were introduced all over New Zealand waters, the Isaak Waltons were out after them. So were the poachers. So were the Maori eel fishers, who welcomed the speckled beauties to their lines and nets.

The laws made by the angling fraternity today are sensible. To reduce poaching, it is forbidden to sell trout or salmon; you have to eat or give away your catch, in some waters restricted to so many fish per man per day. Licences to fish are cheap, but help to maintain the large hatcheries which are necessary to keep up stocks. The Wildlife Branch of the Department of the Interior maintains four: two rainbow trout hatcheries in the North Island, near Lake Taupo and near Lake Rotorua; and two brown trout hatcheries in the South Island, at Lakes Wanaka and Te Anau.

12

The success of these sporting fish overshadows the story of the introduction of smaller pond and stream species, of which perch and the inevitable goldfish are now well established.

Before the coming of the aliens the Maori eagerly hunted their lakes, rivers and streams for the few edible species, using nets, baited hooks and traps and even weirs – as described in Sir Peter Buck's *The Coming of the Maori*. Two species of large eel were a principal catch: the short-finned *Anguilla australia* and the long-finned *A. dieffenbachi*. The Pakeha soon learned that they were delicious, jellied or otherwise prepared for the table with recipes used for European eels. It had been the custom of the Maori to split eels and other fish, caught in large numbers on migration, to the backbone and hang them to dry in the sun for use in the lean days of winter.

The freshwater crayfish, so abundant in clear waters, was trawled up from lakes by the Maori using ingenious dredge nets from their canoes; it was also taken by searching the boulders in streams and in deeper water by diving – a practice soon followed by the Pakeha. Freshwater clams (*Unio* sp.) were raked for in the shallows with a *kapu*, consisting of a wooden frame with teeth, and a net behind to trap the shellfish as they were lifted by the rake.

There are various species or sub-species of *Galaxias*, the native substitute for trout, already referred to, and known as inanga to the Maori. After maturing in lakes and rivers the adult inanga swims down river to deposit its ova on the saltings at high tide; the embryonic galaxias hatch on a subsequent high tide and spend half a year growing in salt water. As 'whitebait' they re-enter estuaries in huge numbers, and are much sought after by Maori and Pakeha. The adult galaxias can grow to about eight inches; and strangely, like the introduced salmon, it can survive and breed in lakes far inland which have no outlet to the sea.

Most important as food for the Maori were the marine animals. Already by the date of Cook's arrival seals were scarce in the North Island, although still plentiful in sombre fiordland sounds. But there were innumerable sea fish which were caught with nets, lines, spears and by diving: fish which Cook gave English names to, and the Pakeha followed the practice – cod, gurnard, hake, sole, mackerel, flounder and so on, most of them totally unrelated to Atlantic species of the same name. The coast-dwelling Maori could never starve so long as the sea was calm enough for him to go fishing. Today the inshore waters still yield fantastic catches with modern equipment. A single haul of the big seine net of a Tauranga power-boat in the Bay of Plenty has enclosed as much as a thousand tons of the gregarious trevalli; fifty or sixty tons is a more usual haul. These figures put in the shade the meagre catches of European fishermen in the overfished and polluted waters of the Eastern Atlantic; whereas the New Zealand fisherman often does not know what to do with his heavy catch.

The sea-crayfish or spiny lobster (also called crawfish) is taken by diving in shallow water by the Maori, and also today by the Pakeha. It is delicious eating, in great demand for export to America, and in calm North Island seas is getting scarcer. In the south Stewart Island men still make good money by netting and trapping them in cages: Robert Traill's son told me that in one day at the crayfishing he might earn enough to keep himself for a month; the stormy local weather was the best friend of the crays because it prevented overfishing.

Along New Zealand's shores will be found tons of discarded shells of mussels, pipis (bivalves), and rock and dredge oysters, evidence of centuries of Maori dependence on shellfish food. The paua, a kind of abilone (*Haliotis* sp.), was much sought after, extremely appetising to eat when beaten like a steak and grilled (as I can testify), but also its iridescent shell was used to liven the wooden carvings and canoes, providing a glittering eye where needed, and its hard edge was used as a knife and chisel. Then there was the *toheroa*, a mollusc living in the sand, a morsel so delicious to the human palate that it has been severely over-hunted and is today strictly protected by a close season and regulations as to catch and size (fifty shells not less than three inches long per person), regulations which ardent gourmets are heavily fined for break-ing every season.

The sea was far more fertile of food for the sustenance of the Maori than the mammal-less land and the vast forests. As a true Polynesian he made full use of everything edible along the shore, paddling and

202 Man Against Nature

diving for fish, including octopus (another delicacy), canoeing out to remote islands, or climbing cliffs after seabirds. Of the 110 native or self-introduced breeding birds on the New Zealand list (page 218) about forty species are marine. In sheer quantity the seabirds easily outnumber the land birds. Banks listed as Maori food such birds as albatross, gannet, shearwater, pintaido (petrel), shag and penguin.

The downy feathers of the albatross were prized by the Maori for personal decoration, and for adorning the gunwale of the war-canoe. As breeding birds in New Zealand albatrosses were too scarce for a regular supply to be obtained from nesting sites. The *toroa*, as the Maori called the albatross, was caught at sea, with the long bird lance, or a special form of hook; it could be attracted within striking range by flesh or fat bait trailed on lines.

Today albatrosses breed on the remote Chatham and other islands to the south. Not until the 1930's did they return to breed on the mainland, at Taiaroa Head, near Dunedin, where they were welcomed and protected. Here detailed studies of this small colony of the royal albatross *Diomedia epomophora*, were begun by L. E. Richdale and continued by others, revealing a fascinating picture of a slow-breeding, long-lived bird. Owing to the fact that it takes more than twelve months to rear a single chick, the royal albatross is unable to breed more than once in two years.

The full story was told to me by Stan Sharpe, the warden in charge of the enclosed area of the albatross sanctuary above Otago Heads. I was fortunate to have been granted a special permit to see the birds, which in that year were low in numbers, only two occupied nests. We walked very slowly right up to where the handsome black and white birds were incubating a single white egg each, in shallow nests on a gentle slope. He sat down alongside one bird, and presently stroked its satin-white head, and with a gentle pressure of his hand invited it to raise its body to reveal the egg. The albatross made no attempt to bite or resist, and afterwards sat down complacently to brood once more. I noticed the ring on its leg.

'You see,' Stan said calmly, 'I know this chap pretty well, and he knows I'm his good friend. He's about thirty years old, according to his ring number; but in any case I know him by his manners and face – as any shepherd knows each sheep in his own flock. Of course he's been away last year, on his biennial holiday, and I won't see him next year. But next year it'll be the turn of the others to come back to Taiaroa; I'm expecting up to nine nesting pairs next year if all those which bred last year return, and maybe one or two young ladies who will be old enough to breed for the first time as well.'

Because breeding comes so late in life and only in alternate years, more than half the royal albatross population is forever at sea. They wander far on the incessant winds of the Roaring Forties – to South America, in fact round the whole world in latitudes 30° to 60° south – as marking them has proved. Stan Sharpe's duties include keeping humans, dogs, cats, ferrets, stoats and other undesirable visitors away. The albatrosses do not lay a second egg if the first is lost. Human egg-collectors have made attempts, but only one egg has been taken by this thief. Out of 48 eggs laid between 1951 and 1959 only 7 were lost from various causes. But of 41 chicks hatched, alas, 19 were lost: 5 through unauthorised human interference, dogs accounted for 6, and a cat and a ferret killed 2 each.

This Taiaroa Head is a fascinating sanctuary. Around its steep sea coast and sandy bays the once severely hunted wild life is strictly protected today. There are massed colonies of shags above holes in the cliffs where the fur seals, almost exterminated by the hunters from the whaling ships 150 years ago, now breed in safety. They are becoming fairly tame, and I could slither down the rocky ledges to photograph these sharp-nosed little sea-lions (for they are not true seals) as they dozed in the sun – or scratched at their heated fur interminably.

Black oyster-catchers piped in Sandfly Bay, where we encountered the tall, handsome, pompous-looking, yellow-eyed penguin *Megadytes antipodes*. It strolled about clumsily, uneasily, as we inspected its two downy chicks hidden under a clump of flax. Close by, in deeper holes on the sloping ground, were the smaller nocturnal blue penguins *Eudyptula minor*. Stan dragged forth the fluffy twin chicks for us to inspect. Mutton birds (sooty shearwaters) were also nesting on the mainland of this Otago Peninsula: we stumbled on the carcases of two, which Stan said must have been killed by cat or ferret.

It was not the first time I had handled plump penguin chicks, which can give a hungry human the sensation of gastronomic possibilities. One can understand why the Maori used to take these substantial nestlings at fledgeling stage. On a small island in the Bay of Plenty, in reaching for petrels in a hole under a pohutukawa root my arm was indignantly pecked by an adult blue penguin nursing her twin chicks. Normally blue penguins never come to land by day, and even those which are at sea dive shyly at the approach of a boat. But they are not so shy at night, marching boldly up to their resting and nesting quarters. These may be at times under the wooden floors of seaside houses and 'baches', even in town suburbs. Their habit of nocturnal conversation by a series of screams, mewing and trumpeting notes is such that only bird-lovers could put up with such a deafening serenade!

A colony of some 250 pairs of blue penguins thrives on Somes Island in the centre of Wellington Harbour Bay, studied by Fred Kinsky of the Dominion Museum. Early in January he took me on one of his rounds. Many of the fledged young had departed and their parents had gone into the sudden and astonishing 'purdah' moult. The feathers come away so rapidly that the penguin is practically naked for a week, and must keep away from the water in a warm, dry burrow. Here for a fortnight, until the new feathers are thick enough, it is like a lobster which has shed its carapace, and awaits a new one in strict hiding, avoiding enemies and fasting. Kinsky carefully drew forth one of his old marked birds; it was covered with a rash of newly-sprouting feather-tips, the whole skin tender, jelly-like, and pulsing with the blood which feeds the new feather growth.

Blue penguins are found around the whole coast of New Zealand, but the black and white penguin we encountered one day, after crossing the new Haast Bridge in the South Island, proved to be a little-studied and local species – the fiordland crested penguin *Eudyptes pachyrhynchus*. It nests in caves and deep cavities under tree-roots in the coastal rain-forest, and is almost as tall as the yellow-crested penguin. This individual barred the way in the centre of the new Haast road, shivering in the pouring rain, immovable, but ready to peck vigorously when I picked it up and transferred it to a drier spot under the forest trees. It was the time of the moult for this nocturnal species, but this individual was in perfect plumage; and we were left with a mystery – it seemed as if this fiordland penguin had been sleep-walking!

Having studied and filmed the Atlantic gannet *Sula bassana* at home, I was curious to see the New Zealand species *Sula serrator*. It proved to be very slightly smaller, with black feathers in the centre of the tail and along the wings, a richer golden head and certainly a softer voice. The young gannet is large, plump and very good eating when nearly ready to fly, before it has developed tough wing muscles. It is certain that it was much hunted in the past by the Maoris, as the Atlantic gannet was in the last century and earlier – and in fact this northern species is still eaten in certain remote islands today.

Probably the Maori hunters exterminated any mainland colonies they found; by the time of Cook's first visit the 'Solan Goose' was confined to the less accessible rocks and steep offshore islets. Banks records that off the North Cape on Christmas Eve 1769 he shot several gannets from the ship's boat, and that on Christmas Day Solan 'Goose pye was eat with great approbation and in the Evening all hands were as Drunk as our forefathers usd to be upon the like occasion.'

At Cape Kidnappers in Hawke's Bay is the only mainland colony of gannets in New Zealand. But Cook does not mention it in 1769 when he recorded an adventure off that headland which resulted in its present name: Maoris in a canoe had seized a Tahitian boy from on board the *Endeavour*, and tried to carry him off; but he escaped by diving as soon as the kidnappers were fired on by Cook's men. Hawke's Bay was thickly populated by natives at that time, and Banks had been shooting seabirds there too, but he does not include gannets. The naturalists Charles Fleming and K. Wodzicki in a recent survey suggest that the first breeding of gannets at Cape Kidnappers was about a hundred years after Cook. At any rate there were for sure about a hundred nests there in 1885, at the time of low Maori numbers.

When I first visited this headland in 1962 there were around three thousand pairs nesting, an increase almost entirely due to protection.

From the more inaccessible stacks and cliffs at Cape Kidnappers the gannets have spread to the level land on the cliff-top. In fact we were driven right up alongside these gannets by Landrover, over twenty miles of track roads bulldozed across the Cape peninsula. A relay system of young voluntary wardens maintains a protective watch over the gannetry by day. But rather surprisingly these New Zealand gannets seem to have no enemies save man. The black-backed gull *Larus dominicanus* has not yet become the persistent egg and chick thief its North Atlantic cousin *Larus marinus* is. The Cape Kidnappers gannets are absurdly tame – but then most New Zealand native birds are.

Just as tame were the gannets farther north in the Bay of Plenty, on White Island, which I visited with a Dominion Museum expedition in 1965, camping for five days with Chris Robertson and Charles Sampson. We sailed from Tauranga in the fishery protection vessel HMNZS *Haku*, a crossing via Whale Island of some eighty miles.

Whale Island, I remembered, was the scene of the massacre in 1831 of Hongi's bloodthirsty Ngapuhi war-party which had been raiding south from Auckland. After a couple of cannibalistic orgies ashore Hongi's men retired to Whale Island, from which the Maori tribal occupants fled. A blind tohunga with the raiders had foretold that large reinforcements would arrive to help the Ngapuhi with further slaughter of the Bay of Plenty tribes. The reinforcements duly arrived, their canoes blackened the water, but they contained the deadly enemies of Hongi gathered together by Te Waharoa (father of the famous Wiremu Tamihana, later known as William Thompson). Enslaved as a child, Te Waharoa had waited long years for this chance to begin his vengeance on those tribes which had so reduced his own. He had persuaded a powerful Tauranga tribe to join him in the assault on Whale Island. No quarter was given. Two warriors were allowed to live to carry the tale of requited utu. The rest were eaten. Even the blind priest was killed, but as a tohunga's blood was tapu, instead of hacking his head off, they pounded him to death with their fists.

Our call at Whale Island was for the purpose of putting ashore three sharpshooters for a similar massacre of the inhabitants – on this occasion the numerous goats which had been destroying the native vegetation.

It is intended to keep this now desolate island as a bird reserve. After sniping off some of the goats as we motored around the sheer north-side cliffs, we put the men ashore and steamed off for White Island, thirty miles away. Hundreds of dolphins, thousands of shearwaters, prions, gulls, shags and gannets enlivened the crossing of this fertile fish-abounding Bay of Plenty.

The snowy appearance of White Island, so named by Cook, is due to the sulphurous lava flows which kill all plant growth around the steaming volcano. But as we drew inshore we saw that the seaward slopes farthest from the thermal cone were clothed in the dark green of pohutakawa forest, with here and there the white triangle of a gannet colony wedged into the shore line.

The ever-present Pacific swell made landing difficult – three journeys in a fibre-glass dinghy manoeuvred by the *Haku*'s imperturbable coxs'n, and we had staggered ashore on the slippery boulders under a gannet colony, with some loss of dignity, but not of equipment. A breeze at that moment was wreathing the volcano's sulphurous steam down upon us as we humped our stores up past the gannets' nests of rotting seaweed, guano and remains of their fish meals. The resulting stench was sickening, but we were to get used to it.

It was better under the pohutukawa trees, which provided plenty of combustible firewood for our supper fire. We encamped near the remains of a former settlement, a number of huts which had tumbled to the ground, their nails rusted through but the wood preserved by the sulphur in the air. It had once been a Pakeha settlement, built by men who attempted to exploit the sulphur and gypsum deposits on this steep island, which is roughly a mile square. One after another three companies had established workmen and machinery, living in huts in the shelter of the forest, and a screening works in the naked crater. But it was difficult to get men to stay near the edge of an active volcano for many months, and the uneasy feeling (which I confess I had from time to time on White Island) they must have had was justified dramatically in 1914, when a huge fall of the volcano wall suddenly blocked the steaming core. Before they could reach safety a party of workmen were buried alive in boiling mud.

Our expedition was for the purpose of counting and marking sea-birds, but we made one journey to the crater. The old miners' trail from the pohutukawa camp up over the high scoria of bare lava is much fallen away where gulleys bisect it, so that we had to use the ice-axe to cut steps from time to time. But at last, after a mile of painful progress, we looked down upon the pits of boiling mud and steam seven hundred feet below. We slithered down the loose wall to where the crater floor was hot with hissing rivulets. We crept nearer the central pits of boiling water which send out the clouds of steam visible fifty miles away. There were about a dozen fumaroles in full blast; these are vents in the ground or the crater wall which shoot forth jets of roaring, sulphurous steam from their butter-yellow jaws. One, known as Noisy Nellie, has been singing her impressive steam-engine song for many decades.

The crater rim rises one thousand feet, but its seaward side is sunk and broken down to sea-level. Gasping, with sulphur in our throats, we retreated to the edge of the sea to gulp fresh air and wash away the dust on a little sandy beach beside the broken concrete jetty. Hot springs make this a warm bathing place. Hard by, the roofless sulphur works are still full of machinery, rusted paper-thin and ready to collapse at the first kick.

The White Island gannetries are larger today. The Maoris may no longer take them as food when they make their periodic visits to collect mutton birds. Since man has kept records there have always been gannets on White Island. The prospectus of the sulphur extraction company, issued in 1926, mentions them as a potential source of guano. Under the present protection their numbers have risen from about two thousand adult birds in 1926 to twelve thousand today.

The mutton bird on White Island is the grey-faced petrel, *Pterodroma macroptera*, about the size of a large pigeon. In the burrows of soft volcanic soil and humus under the evergreen pohutukawa the downy chicks were close to fledging. It was our pleasant evening amusement to sit around the camp fire after a long day scrambling over the island, and fill in the daily records of birds seen (quite a few small birds in the bush areas) and gannets counted. At our feet the tame little kiore rat would scavenge for our crumbs, omnivorously eating fish, bread and fruit. The sea boomed its lullaby on the rocks a dozen yards below. Presently overhead we would hear the crooning calls of the adult mutton birds as they glided in from the sea. With marvellous accuracy each would strike the treetops immediately above its own nest-hole, and flutter down to earth. (This was an operation not without the hazard of being caught by one leg in a fork of the tree and hanging there to die.)

The crops of these adults were loaded with a mess of reddish, oily, semi-digested fish food, chiefly squid. We had to be careful to keep the beak closed to prevent disgorging when we caught and ringed them. The fat youngsters would also eject a stream of oil at us. In pre-European days the Maori used to collect this oil and use it for lamp fuel. The name 'mutton bird' is curious, but it does not originate as might be supposed from the oily fatness of these shearwaters. Vincent Serventy considers that it derives from the early days of the New South Wales colony when the Tasmanian mutton bird was often incorporated in the mutton pies so popular with protein-short settlers.

Mutton bird, grey-faced petrel, shearwater: all these tube-nosed birds have a similar life-history the world over akin to that of the albatross; and it was my good fortune as a young man to lease and live on my own small Welsh island of Skokholm and study the ten thousand or so of the Manx species *Puffinus puffinus* which nested in burrows there. At the fat mutton-birding stage the young shearwater is deserted by its parents, which fly away in the autumn on their long moulting migration, the Skokholm shearwaters crossing the Equator south to the east coast of South America, while the shearwaters of Australia and New Zealand move the other way, into the north Pacific. Thus, sensibly, the shearwaters of both hemispheres (most species) live in perpetual summer – as recoveries of leg-banded birds has proved.

The young shearwater does not breed in its first or second year; some individuals may not breed until they are more than five years old, but in due course these adolescents begin to frequent their birthplaces, chiefly on small islands or high mountain-tops, too late in the spring to do more than familiarise themselves with a locality and its burrows. In this sweethearting stage male and female form a permanent attachment to a vacant burrow, enlarging or cleaning it out in a desultory way, and playing at housekeeping. Although the young pair will not necessarily see each other at sea during the winter, the mate bond has been established and as long as both shall live the attachment to the burrow remains. This is their rendezvous in the spring, when they will accept each other by voice-recognition – for their meeting will be nocturnal – and with considerable ceremonial of bill-fencing, 'necking' and cackling conversation.

Despite the fact that thousands of burrows are concentrated on the small area of breeding ground, and some have become linked together during years of excavation, there are no mistakes of location in the labyrinthine underground. These tube-nosed birds have an uncanny sense of orientation and geographical position. Their migrations over the vast oceans are star-guided. Their return home to the burrow on a pitch dark night with perfect accuracy is accompanied by loud cries; these (in my opinion) may be a form of sonar or sound navigation by echo-location – the incoming bird may recognise the special, familiar echoes it receives from the ground, rocks, trees, etc, which surround its burrow. At any rate there is no calling on moonlit nights when these sharp-eyed birds can see their way home clearly.

For several weeks the mature pair frequent the burrow in early spring, tidying it up, lining a nest and generally laying claim to the site by right of occupation. As soon as the female has laid the single egg the male takes it over. She flies off for a spell of several days of recuperation and feeding at sea. On her return she does not offer her mate any food; but he goes off for a similar long period to refresh himself. Thus incubation is by long shifts of several days each, and takes fifty to sixty days. The new-born chick is covered with a soft down and very helpless for the first ten days. It is tenderly fed on an oily soup of fish food pumped into the baby gullet a little at a time.

These nightly meals become fewer and bulkier as the nestling grows, and soon both parents are away all day collecting food, returning every few nights to stuff their child with rare but enormous loads of fish. About the seventieth day they give up entirely, and fly away on their moulting migration across the Equator; at this age the nestling's feathers are well grown and it actually weighs a good deal more than a worn-out parent. It is extremely fat and needs a period of fasting, during which it comes out of the burrow by night to stretch and exercise its untrained wing muscles, retiring before dawn – and danger from gulls and other diurnal enemies. Then one night about ten days later, its wings still feeble, it flaps awkwardly down to the sea. It cannot fly yet, but if attacked from the air, it dives expertly and swims hurriedly away from the dangers of the shore. Slimming, existing on its reserves of fat, it eventually learns to fish for itself; and the strong autumn winds help it to become airborne. Alone, unguided by the adults, it navigates unerringly thousands of miles to join them in their winter quarters; somewhere in its tiny brain lies the direction-finding equivalent of man's equipment of compass and chronometer and stellar charts which it has inherited to guide its lonely journey.

The mutton birds of White Island were beginning to depart; and the Maoris from the mainland opposite, supplemented by some from the nearby Motiti Island, were preparing to collect them. (When the Maoris ceded their lands to Queen Victoria or the New Zealand Government they reserved the hereditary mutton-birding rights to themselves and their descendants forever. The industry is now restricted to a short killing season.) No longer do the Maoris paddle their swift canoes over the Pacific swell. When we returned to Tauranga, through the vast flocks of shearwaters and schools of dolphins, the *Haku* tied up near a motor trawler which was loading the mutton-birding gang. With much singing, supplies of beer and laughter, it promised to be a festive occasion, a joyous return to the tribal open air life for a week or two.

At Stewart Island the mutton bird is chiefly the sooty shearwater *Puffinus griseus*, about the same size as the White Island mutton bird, but nesting six months later, a summer breeder. Here Rob Traill showed me the various items of equipment used on the off-islets, where mutton-birding is a considerable commercial business still. A short supplejack stick with a sharp wire or nail is used to locate birds in the burrow; by twisting the point into the feathers, a grip is obtained enabling the bird to be dragged out (I noticed several of these weapons lying about White

Island; they resembled the wire – with a sharp chisel point – used on Atlantic Islands to extract rabbits and seabirds from their burrows). Others are collected in the open at night, with torches. As soon as the bird is killed, the oily contents of crop and stomach are squeezed upon the ground, and the head, wings and tail cut off. Plucking takes place while the body is warm, and afterwards it is dipped momentarily in boiling water to loosen the body down. When cooled, some carcases are 'kippered' – opened and salted; but the traditional way is to cook them in their own fat in an iron cauldron or trypot; then place them after cooling in bags made from the local bull-kelp. This seaweed is specially prepared from four-foot fronds which are opened out through their fibrous centre layers, and inflated to form bags. When dried they can hold up to a hundred birds. Each full bag is carefully sealed, after the birds' own fat has been poured in, to exclude air; it is then sheathed externally with totara bark or cabbage tree leaves, and the heavy end lowered into a 'kit' (basket) of woven flax as a further protection against rupture of the precious contents. These keep indefinitely and can be eaten months, perhaps years, later as a very special Maori delicacy.

Probably half a million mutton birds are annually consumed in New Zealand, chiefly by Maoris, but some appear on the market for general sale in the principal towns, and some are imported from Tasmania. In commercially harvesting the mutton bird of the Bass Strait (which is yet another species of shearwater *Puffinus tenuirostris*, somewhat smaller and more slender-billed), the Australian birders collect the strong-smelling oil also. This can be refined for lamp oil and lubricating oil, and more particularly for sun-tan oil – suitably deodorised.

Until 1965 the breeding place of the closely allied Hutton's shear-water *Puffinus huttoni* was undiscovered; then G. Harrow found it nesting in holes on the steep screes well above four thousand feet in the Seaward Kaikoura range, late in the summer. Two larger species also breed on New Zealand mountain ranges: the black petrel *Procellaria parkinsoni*, a summer breeder; and the Westland black petrel *Procellaria westlandica*, which occupies the mountain burrows in winter.

Probably these now rare mountain-breeding shearwaters and petrels were more abundant in the early days of Maori colonisation; there is no history of their hunting the Kaikoura's cold summits, but they took those nesting on the North Island's warmer bush-clad ranges – the fat black petrels of the Taranaki and King Country mountains.

Among the keenest competitors for inshore fish, the abundant shags and cormorants of New Zealand were also killed for food by the Maori, but hardly to a great extent, because Cook and Banks found them numerous and easy to shoot near centres of Maori population; and the *Endeavour*'s crew ate them with relish. But perhaps to the Maori, as to the civilised palate of today accustomed to tender meat, the flesh of these birds is rank. 'Hunger is certainly excellent sauce,' wrote Banks in his diary. 'Old shaggs killed at the nest and as soon broild and eat . . . excellent food I think they were.'

10 Today

From the stone age, in less than two hundred years, the Maori finds himself in the atomic age. How has he taken this change?

'New Zealand belongs to the New Zealanders,' wrote the son of an English settler, enthusiastically opposing federation with Australia seventy years ago. In his loyalty to the land of his birth he overlooked that these words had been the war-cry of the Maori, who at that moment were a conquered and dying race. For by 1896 the white invaders were approaching half a million and the Maori reduced to about 42,000. Fighting, white man's diseases, landlessness had brought about this disintegration. Without strong leaders, without security of tribal territory, a great many were like defeated rabbits, which give up, skulk, and die of sheer chagrin. They had lost the traditional élan, the conquering spirit and alertness which Cook and Banks remarked, even the customary cleanliness of daily bathing and attention to sanitation and health reported by those first white explorers. In short, cut suddenly from their cultural roots, they were in the grip of an inferiority complex: standing helplessly by, they watched the clever Pakeha, the men of the machine age, take over their lands and treat them, politely at times, but nevertheless indubitably, as an illiterate, inferior, dying race. Their diffidence, hesitation and withdrawal in the presence of white people in white settlements has often been noted; in sharp contrast with their behaviour in a purely Maori background, where their personality continues to be expressed with resolution, dignity and authority.

The depopulation was so rapid that in some villages not enough people were left to bury those who had perished from tuberculosis,

A few pairs of the royal albatross nest at Taiaroa Head, a South Island sanctuary for this huge bird–wing span nearly eleven feet

Caspian terns at their communal nesting site

A pair of spotted shags

smallpox, measles, influenza and venereal diseases. But the double
malaise of mental and physical sickness could not be defeated without
strong leaders who could cope with the Pakeha on the same level of
literacy and outlook. The old chiefs, who had fought the white invader,
were either dead or living as pensioners, a few proudly in their native
bush, the rest without self-respect on liquor and credit in or near towns
and other white settlements. Meanwhile land continued to be sold in
reckless haste so that the proceeds could be devoted to more liquor and
the enjoyment of perishable goods sold by the Pakeha, for as long as the
paper money served this debauched appetite.

All was not quite lost, however. There were still a few future leaders
available. Te Aute College, the Anglican school for Maoris, proved that
the young Maori brain could be trained in the field of modern political
thought and the humanities to equal that of the best European scholars.
On leaving Te Aute the literate young men formed an association of old
pupils known as the Young Maori Party, with the avowed object of
Maoritanga: that is, of reviving the condition and morale of their people
as a nation. Three remarkable members of this party eventually became
cabinet ministers, noted for their high integrity: Apirana Ngata,
lawyer and writer; Maui Pomare, doctor and skilled speaker; and Te
Rangi Hiroa (Sir Peter Buck), anthropologist and doctor. By their
literacy and honourable behaviour so acceptable to the European
leaders, these men won the confidence of the Pakeha, and began the
rehabilitation of their own people through the services they were able to
render as legislators and watchdogs of fair laws, of health and hygiene,
and as interpreters of their past who rescued and gloried in Maori
genealogies. Queen Victoria knighted all three, but their greatest
reward was the commendation of their own people.

A new confidence resulted in a fresh attempt to adapt to European
ways, education, hygiene. One indirect result was a remarkable increase
in the birth-rate. It has continued, and as I write this, is double that of
the Pakeha at about 45 per 1,000, while the death-rate has fallen to
around 9 per 1,000. With youth on their side (60 per cent under the
age of 21) the Maoris at this rate have every prospect of building their
numbers to no mean total by the end of the century. Today they are

13

approaching 200,000 out of a total population of about 2,600,000 in the whole of New Zealand.

Looking ahead it is clear that the Maori has moved away from that lethal stage of contact with the white man, which other primitive races experienced and failed to survive. Thanks to modern techniques of inoculation and hygiene more of them live much longer. But this new welfare and increasing longevity has brought other problems. The new sense of physical and political security has in many instances encouraged a natural laziness of these Polynesians in the face of plenty. This has led to a high rate of obesity at an early age, and the accompanying disorders of diabetes, gout and coronary weakness. Pre-European Maoris were noted for their large appetites, in keeping with their active hunting life; it was the custom to eat enormously in times of plenty as an insurance against the lean periods. In the present prosperous age everything encourages over-eating and drinking, which is never frowned upon but even admired within the tribe. Recent statistics show that Maori women suffer more than their men from coronary diseases, probably because of their sedentary existence, and die sooner, thus reversing the present trend of the Pakeha women to outlive their men.

The consumption of vast quantities of beer in a short time is an outstanding feat until recently encouraged by the puritanical Pakeha law of early closing (6 p.m. – recently reverted to 10 p.m.). Essentially gregarious, the Maori loves to celebrate each meeting with friends and relations with long bouts of communal drinking and singing, as in tribal days in the marae. He can earn large pay packets today, chiefly at unskilled and heavy industrial work – as navvy, road operator, docker, etc,; and he spends liberally on beer parties and other indoor communal amusements. This has had an unfortunate result, giving the Maori a name for rowdiness and drunkenness in the towns, a label that also sticks to well-behaved members of their race.

Officially there is no race discrimination in New Zealand. But in fact there are opposing elements which encourage separation. Landless young Maoris, like young Pakehas, must perforce work where the money lies – chiefly in towns. But the Maori people are countrymen at heart. Exiled, they dream of returning to the land, even save money with that aim, but all the same enjoy the amusements of the town – liquor, cinema, sport, lavishing wages upon friends. Even if a Maori saves enough to buy a house – a rare event; he usually rents a flat, or lives in lodgings – he has to be specially courageous in order to take one in the better or 'middle' class part of the town. Despite lip service to equality, white antagonism is sometimes strong behind closed doors. Sensitive to this the average Maori shuns the genteel surburbia of the Pakeha. He mingles instead with the less literate whites, the unskilled workers who live in the back quarters of the town. As a result the Maori is often blamed for the bad behaviour of both races in these back streets.

On his part, out of a naturally generous, happy-go-lucky nature, the average Maori of today is freer of racial prejudice than the average Pakeha, considering himself neither superior nor inferior. He looks for evidence of other levels than colour upon which to judge society. He ranks men by the degrees of their honesty, courage, generosity and helpfulness to their fellow men. He despises cowardice, meanness and drab pessimism. He knows full well his own handicaps to virtue: he is too tolerant, he is lazy, he says 'yes' to please, rather than 'no' to hurt, when he really means 'no' – the broken promise made out of kindness and politeness which you will meet in Wales and Ireland. He follows certain precepts of the Christian teaching more ardently than the missionaries who first introduced the Book in which they are written: Take no thought for tomorrow; Sufficient unto the day is the evil thereof; Silver and gold have I none, but such as I have give I thee; and he is as ready to take as to give; all these were precepts of the pre-Christian Maori too.

There are some New Zealanders who look ahead to complete integration of Maori and Pakeha within the next century, through the middle way – the meat of interbreeding between the sandwich of the two races. It is true that hundreds of half-caste individuals are included in the periodical census of residents, but there is no way of counting these. Officially a New Zealander is either a Maori or European whether he has half, quarter or other fraction of Maori blood in his body. Assimilation of race only goes so far on paper as to bestow upon each registered person the nationality 'New Zealand British'.

In Pakeha society you are accepted as white even if you have Maori blood, provided your skin is fair and your features not Polynesian. But some full-blooded Pakeha whose parents and/or grandparents settled in the North Island's northern province of Auckland often acquire a golden-brown or yellow-tinted complexion and so appear to have Maori blood, even Malayan blood, in their veins; but they have none – the strong sun has burnt them permanently. By contrast in the extreme southern provinces of Otago and Southland, the cool, rainy climate produces white faces, rosy with wind and the cooler summers of a region where few Maoris live.

The Maori problem is a North Island one. Here there is neither *apartheid* nor integration. The Maori language is still spoken freely by the older people in country districts, but seldom in towns where the young people congregate. The average young Maori employee, away from tribal influence, prefers to forget his colour in his legitimate pursuit of happiness in the town; he finds his native language and customs 'old-fashioned', embarrassing, in his contacts with workmates and employers. He will be more ready to remember his ancestry and tribal history as he becomes old; then he may long for the imagined security of the marae in the peace of the country. But he is seldom ambitious; which is perhaps as well for the Pakeha, for it keeps business relations on the harmonious footing of brown employee and white employer.

It was one of the ambitions of the knightly advocates of Maoritanga to raise the Maori above his present category of employee, and see him taking more responsible positions in the upper, ruling strata of society, or at least see him as well distributed among the professional levels as the Pakeha. Sir Apirana Ngata also saw salvation for the Maori in a return to the land. He himself was from the Ngatiporoa tribe inhabiting the east coast of the North Island, an area where many had refused to sell land. He convinced his tribe that the future lay in peaceful, efficient and modern farming, without necessarily destroying their communal way of life. He became Native Minister in charge of the new Department of Maori Affairs, which has ever since continued to support this agrarian policy by advice, credit and State subsidy.

Travelling the lovely north-east coast road lined with yellow lupins in summer one is in a rugged country where nine-tenths of the people are dusky-skinned Maori. The reason is not far to seek – no level pasture or rolling plain coveted by the Pakeha. Inland the Huiarau and Raukumara Ranges are almost as wild and uninhabited as when the first canoes, the *Arawa* and *Tainui,* landed here at Cape Runaway at the time of the Great Fleet migration. The coastwise farmhouses are often rough-looking shacks, the fences poor. Stock stray over the highway, smiling Maoris seem to be forever rounding them up on horseback, with innumerable dogs, in clouds of dust. Mobs of sheep wander, with Jersey cattle, over steep paddocks where sunburned men hunt rabbits, or perhaps carry home a wild pig from the bush, its plump black carcase lolling over the saddle crupper.

An overloaded bus stops at a post office. Stout, grinning wahines in bright print frocks descend and chatter unceasingly, their heavy shopping baskets overflowing with Pakeha prepacked foods. Many are as barefoot as their children. The dusty roads, innocent of tar-seal, are littered with dead opossums and hedgehogs, pecked at by myna, magpie and harrier. Kingfishers and yellowhammers sit on telephone and electricity wires which run from one crooked pole to another. Along the seaward cliffs the pohutukawa trees toss their crimson blossoms in the breeze to the musical calls of the gulls and terns dipping in the clear blue Pacific. Happy, happy people – who should dare despise their carefree sunlit existence because it is not up to 'modern standards'? Who is the happier here – white critic or brown criticised? Are not these people living in something of the Arcadia planned by the visionary Wakefield and other Utopians of the last century?

Alas, all Maoris cannot be so fortunate to live in security on the land – where the worst inconveniences are the occasional drought or storm. Such peace and plenty has encouraged the already very high birth-rate of a philoprogenitive people, who have not taken kindly to modern birth control measures (even the many children born out of wedlock are lovingly cared for by the tribe). There is no permanent work for more than one or two children of the large families of up to ten or more. Of necessity, they drift away to the towns and the factories; or become contract workers, sheep-shearers, wharfies, lumberjacks, etc.

As already mentioned, tribal ownership of land has handicapped those young Maori men who have wished to emulate the Pakeha's success as a stockfarmer. Here and there, however, a few young sons have managed to persuade their fellow landowners to form an 'Incorporation' of shareholders with the object of large scale development of their joint property. In this they can obtain the advice and assistance of the Department of Maori Affairs, and the local Department of Agriculture's advisory staff. In place of the interminable, inconclusive debates of the marae a committee of management makes the executive decisions promptly and effectively. The incorporation can borrow capital from the Government and other sources, on a long-term plan of repayment, and in the pioneering stage forgoes payment of dividends until the project reaches the profit stage some years later.

Near Cape Runaway I met the vigorous Manu Stainton, who in 1952 was appointed manager of 1,400 run-down acres of farmland owned by no less than fifteen sons and daughters of his parents. He had fenced, cleared and reclaimed about a hundred acres each year. For the first years his wife had existed with him in a tiny whare ten feet by eight, with an open fireplace. The holding was stocked at first with what the available money could buy – four hundred ewes and fifty cattle. Between them Manu and his wife did all the work of shearing, building the woolshed, fencing and scrub clearance. The cleared land was top-dressed with superphosphate and sown with clover, grass and turnips, as prescribed by the Department of Agriculture. From the equivalent of four acres to one ewe Manu has raised productivity to four ewes per acre. He now runs two thousand ewes and three hundred cattle. The farm shows a good profit, from which dividends are annually paid. Future development, paid for out of income, is largely contracted out, and Manu can afford to employ a permanent assistant.

And the price to the community? It is hard to assess. At least one Maori family has been rehabilitated on these 1,400 acres, where formerly, two hundred years ago, a dozen families may have existed, working the soil by hand and hunting the bush. And some of Manu's relatives and their families still receive dividends as the result of his labour and the loan of some of their capital. But of course he is not

altogether his own master; in the final assessment he must account to the
family shareholders for his mistakes. So long as he is successful all will
be well (not so long ago the Maori who failed in the eyes of his tribe
would be punished by the seizure of all his goods and possessions); and
as we walked over the reclaimed land it was good to see the healthy
sward and animals content in the new paddocks. There was still the old
problem of erosion, which Manu, a thoroughly enlightened farmer,
feared might be increased by the heightened rate of stocking. In this
country a drought meant overgrazing; then flash-flooding set the soil
in motion. He was planning embankments and ponds to hold flood
water.

Spending Christmas one year by Lake Taupo I visited the hereditary
lands of the famous warrior Te Heu of the Ngati Tuwharetoa, who
had refused to sign the Treaty of Waitangi in 1840, and rejected
Christianity in 1843 because (as he said) it served three conflicting
interests: Anglican, Wesleyan and Roman Catholic. In 1846 he and his
family were buried forever under a great landslide. His successor Te
Heu Heu Tukino, with other Maori chiefs, gave the sacred volcanoes
of Ruapehu, Tongariro and Ngauruhoe to the nation as a sign of peace,
in 1887, on condition that the area remained tapu to all development;
it became the Tongariro National Park. A forest of some 17,000 acres
is now the main portion of Te Heu Heu's lands around Lake Taupo,
still in the possession of the Ngati Tuwharetoa. Six hundred tribal
owners claimed the revenue from the milling of timber on this estate
during the post-war period of high prices. Then the Maori incorporation, founded in 1945 to manage the business, realised in time the need
to utilise this ravished, exhausted land while there was still money from
timber sales to spend. They decided to accept an offer of £1 million for
the whole business and goodwill, and the right to fell the last stands of
millable trees; and planned to spend £25,000 a year on reclamation
for farming.

Pat Hura is the supervisor of this Tuwharetoa tribal organisation.
Discussing the erosion problems on this huge area, he told me his plans.
At that late moment of 1965 work was well advanced in fencing and
clearing the first two thousand acres. The more level land was being

cultivated with grass and clover to carry stock in winter, which is cool here, at around and above two thousand feet above sea-level. Initially the reclaimed land will carry 2½ ewes to each acre. The higher land will be heavily top-dressed, thus encouraging clover, but he did not intend to clear the bush on the highest land, and start off the familiar pattern of erosion. Far-sightedly, his plan was to reclaim and maintain about ten thousand acres of the better, lower land, and concentrate on intensive sheep and beef cattle.

I heard these words of wisdom in the striking new building of Puketapu House, headquarters of the incorporation in busy Taumarunui, in sight of the great Tongariro National Park. Sir Apirana would have approved of this enterprise, with its strong organisation, office and board room, which has retained the land in Maori ownership – one of the all too few successful adaptations to meet the Pakeha challenge.

The rise in numbers of the Maori, the once 'depressed' race, has caused an uneasiness among some Pakeha. They see the high Maori birth-rate, their natural 'get-togetherness', and aloofness in society, as a threat to their own leadership. They even fear that in the years not so far ahead that Maori-dominated territory may be partitioned off, as Ulster has been from the rest of Ireland. They notice, or imagine, an incipient hostility in the new resurgence of the Maori. But these fears are not shared by the many, of both races, who believe in the diversity of mankind, who dislike regimentation, and who advocate the preservation of Maori lands, traditional culture and skills as a welcome part of the New Zealand scene.

Uniformity and assimilation are vastly dull. But at the moment, in spite of attempts to revive the Maori language and arts, it is hard to see any other result of the continuing trend in favour of Pakeha dominance. Only in a few schools is the Maori language taught, and only where there is a majority of Maori children attending; few white parents wish their children to learn a 'dying language', and some will not permit their children to attend such schools. In some country districts there are schools exclusively for Maori children (novels have been written about these schools, notably Miss Ashton-Warner's amusing *Spinster*), who are taught the language and culture of both races. These schools are turning out excellent citizens, although how far they will succeed in higher education and life itself depends on their own energy: all is open to them, if they can overcome their natural laziness and dislike of book-learning. In the towns the Maori language and literature is of no interest to the Pakeha engaged in the absorbing main occupation of the acquisition of personal wealth.

As we have seen, the Maori character is apt to change in long contact with the white overlords of the towns. He wears white man's clothes; he apes white man's habits. He catches the infectious diseases of these palefaces, including that of coveting money and wealth. He sees the greedy, seamy side, perhaps more than the virtues, of the Pakeha. He sees the beautiful country of his fathers and tribe disappear under more and more buildings, more towns, more sprawling suburbs. Each year another twenty thousand European immigrants arrive, their passages subsidized out of taxes raised by the government which he himself must help to support by paying those taxes; he sees that these numbers are enough to continue the process of swamping him and his, to outvote him in parliament and council. And mostly he shrugs his shoulders – after all the Maori is too carefree to care, or to be afraid.

As for the Pakeha, he has no cause now to fear or distrust the Maori as a race – they are too kindly, warm-hearted, and unambitious. If asked what people he fears most the New Zealander, white or brown, will tell you that it is the yellow race from Asia and its islands that he must keep out of Aotearoa.

The gift of the sacred mountains south of Lake Taupo to the nation by the proud chieftains was a gesture of goodwill at the 1887 peace-making which took the New Zealand Government a little off-guard. It came only fifteen years after the long-settled United States of America had established the world's first national park at Yellowstone. It set in train the desire for more, which became an urgent demand as a few far-sighted naturalists and others saw how rapidly native forest and mountain were being abused and exploited by timber merchants and stock-farmers. The government subsequently enlarged the Tongariro National Park to 163,356 acres, by purchases. In 1900 Mount Egmont, an extinct volcano in Taranaki, was secured as a national park by special legislation which preserved 82,380 acres around its 8,260 foot high cone. Both these parks provide good skiing grounds for winter sports.

Special tribute needs to be paid to the continuing efforts of private individuals and conservation societies to secure more national parks, from a government too obsessed with the demands of settlers and timber merchants, which refuses to dedicate an acre of land suitable for either purpose. It was not until 1952 that a proper National Park Authority was created, with both government and private organisations together in one body to co-ordinate the hitherto random efforts to preserve thermal, native forest, and scenic areas for recreation and sporting purposes, and wildlife needs.

There are now ten large national parks, covering five million acres, or one-thirteenth of the total area of New Zealand. This is no mean achievement, since all the designated land is virtually pristine, although partly ravished by the introductions of alien species, and by some forestry operations. But unlike national parks in the United Kingdom and elsewhere, there are no towns, villages or other building development to mar the wilderness, nor are any permitted, save a few hotels, lodges and huts for the visiting public and park personnel.

The largest national park in the world is probably the Fiordland National Park, not quite three million acres of rain-forest, lakes, little known glens, untrodden mountains, and deep indented fiords. It encloses, above Lake Te Anau, the Murchison Mountains, the haunt of the takahe. Nearly another half-million acres adjoining northwards form the Mount Aspiring National Park, so called from the Matterhorn-like peak which reaches 9,959 feet amid icefields. Continuing northwards, beyond the Haast Pass, the majestic Southern Alps rise in breathtaking beauty, as seen on a clear day, to the highest summit in New Zealand, appropriately named Mount Cook, 12,349 feet. This peak was not climbed until 1894. A narrow area, forty miles long, of the highest mountains here forms the Mount Cook National Park of 172,979

acres. Adjoining on the west side, from the divide to the sea is the
Westland National Park of 210,257 acres, enclosing a magnificent
variety of scenery, large and small lakes, snowfields and glaciers. Of the
last the well-known Franz Josef and Fox Glaciers fall towards the
Tasman Sea at a record speed – for glaciers – through steep valleys,
so fast that you can enjoy the unique experience as I did of seeing trees
and bushes within a few yards of your slippery path over the foot of the
glacier. Our guide told us that the glaciers move at the rate of up to
two feet a day, faster in the middle than along the sides. There are few
roads in this huge mountainous group of parks, but there are tracks
and huts for walkers and climbers. For the non-walkers, on fine days,
small amphibian aircraft are available, on regular trips or special hire,
to fly to remote lakes; and small planes fitted with skis make scheduled
flights to land upon the snow-covered icefields under Mount Cook –
another marvellous experience which I enjoyed.

The Urewera National Park in the North Island is the largest remaining area, about half a million acres, of unspoiled native forest in New
Zealand. Lake Waikaremoana, 840 feet deep and two thousand feet
above sea-level, steep or cliff-bound for most of its shore, awe-inspiring
and beautiful, is the focal point for exploring this park where some of the
rarest native birds may still be found (pages 122, 139).

National Parks come under the umbrella of the Department of Lands
and Survey, each with its own Board. Among voluntary organisations
represented on the National Parks Authority which look after wildlife
interests the Royal Forest and Bird Protection Society is noted for its
pioneer work in securing new reserves, and promoting legislation to
protect native species. On the hunting of deer and other noxious animals
the Society sometimes holds views which conflict with those of deer-
stalking and shooters' clubs, also represented on the Authority. From
this field of active interest in the parks is drawn a large corps of voluntary wardens to supplement the full-time services of the paid rangers.
Freedom of access is all-important; restriction of entry only applies to
certain special wildlife reserves.

These come under the same protective Act, which provides for wildlife sanctuaries. Offshore islands and islets containing relict populations

of native fauna and flora are an obvious choice for sanctuaries. Many I have already mentioned: the principal ones are Little Barrier, Poor Knights, Hen and Chickens, Kapiti, Stephens Island, and islets off Stewart Island; as well as all of New Zealand's remote sub-Antarctic islands; and islets in the sub-tropical Kermadecs to the north.

In addition the Reserves and Domains Act of 1953 protects some seven hundred public and private scenic reserves with special natural features, flora and fauna; nearly 700,000 acres of beautiful country secured against development of the wrong sort.

The Forest Service was established in 1920, and began with a programme, not of conserving native forest – these were being felled at an alarming rate at the time – but of planting half a million acres with exotics, chiefly *radiata* pine, to meet the anticipated shortage of mature native trees. The argument for planting radiata is an economic one – this conifer produces fully millable timber in New Zealand in record time, forty years, whereas the native red beech *Nothofagus* takes a hundred, the kauri 150, and the rimu or red pine *Dacrydium* two hundred years to mature to the milling stage. So well does the radiata pine grow that today, from half a million acres, it is yielding more sawn timber than the fourteen million acres of native forest still left – of which, however, part is reserved uncut for scenic-plus-economic reasons of inaccessibility.

Indeed, had these remaining native forests been accessible for timber extraction, they would have been destroyed ere this. New Zealand is fortunate in saving this remnant, and finding a substitute to supply her building needs. The Forest Service is now the principal owner of native woodlands; it can be congratulated upon its vigorous policy of saving these while bowing to a certain extent to the public demand for the unique, handsome native hardwood timber by judicious extraction of a limited cubic footage. Not only do native trees contribute to the characteristic beauty of the mountain scenery and Northland forest but it is recognised that they are the natural protection against erosion and run-off. Research and reafforestation have marched hand in hand, with pleasing results. It was a delight to wander in the Waipoua and other

Northland forests, where 42,000 acres provide a remarkable study area for the forester. Here there are 22,000 inviolate acres of kauri and native trees, 5,000 acres of exotics, and the balance natural regeneration (after exploitation for gum and timber in the last century).

The *pinus radiata* sets its own seed naturally in New Zealand, and under proper management propagates itself without replanting by hand in many areas. In the Marlborough Sounds I saw how it is beginning to reclothe the seaward slopes and fiords, ravished of native bush by the first and later settlers and exploiters. Other conifers also do well, and altogether around one million acres of these are now planted and worked by both public and private interests, about fifty per cent each. Sawn pine for building is usually treated with a preservative, to prevent boring insects and fungoid damage. Apart from the large home consumption, an export trade in timber, wood pulp and news-print brings in a substantial return in foreign currency, now approaching £10 million annually.

The Forest Service provides a useful public benefit in the construction and maintenance within their lands of roads, tracks, river-crossings, sleeping huts and refuges, airstrips and information services for the use of trampers, naturalists, hunters, and others who may enjoy free and unrestricted access to the fine, extensive forests.

Wildlife protection is the concern of the Wildlife Branch of the Department of Internal Affairs. It was established in 1945 as a result of the urgent need to examine problems created largely by the introduction of alien animals which were later branded as noxious. But it also concerned itself with the development of freshwater fisheries, and for this reason was first based on the Hot Lakes district of Taupo and Rotorua. Various acts and orders were passed, to be superseded by the Wildlife Act 1953, six years after the appointment of the first staff biologist. In twenty-five years the study of both native and introduced animals has gone ahead fast. The very considerable results of research and field work on noxious and game animals by a core of devoted and hard-working scientists have been of world-wide interest and value. Basic research on many species of special interest to New Zealand has also been carried out by the Animal Ecology Division of the DSIR in close co-operation with the Wildlife Branch experts. Among useful long-term projects, the ringing or banding of birds is under the direction of the Wildlife Branch, in co-operation with the amateur ornithologists.

Control of deer, opossums and other animals inimical to trees was handed over to the Forest Service in 1956. Rabbit control, however, remains the province of the Rabbit Destruction Council, which also deals with opossums and wallabies where these are found in rabbit country.

The Wildlife Act provides Crown ownership of wild birds, and protects all native birds except a few black-listed species: harrier, kea and black shag (identical with the European cormorant, and world-wide enemy of the trout and fresh-water fishermen). Introduced birds have no protection (save the white or mute swan); they are considered to be tough enough to do without it! Paid and honorary rangers have powers of search and seizure of the weapons and equipment of poachers, who are still a problem in wildlife protection. Game birds (all introduced) are chiefly pheasant, three species of quail and chukor. The last is a substantial Asiatic partridge *Alectoris graeca*, which whirred away from my feet in the foothills of the Southern Alps where it is widespread following its first liberation in 1926. Efforts to establish the European partridge *Perdix perdix* have proved disappointing; at the moment a project in the North Island is persevering with liberations on farmlands resembling those of their English home (where they are dying out from the effects of chemical residues).

The draining of marshes and swamps to produce rich farmland, and the infilling of lakes by eroded soil and gravel have greatly reduced the habitat available for water birds; and the pressure continues. The splendid lagoon of Lake Ellesmere (page 81) is threatened with conversion to farmland, and other lagoons and lakes are in immediate danger of being drained. Native ducks are becoming rarer, and a tighter close season provided; wildfowl are generally excessively tame in New Zealand and badly need this protection; some are gradually learning to fly to refuges as soon as the short shooting season opens.

Many farmers and other landholders have now established ponds and small lakes to provide these refuges for water and wading birds following the appeal of the World Wildlife Fund and the Wildfowl Trust. The Wildlife Branch gives advice on how to construct and develop these through its research and information services.

It is curious that the pukeko or swamp hen *Porphyrio melanotus*, a very handsome bird, smaller and more elegant than its cousin the rare takahe, should be classed as a game bird; for it is essentially a typical moorhen, and moorhens – to my palate at least – are distinctly inedible! Guthrie-Smith, studying it at Tutira, found its family habits most endearing, moral, and happy, and thought that such a nice bird ought not to be persecuted. Others dislike it for its vocal powers, its ear-piercing booming and screeching conversation, as well as its tendency to raid vegetable and farm crops. Unfortunately at the moment it is the shooting fraternity which decides how many may be killed and when; and bird-lovers say the pukeko is now in need of total protection.

11 Tomorrow

Enough has been said in this book about the destruction of forests and the erosion of the soil to weary the reader. If, to New Zealand ears, I have sounded unduly critical in retelling the story of the impact of man upon the virgin country, let me remind them that the events I have described were but a repetition of the universal effect of white man upon the lands of the stone-age peoples remaining in the nineteenth century, and which the present century has seen accelerated. But at first, in the enthusiasm and greed for land and wealth, the sombre words of Cook and other explorers went unheeded: that it would have been better for the land and the people that they had never known white man's civilisation. Now, after the damage has been done, man is endeavouring to remedy some of the worst effects of his impact. In New Zealand it was not until 1941 that the frightening extent of erosion was officially recognised by the setting up of a special body to combat it.

The creation of the Soil Conservation and Rivers Control Council may have been inspired as well by the world-wide publicity given to the notorious dust-bowl effects of arable farming and overgrazing in the United States. The new body was not concerned with saving wildlife, its chief anxieties were the control of rivers, and conservation of farmland by preventing run-off and erosion. Since then it has moved a long way towards understanding the nature of the problem. Its study of New Zealand's special difficulties mainly arising from sudden intense rainstorms and cloudbursts has produced the following recommendations for water control and soil conservation:

The blue duck, or whio, one of the rarest New Zealand waterfowl, lives in fast flowing torrent water

The brilliantly coloured kingfisher
brings food to its nestlings

A pair of silvereyes

The black stilt is
one of the world'
rarest birds

Spelling (retirement from grazing), especially during flowering and seeding, revives both native and sown pastures, producing cover on eroded land which resists erosion and controls water run-off.

Surface sowing of clovers, and in some circumstances grasses, results in the establishment of good pastures even on deteriorated sown and native grassland, when grazing is properly controlled.

Top-dressing with phosphate and trace elements proves to be the biggest factor in promoting clovers and grasses on deteriorated hill country soils.

Rotational grazing of cattle is more effective than sheep grazing in regenerating poor pastures, obviating the need to burn native pastures periodically. When burning and rabbits are eliminated native pastures recover rapidly under controlled cattle grazing.

In areas of high rainfall planted trees are effective in healing unstable eroded land, particularly in gullies, having the same protective effect as native cover regenerated by complete spelling from grazing.

Pasture furrows are valuable to conserve water and reduce scouring of soil.

Graded banks and broad-base terraces are strikingly effective in stopping loss of soil from cultivated slopes by sheet and rill erosion and in greatly reducing uncontrolled run-off.

Wide shallow grassed waterways prove effective in harmlessly disposing of run-off that could not be retained on the land.

Dams capable of temporarily storing floodwaters and regulating their discharge are worth while.

The Control Council has found it helpful to survey and classify each area where soil conservation is necessary, according to its economic capability and physical characters. There are four classes for land suitable for cultivation, three for land only suitable for grazing or forestry, and the eighth class is for high country, or rough, arid or swampy land – suitable only for watershed protection, recreation and wildlife. Plans for the last class, and for the worst of the seventh class of very rough grazing, are for de-stocking altogether, both of domesticated and wild mammals. Here the high country men bring in an opposing argument which I have already recorded (page 100): that the high tops were eroding long before man arrived, to form the rich alluvial plains,

14

and that the real problem is lower down where it can be controlled by
the shelter belts and other measures (above) found effective by the
Control Council; that if tussock and bush are left to regenerate without
judicious burning the fire risk will rise steadily, especially from careless
climbers, hunters and tourists today – one uncontrollable fire in dry
weather could undo the work of a decade of de-stocking.

The main operation on the lower reaches of the river is to train and
stabilise the channel so as to increase its hydraulic efficiency, and the
drainage of the surrounding land. 'Draining works', undertaken chiefly
in the shingle beds when the water is low, include the clearing of unwanted willows (the weeping willow of New Zealand *Salix babylonica*
originated from cuttings from the plantation around Napoleon's tomb
at St Helena; it has been a prodigious success, growing exuberantly to a
great girth, seeding naturally, providing shade for stock and even food
when pollarded in drought when other greenstuff is scarce, and retain-
ing river banks against flood. It is almost an evergreen, shedding its
leaves for only a few weeks in winter). Next, the training of the river
into one easy meandering channel where formerly it trickled through
many 'braids'. Thus confined, and protected by fresh planting
of willow and where necessary by stop-banks with outward-opening
flapgates, the river becomes deeper, more navigable to boats, provides
better fishing, and is controllable for irrigation; and much of the original
wide bed and silt lands will become rich farmland.

In New Zealand everything is changing; and man-made plans and
organisations are no exception. In 1967 a new overall Water Authority
was planned, to put new bite into the reclamation, into reservoir construction, and the allocation of water where it is most needful: for
industry, electricity, recreation and – although this is not mentioned – I
hope, wildlife conservation.

Is it necessary to burn at all? Those tremendous deliberate bush fires
of Samuel Butler's day destroyed the humus of centuries and accelerated
the slow natural erosion to its present uncontrollable degree. At Tara
Hills, far south of Mesopotamia, on the Mount Cook road, I saw how
the Soil Conservation and Rivers Council were implementing their

findings, mentioned above, on this 8,250-acre farm, where the altitude varies between 1,500 and 5,000 feet, and frost-lift of topsoil on the thin, overgrazed runs of this area is a major problem, the rainfall being comparatively light at twenty inches per annum. By prohibiting burning, and by resting the frost-lifted paddocks and hunting the rabbits to a low degree of infestation, a regeneration of the tussock and scrub of the higher slopes was obtained. After topdressings with superphosphate, the large regrowth was winter-grazed with profit by cattle, much to the surprise of the diehards who forecast that cattle would perish without considerable hand-feeding. Instead they have both thriven and opened up the land for sheep, as well as leaving a sufficiency of vegetation to check the effects of frost on the soil. As a farmer myself I could see how the incendiarist runholder would itch to burn this cover when long spells of drought made it possible, and how the fire would run into the very roots underground, leaving the soil powder loose and dry, to blow on the wind or to be swept downhill with the first sudden rainstorms. For rain comes heavily when it does; and at Tara Hills contour ditches have been bulldozed to hold and divert the run-off to irrigate paddocks of lucerne and hay: an admirable example of hill husbandry.

For centuries the incessant westerlies of the Tasman Sea have been piling up black, golden or white sand against the western shoreline, providing more land, especially in the North Island, where you may see wrecks of ships and other jetsam far inland. Considerable success has been achieved by planting these moving dunes with sand-holding marram grass and nitrogen-fixing lupins, followed by pines. At Kawhia, birthplace of the notorious Te Rauparaha (page 73), and along the Ninety-mile Beach in the far north, it was amusing to wander from rows of neatly planted marram into older stands of marram-cum-lupin, and then through the thick growth of five-to ten-year-old pines, and note the fascinating sequence of wildlife abundantly invading the once barren, unstable landscape. Most of the pests which bother the forester here are introduced. Rat and mouse dig up the pine seeds when planted and as they germinate; rabbit and hare cut the seedling pines down. Opossums emerge from cover at night to eat the leaves of lupins and pines. When the cover is high enough – and the lupins here achieve unusual height and girth – deer move in, especially fallow and sambar deer where these are found. Although not widespread at present in the far north, these deer thrive in young plantations, to the delight of local hunters and poachers. The humus builds up in the sand, and more animals and birds move in. The rabbits, rats and mice attract ferrets, stoats and weasels, which vary their diet of small mammals, frogs and insects with an occasional bird, although on the whole they do much good by destroying the rodents.

One of the surprising successes of the dune-reclamation zone is the hedgehog (page 156) which, as Brockie found, is plentiful here and lives on the grubs, snails, slugs, millipedes and other invertebrates harmful to the planted lupins and pines. European birds also serve the forester well, by devouring caterpillars and beetle larvae which attack lupin and pine. I found blackbirds, thrushes, starlings and sparrows plentiful, and a good sprinkling of native warblers, pipits and white-eyes. Yellow-hammers sang from the tops of encroaching furze – which would soon be checked and killed by the vigorous pines. Pheasants strutted through the access avenues, and quail seemed to be abundant in the early stages of marram and lupin growth.

It has become part of the modern tradition of land use to apply insecticides and herbicides as both preventive and curative medicine. At one time DDT was excitedly declared to be the panacea for every sort of insect and grub pest. It has since been shown that these eventually become as resistant as the classic fruit-fly proved to be. Rightly has Dr R. P. Pollinger of Lincoln College recently appealed for a break from this 'shotgun economy' attitude, and demanded more ecological and behaviour studies which could lead to the use of natural methods: for example, the introduction of such enemies of the grassgrub and porina caterpillar as the parasitic wasps which control pasture grubs on the South American pampas.

Fortunately, aerial spraying of forests and hillsides for insect control has not been developed in New Zealand. This indiscriminate method had such disastrous effects in the United States, exterminating the natural enemies of the pest, as well as many birds, useful animals and plants, that the example should be a lesson for all time to New Zealanders. However, residues of DDT or dieldrin insecticide and other herbicides have worked from the land and from the bodies of poisoned invertebrates into the fat and living tissues of farm stock, also into lakes, rivers and sea, affecting fertility, and the palatability of meat and fish. This has caused anxiety and a stricter examination and testing of meat for export; importing nations will reject meat so tainted.

When staying with friends on Lake Rotoiti, I met scientists who were investigating the effects of spraying the alien oxygen weed, which is colonising and covering this and other hot lakes with massive floating rafts, to the detriment of boating and fishing. One hundred acres had been rather too precipitously sprayed, with dubious results. There was talk of importing large water snails to eat down the weed; and the hope that this would also benefit the wild ducks which find a sanctuary here. Anglers told me here that the effects of DDT insecticides making their way into the thermal lakes, including Lakes Rotorua, Rotomahana and Rerewhakaitu, were so serious that the purest strains of rainbow trout which used to flourish here may be wiped out.

As to selective weed-killers, too many are far from selective. They may protect cereals and grasses from competition by broad-leaved plants, but here again, harmful residues accumulate in roots and soil, having a permanently depressive effect on fertility. Moreover the elimination of too many broad-leaved plants or 'weeds' in grass pastures deprives stock of the medicinal qualities (mineral variety) of these herbs, resulting in liver and bowel malfunction. More natural methods of control by rotational grazing, and mechanical cutting of obnoxious plants before seeding, where the terrain permits, are indicated.

The widespread use of poisoned food to kill rabbits, opossums and other pests has not been as successful as it is often made out to be. Pre-baiting with unpoisoned food is usually necessary to achieve a good kill when the poisoned oats, carrots, phosphorized jam, etc, is later put out. Sometimes there is a good kill of the pest, but often there is not; in either case, despite claims to the contrary, many beneficial animals, and sometimes farm stock, also die – and it is not a pleasant death.

Predatory creatures such as wild pig, dog, cat, ferret, stoat and harrier may also die as a result of scavenging poisoned rabbit, hare or opossum. The search continues for a more attractive and successful selective rabbit poison (like warfarin which has been effective and fairly selective against rats and mice, but principally because it can be laid under cover out of range of other animals). Meanwhile a mobile force of sharpshooters using Landrovers at night seems the safest way of keeping rabbits down to innocuous numbers (page 153).

In an effort to save those native species which are close to extinction the government, under pressure from the increasing numbers of nature lovers, amateur naturalists and informed public opinion, agreed to a (disgracefully limited) budget to meet the cost of transferring rare birds from one offshore island to another or to the mainland, or vice versa, in the hope that the conditions (generally man and his introduced mammals) which threaten their extinction at one site will be absent from the other. In addition, again on far too low a capital allowance, the Wildlife Branch has been permitted to set up a Native Bird Reserve at Mount Bruce, near Masterton, with the object of providing a place where rare native birds can be held in restricted freedom, studied and bred if possible, in an effort to prevent their extinction.

Mount Bruce is an acceptable example of the type of spacious zoological gardens which alone should be permitted in future. Zoos should exist today for the purpose of education and research in the conservation of living animals, not for curious visitors to stare at these, miserably confined in small cages. The continued collection of rare animals for the latter purpose is an outrage by adult man on a level with the mentality of the small boy who imprisons living creatures in small boxes; but worse, because those who enjoy, and the many who make their living by, collecting or keeping rare animals in captivity without hope of breeding them are well aware that they are hastening the species on the road to extinction.

The new director of the Mount Bruce Reserve, Colin Roderick, piloted us around the most attractively laid out grounds in the reverted bush and hilly terrain, where he was able to show us several species which are rarely seen in the wild today. It was late spring, and many birds had nested successfully in semi-natural conditions. Others were singing and calling exuberantly against the natural backcloth of native vegetation, wood, pond, stream and swamp. Colin's comments on the rarest species can be summarised as follows:

Takahe (notornis). Nests and lays eggs satisfactorily, but no chicks have yet hatched, either by natural or artificial incubation. Problem of infertility is being studied (page 124).

Kakapo (ground parrot). Only one at Mount Bruce as yet. It is hoped to obtain a breeding pair before it becomes extinct, as is now feared, in its last haunts in fiordland (page 133).

Saddleback. Several broods raised. Transfers to other sites have gone well, all on small islands, but it is hoped to make mainland liberations if they continue to multiply at Mount Bruce.

Stitchbird. Bellbirds are being used to study the honey-feeding habits of the related stitchbird, in readiness for an attempt to breed the latter here. (Survives only on Little Barrier Island.)

Parakeets. Successfully breeding.

Brown duck. This comparatively rare duck is nesting freely.

Eastern or Buff Weka (woodhen). Extinct on mainland. Two pairs have had six clutches. Surplus now available for liberation.

L'ENVOI

New Zealand's problems are not unique. Most of them are shared with the rest of the world. In the midst of his vivid struggle with the elements and their effect upon his management – and mismanagement – of the land, while he complains about authority and taxes – as men have ever so complained – the New Zealander is perhaps not conscious enough of his good fortune in living where he does, in one of the few countries not overpopulated. While most nations are now underfed, he thrives on the fat of his land, possibly a bit too complacent and unconsciously forgetful of world problems in his insular remoteness. But instead of trying to husband his resources by growing more slowly and subsisting on the increment of natural wealth, he is forever eagerly using up capital, borrowing on the future, borrowing money, borrowing population. Why this hurry to saturate the land with men and towns and industry? Isn't the example of impoverished Britain enough? When I have asked the ordinary New Zealander why he encourages so much white immigration, why he does not advocate stricter birth control, so that the world in general, and New Zealand in particular, can have fewer mouths to feed and a better standard of living, the answer has always been that already mentioned bogey of New Zealand nurseries: 'the Yellow Peril!'

On, on, on! With more people than ever now living in the towns, the demand for building sections in new suburbs is almost frantic. The wasteful conurbial growth consumes the fair country with frightful momentum. The monotonous suburbia of London, the bungaloid excrescences of Los Angeles and Sydney, continue to creep over and sterilise forever more and more of New Zealand's most priceless irreplaceable asset, her rich and fertile soil.

How to end this book is my problem. On page 6 I have endeavoured to thank some of the many friends who made special efforts to see that my journeys through New Zealand were so marvellously interesting and comprehensive, who gave me hospitality, and arranged for me to reach places rarely visited. I acknowledge here particularly the aid I have received from the published works of many New Zealand scientists, biologists and naturalists, some of whom I met and talked with, men whose efforts have helped to secure large areas as national parks, islands and mainland sites as nature reserves, and who have fought commercial interests which would destroy more forests, overstock more farms, poison more land and pollute more water with chemicals. Their learning and discussions have reinforced my own impressions and strengthened the theme of this book. They have fully approved the strong emphasis I have been able to lay upon the destructive forces in their midst. (But in the final assessment any mistakes and errors of omission or commission in this book are solely my responsibility.)

A few there were who did not approve my use of strong words such as rape of the land, degraded country. One critic wrote, 'How on earth can you consider that a country can be raped or degraded which has less than a hundredth part even touched by man?' Thereby, I fear, showing a characteristic, complacent, insular attitude; the official estimate of the area of erosion due to Pakeha activity alone is 15,250,000 acres, which is roughly one-quarter of the land surface!

Another said, 'It seems strange, coming from you, a resident of a run-down, worn-out country like Britain. What about your own ugly little black towns, open mines and industrial squalor?'

I could not agree more: that is what this book is trying to warn New Zealand about.

Appendices

I NATIVE BIRDS

NATIVE BREEDING BIRDS OF NEW ZEALAND (North, South and Stewart Isands only)

Species	Status	Breeding Range			
		NORTH I.	SOUTH I.	STEWART I.	AUSTRALIA
Brown Kiwi					
Apteryx australis	common locally	*	*		
Little Spotted Kiwi					
Apteryx oweni	restricted		*		
Great Spotted Kiwi					
Apteryx haasti	restricted, locally common		*		
Yellow-eyed Penguin					
Megadyptes antipodes	restricted, locally common		*	*	
Blue Penguin					
Eudyptula minor	common, all coasts	*	*	*	*
White-flipped Penguin					
Eudyptula albosignata	restricted		*		
Fiordland Crested Penguin					
Eudyptes pachyrhynchus	restricted		*	*	
Crested Grebe					
Podiceps australis	scarce		*		
Dabchick					
Podiceps rufopectus	local	*	*(rare)		
Royal Albatross					
Diomedea epomophora	ca. 12 pairs		*		
Giant Petrel					
Macronectes giganteus	common visitor, all coasts				*(few)*

NATIVE BREEDING BIRDS OF NEW ZEALAND—continued

Species	Status	Breeding Range			
		North I.	South I.	Stewart I.	Australia
Broad-billed Prion *Pachyptila vittata*	restricted		*	*	
Fairy Prion *Pachyptila turtur*	all coasts	*	*	*	*
Flesh-footed Shearwater *Puffinus carneipes*	common, restricted range	*			
Buller's Shearwater *Puffinus bulleri*	common, restricted range	*			
Sooty Shearwater *Puffinus griseus*	world ranging	*	*	*	*
Fluttering Shearwater *Puffinus gavia*	common	*	*		
Hutton's Shearwater *Puffinus huttoni*	restricted mountain breeder		*		
Allied Little Shearwater *Puffinus assimilis*	world-wide species	*			
Black Petrel *Procellaria parkinsoni*	restricted mountain breeder	*			
Westland Black Petrel *Procellaria westlandica*	restricted mountain breeder		*		
Grey-faced Petrel *Pterodroma macroptera*	world-wide species	*			
Mottled Petrel *Pterodroma inexpectata*	ranges whole Pacific		* (doubtful)	*	

NATIVE BREEDING BIRDS OF NEW ZEALAND—continued

Species	Status	Breeding Range			
		North I.	South I.	Stewart I.	Australia
Pycroft's Petrel *Pterodroma pycrofti*	restricted	*			
Cook's Petrel *Pterodroma cooki*	Pacific and Atlantic seas	*	*		
Black-winged Petrel *Pterodroma nigripennis*	Pacific wanderer	*			
White-faced Storm Petrel *Pelagodroma marina*	common	*	*	*	
Diving Petrel *Pelecanoides urinatrix*	fairly common	*	*	*	
Gannet *Sula serrator*	New Zealand & Bass Strait	*	*	*	*
Black Shag (Cormorant) *Phalacrocorax carbo*	world-wide	*	*	*	*
Pied Shag *Phalacrocorax varius*	local	*	*	*	*
Little Black Shag *Phalacrocorax sulcirostris*	local	*			*
Little Shag *Phalacrocorax melanoleucos*	numerous	*	*	*	*
King Shag (several sub- species) *Phalacrocorax carunculatus*	local	*	*	*	
Spotted (and Blue) Shag (2 subspecies) *Stictocarbo punctatus*	local	*	* (Blue)	*	
White-faced Heron *Ardea novaehollandiae*	newcomer (1940), common	*	* (probable)		*

Species		Status				
White Heron	*Egretta alba*	world-wide, only *ca.* 25–100 pairs New Zealand		*		*
Blue Reef Heron	*Egretta sacra*	local	*	*	*	*
Bittern	*Botaurus poiciloptilus*	widespread	*	*	*	*
Royal Spoonbill	*Platalea regia*	newcomer (1940), *ca.* 20 pairs		*		*
Paradise Duck	*Tadorna variegata*	locally common	*	*	*	
Grey Teal	*Anas gibberifrons*	local, increasing	*	*		*
Brown Teal	*Anas chlorotis*	local, decreasing	*	*	*	
Grey Duck	*Anas superciliosa*	universal	*	*	*	
Shoveler	*Anas rhynchotis*	common	*	*		*
Blue Duck	*Hymenolaimus malaco-rhynchos*	restricted	*	*		
Scaup Duck (Black Teal)	*Aythya novaeseelandiae*	common	*	*		
Harrier	*Circus approximans*	widespread, common	*	*	*	*
Falcon	*Falco novaeseelandiae*	scarce	*	*	*	

NATIVE BREEDING BIRDS OF NEW ZEALAND—continued

Species	Status	Breeding Range			
		North I.	South I.	Stewart I.	Australia
Weka *Galliirallus australis*	local	*	*	*	
Banded Rail *Rallus philippensis*	local, rarely seen	*	*	*	*
Spotless Crake *Porzana tabuensis*	widespread, rarely seen	*	*	*	*
Marsh Crake *Porzana pusilla*	widespread, rarely seen	*	*	*	*
Coot *Fulica atra*	cosmopolitan, local in New Zealand	*	*		*
Pukeko *Porphyrio melanotus*	common	*	*	*	
Takahe *Notornis mantelli*	ca. 400 birds (page 130)		*		
Pied Oystercatcher *Haematopus finschi*	inland breeder, common		*		
Black Oystercatcher *Haematopus unicolor*	coast breeder, local	*	*	*	
Spur-winged Plover *Lobibyx novaehollandiae*	new breeder (1940)		*		*
Banded Dotterel *Charadrius bicinctus*	common	*	*	*	
Black-fronted Dotterel *Charadrius melanops*	new breeder (1954), local	*	*		*
Red-breasted Dotterel *Charadrius obscurus*	local	*		*	

Species	Status				
Wrybill *Anarhynchus frontalis*	unique to New Zealand. *ca.* 10,000 birds				
Sub-Antarctic Snipe *Coenocorypha aucklandica*	close to extinction	*			
Pied Stilt *Himantopus leucocephalus*	numerous	*	*	*	
Black Stilt *Himantopus novaezealandiae*	rare, decreasing		*		
Southern Skua *Catharacta lönnbergi*	local breeder		*	*	
Black-backed Gull *Larus dominicanus*	common	*	*	*	
Red-billed Gull *Larus scopulinus*	abundant, mainly coast breeder	*	*	*	*(rare)
Black-billed Gull *Larus bulleri*	common, inland breeder		*	*	
Black-fronted Tern *Chlidonias albostriatus*	common, inland breeder		*	*	
Caspian Tern *Hydroprogne caspia*	cosmopolitan, local in New Zealand		*	*	*
Fairy Tern *Sterna nereis*	very rare, *ca.* 10 pairs?		*		
White-fronted Tern *Sterna striata*	common	*	*	*	
New Zealand Pigeon *Hemiphaga novaeseelandiae*	common locally	*	*	*	

NATIVE BREEDING BIRDS OF NEW ZEALAND—continued

Species	Status	North I.	South I.	Stewart I.	Australia
Kakapo					
Strigops habroptilus	close to extinction		*		
Kaka					
Nestor meridionalis	very local	*	*		
Kea					
Nestor notabilis	locally common		*		
Red-crowned Parakeet					
Cyanoramphus novaezelandiae	local, except islands	*	*	*	
Yellow-crowned Parakeet					
Cyanoramphus auriceps	locally common	*	*	*	
Orange-fronted Parakeet					
Cyanoramphus malherbi	rare, mountain forest only		*		
Shining Cuckoo					
Chalcites lucidus	common migrant	*	*	*	
Long-tailed Cuckoo					
Eudynamis taitensis	less common migrant	*	*	*	
Morepork					
Ninox novaeseelandiae	common	*	*	*	*
Laughing Owl					
Sceloglaux albifacies	probably extinct (last record 1914)	*	*	?	
Kingfisher					
Halcyon sancta	numerous	*	*	*	*
Rifleman					
Acanthisitta chloris	common	*	*	*	
Bush Wren					
Xenicus longipes	local, rare	*	*	*	

Rock Wren
  Xenicus gilviventris — local, mountain dweller

15 Welcome Swallow
  Hirundo neoxena — new breeder (1958), increasing

Fantail
  Rhipidura fuliginosa — numerous

Tomtit
  Petroica macrocephala — common locally

Robin
  Petroica australis — local

Fernbird
  Bowdleria punctata — reduced and local

Brown Creeper
  Finschia novaeseelandiae — local (forests), increasing

Whitehead
  Mohoua albicilla — common

Yellowhead
  Mohoua ochrocephala — local

Grey Warbler
  Gerygone igata — universal

Pipit
  Anthus novaeseelandiae — common

Stitchbird
  Notiomystis cincta — extinct, except Little Barrier I.

Bellbird
  Anthornis melanura — common

NATIVE BREEDING BIRDS OF NEW ZEALAND—continued

Species	Status	Breeding Range			
		North I.	South I.	Stewart I.	Australia
Tui					
Prosthemadera novaeseelandiae	common	*	*	*	
Silvereye (Waxeye)					
Zosterops lateralis	first breeding 1856, common	*	*	*	*
Saddleback					
Philesturnus carunculatus	rare, confined small islands	*			
Huia					
Heteralocha acutirostris	presumed extinct since 1907 (page 120)	*			
Kokoko					
Callaeas cinerea	local (N.I.), rare (S.I.)	*	*		
New Zealand Thrush					
Turnagra capensis	not seen since 1955	?	?		

II. INTRODUCED BIRDS

ESTABLISHED AND BREEDING IN NEW ZEALAND (three main Islands only)

Species	Status	Origin	Breeding Range		
			North I.	South I.	Stewart I.
Canada Goose *Branta canadensis*	increasing	Canada		*	
White (Mute) Swan *Cygnus olor*	local	Europe	*	*	
Black Swan *Cygnus atratus*	abundant	Australia	*	*	*
Mallard *Anas platyrhynchus*	common, increasing	Europe	*	*	?
Australian Brown Quail *Synoicus australis*	local	Australia	*	*	
Californian Quail *Lophortyx californica*	locally common	N. America	*	*	
Bobwhite Quail *Colinus virginianus*	one locality only	N. America	*	*	
Pheasant *Phasianus colchicus*	local	Asia	*	*	
Chukor *Alectoris graeca*	local	Asia	*	*	
Common Partridge *Perdix perdix*	frequent liberations, poor success	Europe	*	*	
Peacock *Pavo cristatus*	very local	Asia	*	*	
Turkey *Meleagris gallopavo*	very local	N. America	*	*	

INTRODUCED BIRDS ESTABLISHED AND BREEDING IN NEW ZEALAND—continued

Species	Status	Origin	Breeding Range		
			North I.	South I.	Stewart I.
Rock pigeon *Columba livia*	largely racing pigeon escapes	Europe	*	*	*
Spotted Dove *Streptopelia chinensis*	Auckland area	Asia	*	*	
Rosella Parakeet *Platycercus eximus*	locally common, increasing	Australia	*	*	
White Cockatoo *Kakatoe galerita*	local	Australia	*	*	
Little Owl *Athene noctua*	local	Europe	*		
Kookaburra *Dacelo gigas*	N. Auckland, local	Australia	*		
Skylark *Alauda arvensis*	abundant	Europe	*	*	*
Song Thrush *Turdus philomelos*	numerous	Europe	*	*	*
Blackbird *Turdus merula*	abundant	Europe	*	*	*
Dunnock *Prunella modularis*	numerous	Europe	*	*	*
Greenfinch *Chloris chloris*	numerous	Europe	*	*	*
Goldfinch *Carduelis carduelis*	common	Europe	*	*	*

	Status	Origin			
Redpoll *Carduelis flammea*	common, even above tree-line	Europe	*	*	*
Chaffinch *Fringilla coelebs*	numerous	Europe	*	*	*
Yellowhammer *Emberiza citrinella*	common	Europe	*	*	*
Cirl Bunting *Emberiza cirlus*	rare N.I., local S.I.	Europe		*	*
House Sparrow *Passer domesticus*	abundant	Europe	*	*	*
Starling *Sturnus vulgaris*	abundant	Europe	*	*	*
Myna *Acridotheres tristis*	common, N. half of N.I.	Asia			*
Rook *Corvus frugilegus*	local	Europe		*	*
Australian Magpie (2 species) *Gymnorhina* spp.	widely spread, inter-breeding, increasing	Australia		*	*

III INTRODUCED MAMMALS

		DISTRIBUTION		
	ORIGIN, YEAR INTRODUCED	NORTH I.	SOUTH I.	STEWART I.
Opossum *Trichosurus vulpecula*	Australia 1858	*	*	*
White-throated (Parma) Wallaby *Macropus parma*	Australia 1870	* Kawau I. only		
Black-striped Wallaby *Macropus dorsalis*	Australia 1870	* Kawau I. only		
Dama Wallaby *Macropus eugenii*	Australia 1870	* Kawau and Rotorua		
Swamp Wallaby *Macropus bicolor*	Australia 1870	* Kawau I. only		
Scrub Wallaby *Macropus rufogrisea*	Australia 1870	* Kawau I. only	* Restricted	
Rock Wallaby *Macropus penicillata*	Australia 1870	* Kawau and Rangitoto Is.		
Hedgehog *Erinaceus europaeus*	Europe *ca.* 1890	*	*	*
Cat (feral) *Felis catus*	Europe *ca.* 1800	*	*	*
Stoat *Mustela erminea*	Europe 1885	*	*	
Weasel *Mustela nivalis*	Europe 1885	*	*	

Common name	Scientific name	Origin & date			
Ferret	*Putorius putorius*	Europe 1885	*	*	
Kiore (Polynesian) Rat	*Rattus exulans*	Polynesia 10th cent.?	*	*	*
Black (Ship) Rat	*Rattus rattus*	Europe late 18th cent.	*	*	*
Brown Rat	*Rattus norvegicus*	Europe early 19th cent.	*	*	*
House Mouse	*Mus musculus*	Europe early 19th cent.	*	*	*
European Hare	*Lepus europaeus*	Europe 1867	*	*	
Rabbit	*Oryctolagus cuniculus*	Europe 1838	*	*	
Goat	*Capra hircus*	Europe 18th cent.		*	*
Chamois	*Rupicapra rupicapra*	Europe 1907		* high mtns.	
Thar	*Hemitragus jemlahicus*	Asia 1904		* high mtns.	
Red Deer	*Cervus elaphus*	Europe 1851	*	*	*
Sambar Deer	*Cervus unicolor*	Asia 1875	*		
Java Rusa Deer	*Cervus timoriensis*	Java 1907	*		
Wapiti	*Cervus canadiensis*	N. America 1905		* restricted	

INTRODUCED MAMMALS—continued

| | ORIGIN, YEAR INTRODUCED | DISTRIBUTION | | |
		NORTH I.	SOUTH I.	STEWART I.
Japanese Deer *Cervus nippon*	Asia 1885	*		
Fallow Deer *Dama dama*	Europe 1864	*	*	
Moose *Alces americana*	N. America 1900		*	
Virginia Deer *Odocoileus virginianus*	N. America 1901		rare	*
Pig *Sus scrofa*	Europe 18th cent.	*	*	

(The above list excludes gone-wild sheep and cattle, which are sometimes a nuisance to land-holders)

Index

Olearia 161
Opossum 99, 137, 162, 165–70, 197, 206, 211
Orbell, W. R. B. 124
Orielton 88, 90, 97
Otago 30, 132, 196
Overstocking 150, 162
Owls 22, 122, 129
Oxygen weed 213
Oystercatcher 99, 181
Oysters 179

Pakeha (white settler) 57 *et seq*
Parakeets 137, 215
Parengarenga Sands 84
Partridges 206
Paterson Inlet 137
Paua 54, 179
Peafowl 149
Penguins 81, 181
Pheasant 19, 94, 149, 206, 212
Pig 61, 64, 89, 99, 108, 118, 145
Pigeon, native, 170
Pine forest 83, 115, 204
Piopio thrush 122
Pipis 179
Pipit 18, 115, 127, 212
Plover, golden, 25
Pohutukawa 32, 70, 82, 185, 197
Poison baits 213
Pollinger, R. P., 212
Polynesian people 41, 51
Pomare of the Ngatiawa 67
Poor Knights Islands 204
Porpoises 22
Poverty Bay 60
Pukeko (swamp hen) 207
Puketea tree 112

Puketi Reserve 83

Quail 94, 99, 119, 206, 212

Rabbit 92, 148–55, 206, 211
Rabbit Acts 93, 153
Rain-forest 21, 25, 30, 182
Rangitata river 89
Rangitoto Island 171
Rata 21, 32, 137, 169
Rat, black, 64, 138, 140
  brown, 64, 141, 211
  native (see kiore)
Raukumara Range 197
Rauparaha, Chief Te, 73
Redpoll 125, 173
Reserves 133, 204–7, 214
Resolution Island 134
Richdale, L. E., 180
Rifleman 127
Rimu (red pine) 21, 204
River control 210
Robertson, Chris, 184
Robin (native) 99, 116
Roderick, Colin, 136, 214
Romney Marsh sheep 110
Rook 94
Roturua 171
Royal Forest & Bird Prot. Socy. 203
Ruahine Range 120
Ruapehu 199

Saddleback 138, 215
Salmon 94, 175
Sampson, Charles, 184
Scenic reserves 85, 209
Sea-birds 81

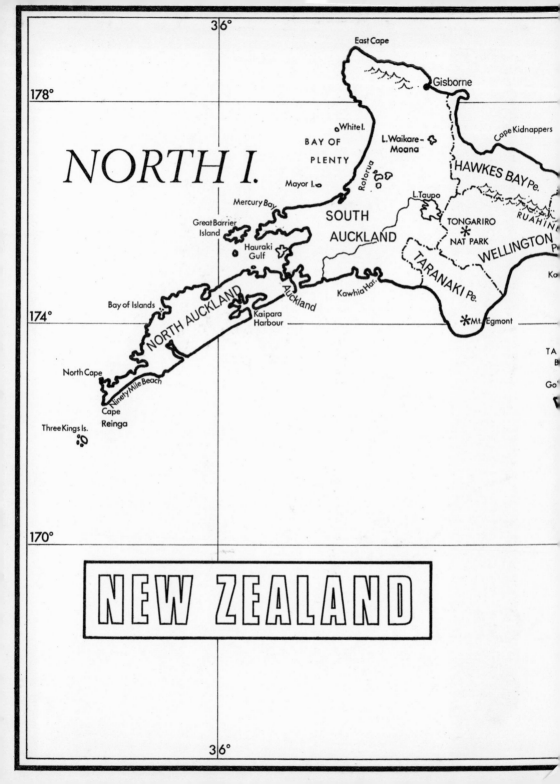